T. McLemore
7-14-94

To Reuben Jordan,

May God richly
bless you as you
rest upon the promise
of His Word.

With love,
The Warrens
John, Mary Beth,
Lydia and Johnny
—1980—

1 Pet. 5:10
2 Tim. 3:16-17
2 Pet. 1:5-8
Phpe. 1:20-21
and especially—
John 3:16

Given in thankfulness to God for your Christian fellowship.

# A HARMONY OF THE
# WESTMINSTER PRESBYTERIAN STANDARDS

## WITH EXPLANATORY NOTES

# A Harmony *of the*
# Westminster Presbyterian Standards

WITH EXPLANATORY NOTES

*by*

## James Benjamin Green

*Professor Emeritus of Systematic Theology and Homiletics*
*Columbia Theological Seminary, Decatur, Georgia*
*Author of Studies in the Holy Spirit*

COLLINS WORLD

*Seventh printing, 1976*

TO MY WIFE
*without whose competent assistance this work would
never have been finished, and*

TO MY STUDENTS
*without the knowledge of whose needs this work would
never have been begun*

THIS HARMONY
*is with grateful memories and prayerful hopes*

AFFECTIONATELY DEDICATED

# Preface

THE idea of the Harmony of the Standards was born in the classroom at Columbia Seminary. Ever since the transfer of the Seminary from Columbia, South Carolina, to its new campus in this suburb of Atlanta, the last quarter of the course in theology has been devoted to a study of the Westminster Standard. The method of study has been that of analysis and comparison. Each part of the threefold Standards has been studied analytically, and then compared with the other two. Thus the Confession of Faith and the Catechisms have been laid alongside one another, and their contents considered separately and together. In our efforts to accomplish a synthesis of the documents and obtain a synoptic view of the whole, teacher and students have had to put their fingers at three places in the book, and turn from one to another, comparing and combining.

It was while thus engaged that the idea of the harmony came to me. I said to myself, If the Standards were only printed with their corresponding parts side by side on the same page, a comparison of their contents would be greatly facilitated. The sense of the need and value of such an arrangement has been deepened with every repetition of the course. Finally I decided to undertake the preparation of a harmony of the Standards for my own convenience. Then it occurred to me that a harmony might be useful to others as well as to myself. So after sharing my idea with men of judgment and receiving their encouragement, I decided to venture into print with an Annotated Harmony of the Presbyterian Standards.

But why study the Confession of Faith and the Catechisms? If they are to be studied, all will agree that a parallel arrangement of their parts would be an aid to comprehension. But why study them? For two reasons.

First, because they are important historic documents. They belong to the literature of Christianity. They arose out of the life of the Church, and have profoundly affected the course and character of that life. Is a man interested in history? Does he find value in the records of the past? Then the Standards have a claim on his attention. For out of history they have come, and into history they have gone and are still going. So even if the Standards be old and out of date, as some seem to think, they are worthy of study. But they are neither ancient nor antiquated, being only three hundred years old. The Bible is far older, yet men do not discard it on account of its age.

No right-thinking person wishes to break with the past. He wants to consecrate it, not sacrifice it. The only way to consecrate and conserve the past is to preserve and perpetuate its values.

This leads me to say, in the second place, that the Standards should be studied because they have present-day value. They contain a system of doctrine, a creed. A creed, a system of doctrine, is a necessity. It is a necessity of thought. It is a necessity of character. It is a necessity of instruction. It is a necessity of fellowship and co-operation. A cogent system of doctrine is an intellectual and educational necessity. If the Church would edify her people, unify and mobilize them, she must educate them after a thorough manner in her creed. Some are not of this way of thinking, they decry creeds; they demand a creedless Christianity, a religion without a theology. This demand has been called pious nonsense. Leave off the pious — call it simply nonsense. To say of a man that he has no creed is tantamount to saying that he has no intelligence and no character.

In getting a creed a man may follow one of two courses. He may be independent and original; he may do his own thinking and construct his own creed. Or he may recognize the labors of others in this field, and, without sacrificing his independence, use the materials furnished to his hand. He would save time and labor, and probably arrive at a better result, if he should employ the second method.

These Westminster Standards present a ready-made theology, a creed formulated and finished. But they are not necessarily final. This creed is not placed in anybody's hands to be swallowed whole; but to be chewed, digested, and assimilated, if found to be proper food. "A creed is not a goal but a landmark." Start with the Church's creed. Accept it if you can. Reject it if you must. If you see light beyond it or to the right or the left, follow the gleam and share your vision with others.

I am making a plea for the study of the Standards. And I am saying that no man has a right to an opinion in regard to them who has not studied them, and studied them as a whole. As the Standards are in three parts which present the same system of doctrine in different degrees of fullness, they are best studied comparatively. For they supplement and illuminate one another. We come to a correct and full knowledge of revealed truth by comparing and combining Scripture with Scripture. So we obtain a sound and whole view of our creed by looking at each part in the light of the other two.

In constructing the Harmony I have followed the order of the Confession of Faith and retained its chapter numbers and titles. For the Confession is more complete in its scope; that is, it treats more subjects than the Catechisms. The three symbols parallel one another down to Chapter VIII of the Confession, Question 56 of the Larger Catechism, and Question 28 of the Shorter Catechism. From these points onward similar matters are sometimes found in different connections in the threefold formulation. In the notes which accompany the Harmony, attention is called to these differences of order.

In order to reduce the size and cost of the volume the supporting Scriptures are not printed, but ref- erences to those Scriptures are given in large, readable type. The Scriptures cited in proof of the Confessional statements are given in immediate connection with the sections to which they belong, and not at the bottom of the page, as in other editions of the Standards.

This Harmony with its analyses and explanations is sent forth in the hope that it will prove useful in reviving interest in the Standards and in rescuing them from neglect; in making them more intelligible to laymen and more usable by ministers in giving courses of instruction in these fundamentals of our religion.

With grateful appreciation I wish to inscribe upon this page the name of my niece, Mrs. Rachel Norris Dickerson, who rendered valuable service in preparing the manuscript for the printer. She amazed the author by her ability to read almost without error his illegible script.

Another name I fain would inscribe on this page in letters of gold. But I am restrained by her request that her name be not published. What she has done can and ought to be published. She in part — large part — subsidized the publication of this volume, did it without solicitation. Seeing the need and the opportunity she volunteered a generous donation. The gift was so unexpected, unusual, and withal so beautiful that it thrilled all who witnessed it or afterwards heard of it. Wherever this Harmony of the Presbyterian Standards shall be read, that also which this woman has done shall be spoken of for a memorial of her. I cannot tell you her name, but I can give you her address. The home of this Elect Lady is in Dalton, Georgia. The Lord multiply her kind, and reward her in His own great way!

# Table of Contents

# CHAPTER I

# Of the Holy Scripture

CONFESSION OF FAITH I:1-10 · LARGER CATECHISM 1-6 · SHORTER CATECHISM 1-3

---

## THE WESTMINSTER CONFESSION OF FAITH

ALTHOUGH the light of nature, and the works of creation and providence, do so far manifest the goodness, wisdom, and power of God, as to leave men inexcusable;[1] yet are they not sufficient to give that knowledge of God, and of his will, which is necessary unto salvation;[2] therefore it pleased the Lord, at sundry times, and in divers manners, to reveal himself, and to declare that his will unto his church;[3] and afterwards for the better preserving and propagating of the truth, and for the more sure establishment and comfort of the church against the corruption of the flesh, and the malice of Satan and of the world, to commit the same wholly unto writing;[4] which maketh the Holy Scripture to be most necessary;[5] those former ways of God's revealing his will unto his people being now ceased.[6]

---

## THE WESTMINSTER LARGER CATECHISM

Q. 1. *What is the chief and highest end of man?*

A. Man's chief and highest end is to glorify God,[1] and fully to enjoy him forever.[2]

GENERAL NOTE: — At several points the Larger Catechism is more specific in its statements than the Scriptures. These statements are inferences from the Scriptures, or from statements based on the Scriptures, or from the experience and observation of the Church. In such cases no texts are cited; but reference is made to this general note.
(1) Rom. 11:36; I Cor. 10:31.
(2) Psa. 73:24, 25, 26; John 17:22, 24.

Q. 2. *How doth it appear that there is a God?*

A. The very light of nature in man, and the works of God, declare plainly that there is a God;[1] but his word and Spirit only, do sufficiently and effectually reveal him unto men for their salvation.[2]
(1) Rom. 1:19, 20; Psa. 19:1-4.
(2) I Cor. 1:21; I Cor. 2:9, 10.

---

## THE WESTMINSTER SHORTER CATECHISM

Q. 1. *What is the chief end of man?*

A. Man's chief end is to glorify God,[1] and to enjoy him forever.[2]
(1) I Cor. 10: 31; Rom. 11:36.
(2) Psa. 73:24, 25, 26; John 17:22, 24.

| THE WESTMINSTER CONFESSION OF FAITH | THE WESTMINSTER LARGER CATECHISM | THE WESTMINSTER SHORTER CATECHISM |
|---|---|---|

GENERAL NOTE: — At several points the Confession of Faith is more specific in its statements than the Scriptures. These statements are inferences drawn from the Scriptures or from statements based on the Scriptures, or from the experience and observation of the Church. In such cases no texts are cited, but reference is made to this General Note.

(1) Rom. 1:19, 20; Rom. 2:14, 15; Rom. 1:32.
(2) I Cor. 1:21; I Cor. 2:13, 14; I Cor. 2:9-12; Acts 4:12; Rom. 10:13, 14.
(3) Heb. 1:1, 2; Gal. 1:11, 12; Deut. 4:12-14.
(4) Luke 24:27; II Tim. 3:16; Rom. 15:4; II Pet. 3:15, 16.
(5) Luke 16:29, 30, 31; Heb. 2:1-3; II Tim. 3:15, 16; II Pet. 1:10.
(6) See General Note above.

2. Under the name of Holy Scripture, or the word of God written, are now contained all the books of the Old and New Testaments, which are these:

*Of the Old Testament*

Genesis. Exodus. Leviticus. Numbers. Deuteronomy. Joshua. Judges. Ruth. Samuel, I. Samuel, II. Kings, I. Kings, II. Chronicles, I. Chronicles, II. Ezra. Nehemiah. Esther. Job. Psalms. Proverbs. Ecclesiastes. The Song of Songs. Isaiah. Jeremiah. Lamentations. Ezekiel. Daniel. Hosea. Joel. Amos. Obadiah. Jonah. Micah. Nahum. Habakkuk. Zephaniah. Haggai. Zechariah. Malachi.

*Of the New Testament*

The Gospel according to Matthew. Mark. Luke. John. The Acts of the Apostles. Paul's Epistles to the Romans. Corinthians, I. Corinthians, II. Galatians. Ephesians. Philippians. Colossians. Thessalonians, I. Thessalonians, II. To Timothy, I. To Timothy, II. To Titus. To Philemon. The Epistle to the Hebrews. The Epistle of James. The first and second Epistles of Peter. The first, second, and third Epistles of John. The Epistle of Jude. The Revelation.

All which are given by inspiration of God, to be the rule of faith and life.

Q. 3. *What is the word of God?*

A. The holy Scriptures of the Old and New Testaments are the word of God, the only rule of faith and obedience.[1]

(1) Gal. 1:8, 9; Isa. 8:20; Luke 16:29, 31; II Tim. 3:15-17.

Q. 2. *What rule hath God given to direct us how we may glorify and enjoy him?*

A. The word of God, which is contained in the Scriptures of the Old and New Testaments, is the only rule to direct us how we may glorify and enjoy him.[1]

(1) Gal. 1:8, 9; Isa. 8:20; Luke 16:29, 31; II Tim. 3:15-17.

## THE WESTMINSTER
## CONFESSION OF FAITH

## THE WESTMINSTER
## LARGER CATECHISM

## THE WESTMINSTER
## SHORTER CATECHISM

3. The books commonly called Apocrypha, not being of divine inspiration, are no part of the canon of the Scripture; and therefore are of no authority in the Church of God, nor to be any otherwise approved, or made use of, than other human writings.[7]

(7) The Canon of Scripture is not established by explicit passages, but by the testimony of Jesus and His Apostles; of ancient manuscripts and versions; of ancient Christian writers and church councils, and by the internal evidence exhibited in the separate books.

4. The authority of the Holy Scripture, for which it ought to be believed and obeyed, dependeth not upon the testimony of any man or church, but wholly upon God (who is truth itself), the author thereof; and therefore it is to be received, because it is the word of God.[8]

(8) I Thess. 2:13; II Tim. 3:16; II Pet. 1:21; Gal. 1:11, 12.

5. We may be moved and induced by the testimony of the church to an high and reverent esteem for the Holy Scripture; and the heavenliness of the matter, the efficacy of the doctrine, the majesty of the style, the consent of all the parts, the scope of the whole (which is to give all glory to God), the full discovery it makes of the only way of man's salvation, the many other incomparable excellencies, and the entire perfection thereof, are arguments whereby it doth abundantly evidence itself to be the word of God; yet, notwithstanding, our full persuasion and assurance of the infallible truth and divine authority thereof, is from the inward work of the Holy Spirit, bearing witness by and with the word in our hearts.[9]

(9) I Cor. 2:10, 11; John 16:13, 14; I Cor. 2:6-9.

6. The whole counsel of God, concerning all things necessary for

---

Q. 4. *How doth it appear that the Scriptures are the word of God?*

A. The Scriptures manifest themselves to be the word of God, by their majesty and purity; by the consent of all the parts, and the scope of the whole, which is to give all glory to God; by their light and power to convince and convert sinners, to comfort and build up believers unto salvation.[1] But the Spirit of God, bearing witness by and with the Scriptures in the heart of man, is alone able fully to persuade it that they are the very word of God.[2]

(1) See General Note, question 1 of Larger Catechism.

(2) John 16:13, 14; I Cor. 2:6-9.

THE WESTMINSTER
## CONFESSION OF FAITH

THE WESTMINSTER
## LARGER CATECHISM

THE WESTMINSTER
## SHORTER CATECHISM

his own glory, man s salvation, faith, and life, is either expressly set down in Scripture, or by good and necessary consequence may be deduced from Scripture:[10] unto which nothing at any time is to be added, whether by new revelations of the Spirit, or traditions of men.[11] Nevertheless we acknowledge the inward illumination of the Spirit of God to be necessary for the saving understanding of such things as are revealed in the word;[12] and that there are some circumstances concerning the worship of God, and government of the church, common to human actions and societies, which are to be ordered by the light of nature and Christian prudence, according to the general rules of the word, which are always to be observed.[13]

(10) Mark 7:5, 6, 7.
(11) This statement is an inference from the sufficiency of the Scriptures.
(12) John 6:45; I Cor. 2:9, 10, 12.
(13) I Cor. 14:26, 40; I Cor. 11:13, 14.

7. All things in Scripture are not alike plain in themselves, nor alike clear unto all;[14] yet those things which are necessary to be known, believed, and observed, for salvation, are so clearly propounded and opened in some place of Scripture or other, that not only the learned, but the unlearned, in a due use of the ordinary means, may attain unto a sufficient understanding of them.[15]

(14) II Pet. 3:16; John 16:17; John 6:60.
(15) Psalm 119:105, 130; Acts 17:11, 12.

8. The Old Testament in Hebrew (which was the native language of the people of God of old), and the New Testament in Greek (which at the time of the writing of it was most generally known to the nations), being immediately inspired by God,[16] and by his singular care and providence kept pure in all ages, are therefore authentical;

| THE WESTMINSTER CONFESSION OF FAITH | THE WESTMINSTER LARGER CATECHISM | THE WESTMINSTER SHORTER CATECHISM |
|---|---|---|

so as in all controversies of religion the church is finally to appeal unto them.[17] But because these original tongues are not known to all the people of God who have right unto, and interest in, the Scriptures, and are commanded, in the fear of God, to read and search them,[18] therefore they are to be translated into the language of every people unto which they come, that the word of God dwelling plentifully in all, they may worship him in an acceptable manner, and, through patience and comfort of the Scriptures, may have hope.[19]

(16) See note under Section 3, figure 7, above.
(17) Isa. 8:20; Acts 15:14-18.
(18) John 5:39; II Tim. 3:14, 15; II Pet. 1:19.
(19) I Cor. 14:6, 9, 11, 12, 24, 27, 28; Matt. 28:19, 20; Col. 3:16; Rom. 15:4.

9. The infallible rule of interpretation of Scripture, is the Scripture itself; and therefore, when there is a question about the true and full sense of any scripture (which is not manifold, but one), it may be searched and known by other places that speak more clearly.[20]

(20) Matt. 4:5, 6, 7; Matt. 12:1, 2, 3, 4, 5, 6, 7.

10. The Supreme Judge, by which all controversies of religion are to be determined, and all decrees of councils, opinions of ancient writers, doctrines of men, and private spirits, are to be examined, and in whose sentence we are to rest, can be no other but the Holy Spirit speaking in the Scripture.[21]

(21) Matt. 22:29, 31; Acts 28:25; Luke 10:26.

Q. 5. *What do the Scriptures principally teach?*

A. The Scriptures principally teach, what man is to believe concerning God, and what duty God requires of man.[1]

(1) See General Note, question 1 of **Larger Catechism.**

Q. 3. *What do the Scriptures principally teach?*

A. The Scriptures principally teach, what man is to believe concerning God, and what duty God requires of man.[1]

(1) Micah 6:8; John 20:31; John 3:16.

| THE WESTMINSTER CONFESSION OF FAITH | THE WESTMINSTER LARGER CATECHISM | THE WESTMINSTER SHORTER CATECHISM |
|---|---|---|

WHAT MAN OUGHT TO BELIEVE CONCERNING GOD

Q. 6. *What do the Scriptures make known of God?*

A. The Scriptures make known what God is,[1] the persons in the Godhead,[2] his decrees,[3] and the execution of his decrees.[4]

(1) John 4:24; Ex. 34:6, 7.
(2) Matt. 28:19; II Cor. 13:14.
(3) Eph. 1:11.
See the Context.
(4) Acts 4:27, 28; Isa. 42:9.

# EXPLANATORY NOTES

THE Confession and Catechisms agree in presenting the Scripture as the first object of faith. Note the singular "Scripture" in the Confession and the plural "Scriptures" in the Catechisms. The singular expresses unity; the plural denotes variety and diversity.

Why is faith in the Scripture placed in the forefront of our creed? Because what we believe about the Scripture determines what we believe about other matters pertaining to religion.

The first object of Satan's attack was the word of God. (Genesis 3:1-5.) Peter tells us that Christ was a stone of stumbling and a rock of offense to some because they stumbled at the word. (I Peter 2:8.)

## L.C. 1; S.C. 1

Both Catechisms approach the subject of the Scriptures by a preliminary question to which they give memorable answers.

The answers *imply* two things:

1. The true idea of God as alone in His Godhood, the one grand object of religion.
2. The true idea of man as religious and immortal in his nature, the great subject of religion.

The answers *assert* two things:

1. The duty of man, "to glorify God."
2. The destiny of man, "to enjoy Him."

Duty first; destiny follows.

Where, then, is human life properly centered? The life of the irreligious and ungodly is eccentric, out of focus. What is the circumference of a God-centered life? Of a self-centered life?

Why is this a good question and answer to lodge first in the heart of a child? Because it is designed to put the child at once in right relation to the Supreme Being. The first lesson of the Reformed creed is that man's first and final concern is not his own salvation but his service to the Sovereign God.

*Moffatt*: "The supreme interest in religion is conceived to be not the human soul in relation to its destiny, but the glory or the will of God." (*History of the Presbyterian Churches,* p. 177.)

*Augustine*: "Thou hast made us for Thyself, O God; and our heart is restless till it finds its rest in Thee." (*Confessions.* Bk. I, Ch. I.)

*Carlyle*: "The older I grow, and I am now upon the brink of Eternity, the more comes back to me the first sentence of the Catechism which I learned when a child, and the fuller and deeper its meaning becomes."

Thus the first statements of the Catechisms strike the keynote of Calvinism. They condense into pregnant sentences the Reformed conception of the significance of human life.

The virtue of the opening questions and answers of the Catechisms is the height of the plane upon which they move.

God who is the Beginning is also the Goal.

## CONF. 1:1; L.C. 2

The first section of the Confession and the second statement of the Larger Catechism name two sources of general religious knowledge: nature and human nature. "The light of nature" (Conf.); "The very light of nature in man" (L.C.).

The value of natural revelation is admitted, but its insufficiency is declared. It is sufficient to make known the existence of God and certain of His attributes, and to leave man inexcusable for his unbelief and idolatry; yet it is not sufficient for his salvation. Therefore it pleased God to provide two other sources of religious knowledge, namely, His Word and His Spirit.

So these parts of the Standards answer two important questions about the Word of God.

1. Why it was given.
2. Why it was written.

Our first concern is to know that God has spoken. "God . . . hath . . . spoken." (Heb. 1:1-2.)

## CONF. 1:2; L.C. 3; S.C. 2

Our second concern is to know what He has said.

The second section of the Confession, the third statement of the Larger Catechism, and the second statement of the Shorter tell us first what the Word of God is (the Scriptures of the Old and New Testaments); second, how it was given (by inspiration, Conf.); and third, why it was given (to be the rule of faith and life).

## CONF. 1:3

Section 2 is inclusive, specifying the books which are included in the canon. Section 3 is exclusive, specifying certain books which are excluded from the canon. Both the inclusion and the exclusion are justified (1) by internal evidence; that is, evidence furnished by the books themselves; (2) by external evidence; that is, evidence furnished by history, by the testimony of both Jews and Christians.

## CONF. 1:4

This section answers both negatively and positively this important question: On what does the authority of the Scripture depend? It depends upon its being the very word of God. The Scripture is authoritative just to the extent that it is true; and it is true just to the extent that it is the word of God.

## CONF. 1:5; L.C. 4

Herein is given the warrant for believing that the Scripture is the very word of God. The warrant is not single but double, nay, triple: the witness of the Scripture, the witness of the Spirit, and the witness of the heart of man. It is this conjoint testimony that convinces and satisfies. Where the Book and the breast agree, there the soul in safety may rest.

Mark the clause in the Larger Catechism: "The Scriptures manifest *themselves* to be the word of God." That is, they are self-evidencing, seen to be true in their own light — the light of what they are and what they do. The word "scope" as used here is archaic, and signifies purpose or design.

"When you have read the Bible, you will know that it is the Word of God, because you will have found the key to your own heart, your own happiness, and your own duty." (Woodrow Wilson.)

## CONF. 1:6-10

As the vacant parallel columns show, there is nothing in the Catechisms that corresponds to sections 6-10 in the Confession. These sections are added to combat Romish errors and complete the Protestant doctrine.

To this point the nature of Scripture is set forth; from here to the end of the chapter the sufficiency of the Scripture is the theme. Sufficiency includes fullness, clearness, and finality.

## CONF. 1:6

Section 6 teaches that the Scripture is sufficient in its content, being the "whole counsel of God," unto which nothing at any time needs to be added. This section admits that not everything allowable in the worship of God has been prescribed. In other words, not everything is proscribed which has not been prescribed. The church could easily make too free a use of this doctrine of expediency. Yet see end of section 1 in Chapter XXIII.

## CONF. 1:7

Section 7 relates to the clearness of Scripture. It distinguishes between "things plain" and "things not plain," and affirms that those things which are necessary to be known, believed, and observed for salvation are among the "plain." So that the un-learned, in the due use of the ordinary means, may find the way of life. The Bible is addressed to all men, and in its essential message is level to the un-derstanding of every sincere soul.

"Protestants affirm and Romanists deny (1) that every essential article of faith and rule of practice may be learned from the Scripture; and (2) that private and unlearned Christians may be safely al-lowed to interpret Scripture for themselves." (Hodge on the Confession, p. 63.)

## CONF. 1:8

Section 8 teaches (1) that the Old and New Tes-taments in their original languages were inspired, and therefore free from error; and therefore full and final in their authority; and (2) that while translations into the languages of all peoples are necessary, in religious controversies final appeal is not to be made unto them, but unto the Scripture in the language of inspiration. This paragraph is pointed against Catholics whose appeal is to the Latin Vulgate and the Church.

The accuracy of the statement that the Scrip-tures have been "kept pure in all ages" may be questioned by some who know that the Scriptures have been corrupted in not a few places Yet, not-withstanding, it can be truthfully said that the im-purities of the sacred text are not such as to affect in the least either the doctrines or the design of the Book. The authority and infallibility of Scrip-ture are not impaired by the imperfections and vari-ations of the manuscripts: just as the sovereign rule and service of the sun are not impaired by the spots on its surface.

## CONF. 1:9-10

Sections 9 and 10 relate to interpretation and teach that the Scriptures are self-interpreting when studied comparatively with the aid of the divine Spirit, who is the Supreme Judge in all matters of religious debate and doctrine.

This is a phase of the doctrine of the sufficiency of the Scriptures.

### SUMMARIES AND QUESTIONS

The Catechisms set before us:

1. The chief end of man.
2. The chief end of Scripture.
3. The chief content of Scripture.

As to the revelation of God in the Scripture the Standards teach:

1. The necessity of it.
2. The authority of it.
3. The completeness of it.
   Completeness includes clearness, fullness, and finality. "The whole counsel of God," "to commit . . . wholly unto writing." Find those phrases.

What do the Standards teach as to inspiration? Is it true, as sometimes alleged, that the Standards contain no theory of inspiration? What is the dif-ference between the doctrine and the theory of in-spiration? Consider the following questions: Do the Standards teach

1. The fact of inspiration?
2. The nature of it?
3. The extent of it?
4. The design and effect of it?

Is the Confessional treatise on the Scriptures ade-quate for today? Is the doctrine of Scripture con-tained in the Standards defensible today?

**L.C. 5; S.C. 3**

Above, under Confession I:2, L. C. 3, and S.C. 2 we have "the only rule" of the Christian religion in its matter: the Word of God. Here we have the only rule in its principal parts:

1. Truth to be believed.
2. Duty to be done.

That is, the Scriptures are mainly occupied with two matters: doctrine and duty, faith and life; these are for God's glory and man's good.

The answers to questions 5 and 3 of the Catechisms furnish the basis for the major divisions of the catechetical treatises. Questions 1-90 of the Larger Catechism and 1-38 of the Shorter Catechism are concerned with matters of faith, while questions 91-196 of the Larger Catechism and questions 39-107 of the Shorter deal with matters of practice.

The chapters of the Confession may be conveniently grouped under three heads:

1. Matters of faith (doctrine). I-XX, XXXIV-XXXV.
2. Matters of practice (life). XXI, XXVI.
3. Matters of administration and discipline (polity). XXVII-XXXIII

**L.C. 6**

The Larger Catechism opens its discussion of the question, What Man Ought to Believe Concerning God, by distributing the Bible teaching about God into four parts. Name them. Does man need to know any other thing about God?

# CHAPTER II

# Of God, and of the Holy Trinity

CONFESSION OF FAITH II:1-3
LARGER CATECHISM 7-11 · SHORTER CATECHISM 4-6

## THE WESTMINSTER CONFESSION OF FAITH

THERE is but one only living and true God,[1] who is infinite in being and perfection,[2] a most pure spirit,[3] invisible,[4] without body, parts, or passions,[5] immutable,[6] immense,[7] eternal,[8] incomprehensible,[9] almighty;[10] most wise,[11] most holy,[12] most free,[13] most absolute,[14] working all things according to the counsel of his own immutable and most righteous will,[15] for his own glory;[16] most loving,[17] gracious, merciful, long-suffering, abundant in goodness and truth, forgiving iniquity, transgression, and sin;[18] the rewarder of them that diligently seek him;[19] and withal most just and terrible in his judgments;[20] hating all sin,[21] and who will by no means clear the guilty.[22]

(1) Deut. 6:4; I Cor. 8:4, 6; I Thess. 1:9; Jer. 10:10.
(2) Jer. 23:24; Psa. 147:5; I Kings 8:27; Psa. 139.
(3) John 4:24.
(4) I Tim. 1:17.
(5) Luke 24:39; Deut. 4:15, 16.
(6) James 1:17.
(7) I Kings 8:27; Jer. 23:23, 24.
(8) Psa. 90:2; I Tim. 1:17.
(9) Rom. 11:33; Psa. 145:3.
(10) Rev. 4:8.
(11) Rom. 16:27.
(12) Isa. 6:3; Rev. 4:8.
(13) Psa. 115:3.
(14) Isa. 44:6; Acts 17:24, 25.
(15) Eph. 1:11.
(16) Rom. 11:36; Rev. 4:11.
(17) I John 4:8, 9, 10.
(18) Ex. 34:6, 7.
(19) Heb. 11:6.
(20) Neh. 9:32, 33.
(21) Hab. 1:13; Psa. 5: 5, 6.
(22) Ex. 34:7; Nahum 1:2, 3.

## THE WESTMINSTER LARGER CATECHISM

Q. 7. *What is God?*

A. God is a Spirit,[1] in and of himself infinite in being,[2] glory, blessedness, and perfection;[3] all-sufficient,[4] eternal,[5] unchangeable,[6] incomprehensible,[7] everywhere present,[8] almighty;[9] knowing all things,[10] most wise,[11] most holy,[12] most just,[13] most merciful and gracious, long-suffering, and abundant in goodness and truth.[14]

(1) John 4:24.
(2) I Kings 8:27; Isa. 40:20.
(3) See General Note, under question 1 of Larger Catechism.
(4) Acts 17:24, 25.
(5) Psa. 90:2.
(6) Mal. 3:6; James 1:17.
(7) Rom. 11:33.
(8) Jer. 23:24; Psa. 139.
(9) Rev. 4:8.
(10) Heb. 4:13; Psa. 147:5.
(11) Rom. 16:27.
(12) Isa. 6:3; Rev. 15:4.
(13) Deut. 32:4.
(14) Ex. 34:6.

Q. 8. *Are there more gods than one?*

A. There is but one only, the living and true God.[1]

(1) Deut. 6:4; I Cor. 8:4, 6; Jer. 10:10.

## THE WESTMINSTER SHORTER CATECHISM

Q. 4. *What is God?*

A. God is a Spirit,[1] infinite, eternal, and unchangeable, in his being,[2] wisdom,[3] power,[4] holiness,[5] justice,[6] goodness,[7] and truth.[8]

(1) John 4:24.
(2) Ps. 90:2; Mal. 3:6; James 1:17; I Kings 8:27; Jer. 23:24; Isa. 40:22.
(3) Psa. 147:5; Rom. 16:27.
(4) Gen. 17:1; Rev. 19:6.
(5) Isa. 57:15; John 17:11; Rev. 4:8.
(6) Deut. 32:4.
(7) Psa. 100:5; Rom. 2:4.
(8) Exod. 34:6; Psa. 117:2.

Q. 5. *Are there more gods than one?*

A. There is but one only, the living and true God.[1]

(1) Deut. 6:4; Jer. 10:10.

| THE WESTMINSTER CONFESSION OF FAITH | THE WESTMINSTER LARGER CATECHISM | THE WESTMINSTER SHORTER CATECHISM |
|---|---|---|

2. God hath all life, glory, goodness, blessedness, in and of himself;[23] and is alone in and unto himself all-sufficient, not standing in need of any creatures which he hath made, nor deriving any glory from them, but only manifesting his own glory in, by, unto, and upon them;[24] he is the alone fountain of all being, of whom, through whom, and to whom, are all things;[25] and hath most sovereign dominion over them, to do by them, for them, or upon them, whatsoever himself pleaseth.[26] In his sight all things are open and manifest;[27] his knowledge is infinite, infallible, and independent upon the creature;[28] so as nothing is to him contingent or uncertain.[29] He is most holy in all his counsels, in all his works, and in all his commands.[30] To him is due from angels and men, and every other creature, whatsoever worship, service, or obedience he is pleased to require of them.[31]

(23) John 5:26; Acts 7:2; Psa. 119:68; I Tim. 6:15; Rom. 9:5.
(24) Acts 17:24, 25.
(25) Rom. 11:36; Isa. 40:12-17.
(26) Dan. 4:25; Eph. 1:11.
(27) Heb. 4:13.
(28) Rom. 11:33, 34; Psa. 147:5.
(29) Isa. 46:9, 10, 11; Acts 15:18; Ezek. 11:5.
(30) Psa. 145:17; Rom. 7:12.
(31) Rev. 7:11, 12; Rev. 5:12-14.

3. In the unity of the Godhead there be three persons of one substance, power, and eternity: God the Father, God the Son, and God the Holy Ghost.[32] The Father is of none, neither begotten nor proceeding; the Son is eternally begotten of the Father;[33] the Holy Ghost eternally proceeding from the Father and the Son.[34]

(32) Matt. 28:19; II Cor. 13:14; Matt. 3:16, 17.
(33) John 1:14, 18; John 17:24.
(34) Gal. 4:6; John 15:26.

**Q. 9.** *How many persons are there in the Godhead?*

**A.** There be three persons in the Godhead: the Father, the Son, and the Holy Ghost; and these three are one true, eternal God, the same in substance, equal in power and glory: although distinguished by their personal properties.[1]

(1) Matt. 3:16, 17; Matt. 28:19; II Cor. 13:14.

**Q. 6.** *How many persons are there in the Godhead?*

**A.** There are three persons in the Godhead: the Father, the Son, and the Holy Ghost; and these three are one God, the same in substance, equal in power and glory.[1]

(1) II Cor. 13:14; Matt. 28:19; Matt. 3:16, 17.

| THE WESTMINSTER CONFESSION OF FAITH | THE WESTMINSTER LARGER CATECHISM | THE WESTMINSTER SHORTER CATECHISM |
|---|---|---|
| | Q. 10. *What are the personal properties of the three persons in the Godhead?* | |
| | A. It is proper to the Father to beget the Son,[1] and to the Son to be begotten of the Father,[2] and to the Holy Ghost to proceed from the Father and the Son, from all eternity.[3]<br>(1) Heb. 1:5, 6.<br>(2) John 1:14.<br>(3) Gal. 4:6; John 15: 26. | |
| | Q. 11. *How doth it appear that the Son and the Holy Ghost are God equal with the Father?* | |
| | A. The Scriptures manifest that the Son and the Holy Ghost are God equal with the Father, ascribing unto them such names,[1] attributes,[2] works,[3] and worship,[4] as are proper to God only.<br>(1) Jer. 23:6; I John 5:20; Psa. 45:6; Acts 5:3, 4.<br>(2) John 1:1; Isa. 9:6; John 2:24, 25; I Cor. 2:10, 11; Heb. 9:14.<br>(3) Col. I:16; Gen. 1:2; Psa. 104:30; John 1:3.<br>(4) Matt. 28:19; II Cor. 13:14. | |

## EXPLANATORY NOTES

HERE we have the first two things which the Larger Catechism says (under question 6) the Scriptures teach about God:

1. What He is.
2. The Persons in the Godhead.

Note that the first question of the Standards about God is not, Is He? but, What is He? The Bible at Genesis 1:1 and elsewhere assumes that the being of God is too evident to need either assertion or argument, proof or proclamation.

### CONF. II:1; L.C. 7; S.C. 4

The Confession and the two Catechisms here tell us what God is in Himself — in His nature and attributes.

Of the three statements, which is the most impressive? As a definition of indefinable Deity, the Shorter Catechism is unexcelled, unequaled by any other word of man. When one compares the Shorter Catechism with the other two Standards at this point, one is reminded of the saying that the adjective is the enemy of the noun.

1. Note the superlatives in the Confession and the Larger Catechism.
2. Find the words which express the nature of God.
3. Gather the adjectives descriptive of His attributes under the following heads:
   a. Essential (those descriptive of His essence).
   b. Intellectual.
   c. Moral.
   d. Emotional.

## CONF. II:2

This section makes known what God is in relation to other existences. In the first half it is affirmed that God is

1. Self-existent.
2. Self-sufficient.
3. The sole source and end of all things.
4. Sovereign over all things.

In the second half it is affirmed that God is

1. All-knowing — omniscient.
2. All-holy — morally perfect.
3. All-worshipful — entitled to require and receive the worship and service of all creation.

Does not the second section repeat some ideas expressed in the first section?

## CONF. II:3a; L.C. 8-9; S.C. 5-6

After the question, What is God? comes the question, How is God? What is the manner of His existence?

God is one, yet three; three, yet one. Is this a mathematical absurdity? As the Unitarians state it, Yes; as we state it, No. God is not one *and* three. One and three make four. God is one *in* three. He is not one in the same sense as He is three. He is one in being, in nature; threefold in the manner of His being. In the one nature is a threefold personal distinction.

The truth about God is the reverse of the truth about man. Man is two natures (body and soul) in one person; God is one nature in three Persons.

In other words, man is plural in his nature but singular in his personality, while God is singular in His nature and plural in His personality. Is triplicity of personality in unity of substance any more absurd than duality of substance in unity of personality?

We — Unitarians with the rest — accept the doctrine of man in spite of its mystery. May we not rationally do the same with respect to the doctrine of God?

## CONF. II:3b; L.C. 10

What is the difference between attribute and property? Popularly there is no difference, but technically there is. Attributes are common to the Persons, whereas properties are peculiar to the Persons. All the attributes of God belong to each Person of the Godhead, but each Person has a property which He does not share with the other two.

The property of the first Person is fatherhood, begetting, generation — three ways of saying the same thing.

The property of the second Person is sonship or filiation.

The property of the third Person is procession.

How are the three Persons related to the divine activity in creation, providence, and redemption?

In all acts outside the Godhead the three concur. But there is an order of operation which is invariable. The Father sends the Son and the Spirit, and works through them. The Son sends the Spirit, and works through Him. This order is never reversed.

### SUMMARY
### SUBJECT: GOD

1. Is He? He is.
2. What is He? He is Spirit. He is infinite in His perfections.
3. How is He? He is one in His threeness; He is three in His oneness.
   His name in His unity: God.
   His name in His trinity: Father, Son, Spirit.
4. How are the persons distinguished?
   Not by difference of substance,

Not by difference of attributes,
Not by difference of power and glory;
But by difference of properties,
And by difference of operations.

5. How are the Persons related to one another?
Same in substance,
Equal in rank,
Subordinate in office or function. (The Holy
Spirit is subordinate to the Father and the Son;
the Son is subordinate to the Father only. The
Father is always first, the Son second, and the
Spirit third. The subordination is of office or
function, not of Person; and it is in the inter-
est of economy and efficiency.)

Such is the picture of God as presented by our
Standards. Is it an attractive portrait? It is both
winsome and awesome; it allures while it alarms.
The only way to escape Him is to flee to Him.

## L.C. 11

The Larger Catechism goes beyond the Confession
and Shorter Catechism in that it outlines an argument for the deity of the Son and of the Holy
Spirit. The argument is fourfold. The only way to
prove that the Father is God is by His names, attributes, works, and worship. By the same method
it can be shown that the Son is God and that the
Spirit is God. If they are the owners of the same
names and attributes, the authors of the same
works, and the objects of the same worship, it ought
not to be doubted that they are God — equal with
the Father.

# CHAPTER III

# Of God's Eternal Decrees

CONFESSION OF FAITH III:1-8*
LARGER CATECHISM 12-13 · SHORTER CATECHISM 7

| THE WESTMINSTER CONFESSION OF FAITH | THE WESTMINSTER LARGER CATECHISM | THE WESTMINSTER SHORTER CATECHISM |
|---|---|---|

GOD from all eternity did by the most wise and holy counsel of his own will, freely and unchangeably ordain whatsoever comes to pass;[1] yet so as thereby neither is God the author of sin;[2] nor is violence offered to the will of the creatures, nor is the liberty or contingency of second causes taken away, but rather established.[3]

(1) Eph. 1:11; Acts 4:27, 28; Matt. 10:29, 30; Eph. 2:10.
(2) James 1:13; I John 1:5.
(3) Acts 2:23; Matt. 17:12; Acts 4:27, 28; John 19:11; Prov. 16:33; Acts 27:23, 24, 34, 44.

2. Although God knows whatsoever may or can come to pass, upon all supposed conditions;[4] yet hath he not decreed anything because he foresaw it as future, or as that which would come to pass, upon such conditions.[5]

(4) I Sam. 23:11, 12; Matt. 11:21, 23; Psa. 139:1-4.
(5) Rom. 9:11, 13, 16, 18; II Tim. 1:9; Eph. 1:4-5.

3. By the decree of God, for the manifestation of his glory, some men and angels are predestinated unto everlasting life,[6] and others fore-ordained to everlasting death.[7]

(6) I Tim. 5:21; Acts 13:48; Rom. 8:29, 30; John 10:27-29.
(7) Matt. 25:41; Rom. 9:22, 23; Jude 4.

4. These angels and men, thus predestinated and fore-ordained, are particularly and unchangeably designed; and their number is so cer-

Q. 12. *What are the decrees of God?*

A. God's decrees are the wise, free, and holy acts of the counsel of his will, whereby, from all eternity, he hath, for his own glory, unchangeably foreordained whatsoever comes to pass in time,[1] especially concerning angels and men.

(1) Eph.1:4, 11; Acts 4:27, 28; Psa. 33:11.

Q. 13. *What hath God especially decreed concerning angels and men?*

A. God, by an eternal and immutable decree, out of his mere love, for the praise of his glorious grace, to be manifested in due time, hath elected some angels to glory;[1] and, in Christ, hath chosen some men to eternal life, and the means thereof;[2] and also, according to his sovereign power, and the unsearchable counsel of his own will (whereby

Q. 7. *What are the decrees of God?*

A. The decrees of God are, his eternal purpose, according to the counsel of his will, whereby, for his own glory, he hath foreordained whatsoever comes to pass.[1]

(1) Eph. 1:11; Acts 4:27, 28; Psa. 33:11; Eph. 2:10; Rom. 9:22, 23; 11:33.

*The One Hundred First General Assembly (April, 1961) received the Report of the Ad Interim Committee on Possible Revision of Chapter III of the Confession of Faith and approved its recommendations, including the following:

"That the General Assembly declare that in its judgment the doctrine of fore-ordination to everlasting death as formulated in the Confession is not an adequate statement of Christian faith . . ."

For full report of the Ad Interim Committee, see Minutes of the One Hundred First General Assembly of the Presbyterian Church in the United States, pages 39, 132-139.

THE WESTMINSTER
## CONFESSION OF FAITH

THE WESTMINSTER
## LARGER CATECHISM

THE WESTMINSTER
## SHORTER CATECHISM

tain and definite that it cannot be either increased or diminished.[8]

(8)  John 10:14, 15, 16, 27, 28, 29; John 6:37, 38, 39; John 13:18; Acts 13:48; II Tim. 2:19.

5. Those of mankind that are predestinated unto life, God, before the foundation of the world was laid,[9] according to his eternal and immutable purpose,[10] and the secret counsel and good pleasure of his will,[11] hath chosen in Christ,[12] unto everlasting glory,[13] out of his free grace and love alone, without any foresight of faith or good works, or perseverance in either of them, or any other thing in the creature, as conditions, or causes moving him thereunto;[14] and all to the praise of his glorious grace.[15]

(9)  Eph. 1:4.
(10) Eph. 1:11.
(11) Eph. 1:9.
(12) II Tim. 1:9.
(13) Rom. 8:30; I Pet. 5:10.
(14) II Tim. 1:9; Eph. 1:6; Eph. 2:8, 9.
(15) Eph. 1:5, 6, 12.

6. As God hath appointed the elect unto glory, so hath he, by the eternal and most free purpose of his will, fore-ordained all the means thereunto.[16] Wherefore they who are elected being fallen in Adam, are redeemed by Christ,[17] are effectually called unto faith in Christ by his Spirit working in due season;[18] are justified,[19] adopted,[20] sanctified,[21] and kept by his power through faith unto salvation.[22] Neither are any other redeemed by Christ, effectually called, justified adopted, sanctified, and saved, but the elect only.[23]

he extendeth or withholdeth favor as he pleaseth) hath passed by, and foreordained the rest to dishonor and wrath, to be for their sin inflicted, to the praise of the glory of his justice.[3]

(1)  I Tim. 5:21.
(2)  Eph. 1:4, 5, 6; II Thess. 2:13, 14; I Pet. 1:2.
(3)  Rom. 9:17, 18, 21, 22; Jude 4; Matt. 11:25, 26; II Tim. 2:20.

| THE WESTMINSTER **CONFESSION OF FAITH** | THE WESTMINSTER **LARGER CATECHISM** | THE WESTMINSTER **SHORTER CATECHISM** |
|---|---|---|

(16) Eph. 2:10; II Thess. 2:13; I Pet. 1:2; Eph. 1:4.

(17) Rom. 5:19; I Thess. 5:9, 10; Tit. 2:14.

(18) Rom. 9:11; II Thess. 2:13, 14; I Cor. 1:9.

(19) Rom. 8:30.

(20) Eph. 1:5.

(21) Eph. 1:4; I Thess. 4:3; II Thess. 2:13.

(22) I Pet. 1:5; John 10:28.

(23) John 17:9; John 6:64, 65; John 8:47; John 10:26; Acts 13:48; I John 2:19.

7. The rest of mankind, God was pleased, according to the unsearchable counsel of his own will, whereby he extendeth or withholdeth mercy as he pleaseth, for the glory of his sovereign power over his creatures, to pass by,[24] and to ordain them to dishonor and wrath for their sin,[25] to the praise of his glorious justice. [26]

(24) Matt. 11:25, 26.

(25) Rom. 2:8, 9; II Thess. 2:10, 11, 12; Rom. 9:14-22.

(26) Rev. 15:3, 4.

8. The doctrine of this high mystery of predestination is to be handled with special prudence and care, that men attending the will of God revealed in his word, and yielding obedience thereunto, may, from the certainty of their effectual vocation, be assured of their eternal election. So shall this doctrine afford matter of praise, reverence, and admiration of God; and of humility, diligence, and abundant consolation to all that sincerely obey the gospel.[27]

(27) See General Note, Confession of Faith, Chapter 1, Section 1.

## EXPLANATORY NOTES

THIS is the third of the four things which the Scriptures teach about God, according to the Larger Catechism under question 6.

This is one of the hard articles of our Creed. There is mystery in it. Let no one enter here who is unwilling to put the shoes from his feet. If a man cannot accept what he cannot understand, he can find no standing room here. Indeed, he can find no standing room anywhere in the Bible or in the world.

Let the student give diligence to ascertain just what the Standards do say on the subject of the decrees, and then consider whether what they say is derived from Scripture. It is well to recall here that the framers of the Standards bound themselves by an oath not to propose or approve anything for inclusion in the Creed which is not contained in the Scriptures explicitly or by good and necessary inference deducible therefrom. The contents of these Confessional statements were drawn from the Scriptures and defended by the Scriptures.

Sections 3 and 4 of this chapter of the Confession offend some by the baldness of their statements. They contain no intimation that the angels and men foreordained to everlasting death were contemplated as fallen. The Standards elsewhere make it clear that both election and preterition presuppose creation and the fall; but the sections before us contain no such implication. Their form was probably due to supralapsarian influence. These sections should not be read by themselves but in the context of the rest of the Standards. I have thought and still think that these sections may be omitted without loss of or detriment to any principle essential to the integrity of the Calvinistic system.

### CONF.III:1-2; L.C. 12; S.C. 7

Do not stumble at the word "decrees." It has evil associations when used of men, but not when used of God. The decrees of God are defined by the Shorter Catechism as "His eternal purpose." Purpose and plan are familiar words, and free from objection. When it is understood that the decree of

God is His purpose and plan, the doctrine of the decree should be less contested and detested.

The Confession and the Shorter Catechism regard the decrees of God in their unity: they are His purpose, not purposes. The Larger Catechism, on the other hand, regards the decrees in their plurality: they are the "acts of the counsel of His will." So it is proper to speak of God's decree or of God's decrees. His decrees are one, and also many; one whole of many parts.

The Shorter Catechism sets forth the decree or purpose of God in its broadest scope. The Confession and the Larger Catechism present it in both the broad and narrow aspects. The name for God's purpose in its general reference is foreordination. The name for that purpose in its specific reference is predestination; though foreordination is sometimes used in this restricted sense.

Predestination is God's will as it affects the destiny of moral agents: angels and men. In the Standards it is applied only to the elect — foreordained is the word used of the non-elect. Those who are predestinated to life are said to be chosen (section 5); while those who are foreordained to death are said to be passed by (section 7).

Now this purpose of God neither in its positive nor in its negative aspect is arbitrary or capricious. It is said to be "according to the unsearchable counsel of His own will," *i.e.*, conceived in wisdom.

The purpose of God as it relates both to the chosen and the passed by is described in the Standards:

1. As eternal.
   The purpose He now has with respect to His rational creatures He has always had and always will have.

2. As most wise and holy.
   It is consistent with His character and with the nature of His creatures.

3. As unchangeable.
   He cannot change it for the better, as it is most wise and holy; and He will not change it for the worse.

4. As all-comprehending.

It includes whatsoever comes to pass.

5. As unconditional.

That is, it is not conditioned by anything outside of God, by anything in the creature. All God's actions are conditioned by His character and His self-chosen ends.

6. As effectual.

This means that His purpose and plan will certainly work out to their predestined end. This eternal purpose of God means certainty, though not fate or necessity.

## CONF. III:3-7; L.C. 13

These statements analyzed yield the following points about God's predestination or foreordination of men and angels.

1. The time of it. It took place before time began.

2. The nature of it. The act, whether of choice or of passing by, was free, sovereign, personal, and final.

The choice was an act of grace; the passing by, an act of justice.

3. The ground of it.

That is, the basis or reason of the act in either case. "The . . . good pleasure of His will." The election was not based on the foresight of good in those chosen. The passing by was not based on the foresight of evil in those left. The reason for God's act of discrimination is in Him, not in man; and it hath not pleased Him to disclose it. It is useless to speculate about it. It is irreverent to find fault with the divine will. The only right thing to do is to uncover and bow our heads, and say with Jesus, "Yea, Father, for so it was well-pleasing in thy sight." (Matt. 11:26;* Deut. 29:29.)

---

*This and other quotations from the American Standard Version are copyrighted by the International Council of Religious Education and used by permission.

4. The end or purpose of it.

The praise of His grace on the one hand and the praise of His justice on the other.

5. The means appointed for the carrying of His purpose of election into effect. Name them. (Section 6.)

6. The certainty of the application of these means and the results in experience. (Section 6.)

Christ's work was done not merely nor mainly to make the salvation of all men possible, but to make the salvation of some men certain.

7. One feature of the Confession and Larger Catechism under this head remains to be noticed. Elect men are said to be chosen "in Christ." That is the language of Scripture. What does it mean? It cannot mean that they were in Christ before they were chosen. We believe that union with Christ is a consequence of election, not the cause or condition of it. With my present light the best I can say is this: When the Standards and the Scripture say that elect men were chosen in Christ, the meaning is that Christ was the medium of their choice. They were chosen with reference to His mediation. Elect angels were not so chosen. God's choice of them was supralapsarian, while His choice of men was sublapsarian. That is, elect angels were chosen before they fell not to fall but to stand. Elect men were chosen after they had fallen to rise from this fall. The words "before" and "after" here are not temporal but logical; they denote not sequence of time but of thought. These acts of God antedate time.

## CONF. III:8

This section tells us:

1. How the mysterious doctrine of predestination should be preached — with care.

2. To whom it should be preached — to those attending, and yielding obedience; that is, to Christians or saints.

3. Why it should be preached — for assurance and comfort.

# CHAPTER IV

# Of Creation

CONFESSION OF FAITH IV:1-2
LARGER CATECHISM 14-17 · SHORTER CATECHISM 8-10

| THE WESTMINSTER **CONFESSION OF FAITH** | THE WESTMINSTER **LARGER CATECHISM** | THE WESTMINSTER **SHORTER CATECHISM** |
|---|---|---|
| | Q. 14. *How doth God execute his decrees?* | Q. 8. *How doth God execute his decrees?* |
| | A. God executeth his decrees in the works of creation and providence, according to his infallible foreknowledge, and the free and immutable counsel of his own will.[1] | A. God executeth his decrees in the works of creation and providence.[1] |
| | (1) Eph. 1:11; I Pet. 1:1, 2. | (1) Rev. 4:11; Eph. 1:11. |
| It pleased God the Father, Son, and Holy Ghost, for the manifestation of the glory of his eternal power, wisdom, and goodness, in the beginning, to create or make of nothing the world, and all things therein, whether visible or invisible, in the space of six days, and all very good.[1] | Q. 15. *What is the work of creation?* | Q. 9. *What is the work of creation?* |
| | A. The work of creation is that wherein God did in the beginning, by the word of his power, make of nothing, the world and all things therein for himself, within the space of six days, and all very good.[1] | A. The work of creation is, God's making all things of nothing, by the word of his power, in the space of six days, and all very good.[1] |
| (1) Gen. 1:1, 2, 3; Ex. 20:11; Jer. 10:12; Col. 1:16; John 1:2, 3; Heb. 1:2; Heb. 11:3; Psa. 104:24; Gen., chapter 1. | (1) Heb. 11:3; Rev. 4:11; Gen. 1. | (1) Heb. 11:3; Rev. 4:11; Gen. 1:1-31. |
| | Q. 16. *How did God create angels?* | |
| | A. God created all the angels, spirits,[1] immortal,[2] holy,[3] excelling in knowledge,[4] mighty in power;[5] to execute his commandments, and to praise his name,[6] yet subject to change.[7] | |
| | (1) Psa. 104:4; Col. 1:16.<br>(2) Luke 20:36.<br>(3) Gen. 1:31.<br>(4) Matt. 24:36.<br>(5) II Thess. 1:7.<br>(6) Psa. 103:20, 21.<br>(7) II Pet. 2:4. | |
| 2. After God had made all other creatures, he created man, male and female,[2] with reasonable and im- | Q. 17. *How did God create man?*<br>A. After God had made all other creatures, he created man, male and | Q. 10. *How did God create man?*<br>A. God created man, male and female, after his own image,[1] in |

| THE WESTMINSTER CONFESSION OF FAITH | THE WESTMINSTER LARGER CATECHISM | THE WESTMINSTER SHORTER CATECHISM |
|---|---|---|

mortal souls,[3] endued with knowledge, righteousness, and true holiness after his own image,[4] having the law of God written in their hearts,[5] and power to fulfill it; and yet under a possibility of transgression, being left to the liberty of their own will, which was subject unto change.[6] Besides this law written in their hearts, they received a command not to eat of the tree of the knowledge of good and evil;[7] which while they kept they were happy in their communion with God,[8] and had dominion over the creatures.[9]

(2) Gen. 1:27.
(3) Psa. 8:5, 6; Gen. 2:19, 20; Luke 23:43; Matt. 10:28.
(4) Gen. 1:26; Col. 3:10; Eph. 4:24.
(5) Rom. 2:14, 15.
(6) Gen. 2:16, 17; Gen. 3:6, 17.
(7) Gen. 2:16, 17.
(8) Gen. 2:17; Gen. 3:8, 9, 10, 11, 23.
(9) Gen. 1:28; Psa. 8:6-8.

female;[1] formed the body of the man of the dust of the ground,[2] and the woman of the rib of the man;[3] endued them with living, reasonable, and immortal souls;[4] made them after his own image,[5] in knowledge,[6] righteousness and holiness,[7] having the law of God written in their hearts,[8] and power to fulfill it, with dominion over the creatures;[9] yet subject to fall.[10]

(1) Gen. 1:27.
(2) Gen. 2:7.
(3) Gen. 2:22.
(4) Gen. 2:7; Matt. 10:28; Luke 23:43.
(5) Gen. 1:27.
(6) Col. 3:10; Gen. 2:19, 20.
(7) Eph. 4:24.
(8) Rom. 2:14, 15.
(9) Gen. 1:28.
(10) Gen. 2:16, 17; Gen. 3:6.

knowledge, righteousness, and holiness,[2] with dominion over the creatures.[3]

(1) Gen. 1:27.
(2) Col. 3:10; Eph. 4:24.
(3) Gen. 1:28.

# EXPLANATORY NOTES

## L.C. 14; S.C. 8

Here we come to the last of the four things which the Scriptures make known of God; namely, the execution of His decrees. God executes His decrees in two major works — those of creation and providence. Redemption, His greatest work, is not mentioned here. Why? Because it is included under the head of providence.

## CONF. IV:1; L.C. 15; S.C.9

As the statement in the Confession contains all that is in the Catechisms and more, we may pass at once to the analysis of section 1. The subject of this section is the creation of the world. Here we find the best answer anywhere to be found to the following questions:

1. How did the world come to be?

   The answers which have been given to this question may best be given in this order:

   a. The world is a chance formation: atomistic, materialistic, monistic.

   b. Conscious formation: platonic, dualistic. Matter as well as mind is eternal. God, who is mind, took matter in hand and formed the best world He could out of it.

   c. Voluntary yet unconscious emanation: pantheistic, monistic, practically atheistic.

   d. Conscious, purposive creation: monistic (before creation, dualistic after creation); Mosaic, theistic, Christian.

2. Who created (or made) the world?

3. How did He make it?

4. Why did He make it?

"For Himself." (Larger Catechism.)

Mark the attributes glorified in creation. (Confession.)

Note the classification of things made.

## L.C. 16

The Larger Catechism is peculiar in devoting a question and answer to the creation of angels. This brief statement tells us several things about these heavenly beings.

1. Their nature.

Angels are not a race, but a company. There is no kinship among them; each is a separate creation.

2. Their excellency. Whom do they excell and how?

3. The purpose of their creation.

4. Their mutability — liability to change.

## CONF. IV:2; L.C. 17; S.C. 10

The topic here is the creation of man. These parts of the Standards introduce us to the great subject of religion. We have seen that God is the object of religion; all religious acts and thoughts are directed toward Him. Man is the subject of religion; the seat of it is in him, and from him it proceeds.

Man is second of three major interests of Scripture: God, man, the God-man; the second of four major interests, if we include the Spirit: God, the Creator; man, the highest earthly creature, lord of creation; Jesus Christ, the divine-human Redeemer; the Holy Spirit of wisdom and power, the Regenerator and Finisher.

These statements of the Standards supply important information on the following points:

1. Man's place in creation. "After" — the last for which the first was made. The Bible is frankly anthropocentric in its representation of man's place in the universe. In the present state of scientific knowledge, no man can afford to dispute its accuracy. (See *Doctrine of Redemption* by Knudsen, p. 75.)

2. Man's nature. Male and female; a species, a race; dual — soul and body; personal, immortal.

3. Man's original character. Moral, upright.

4. Man's dignity. "With dominion over the creatures." Standing at the apex he was given lordship over all beneath him. (Gen. 1:28.)

5. Man's probation.

He was placed under law, moral and positive, with two possible issues. Distinguish between moral and positive laws, and define the possible issues of the probation.

The best knowledge is the knowledge of God. The next best is the knowledge of man. The Jew came saying, Know thy God. The Greek came saying, Know thyself. The Christian comes saying, Know thy God and thyself in Jesus Christ. The union of the two kinds of knowledge makes for perfect wisdom. (Calvin in *Institutes of the Christian Religion*, Bk. I, Ch. 1.)

# CHAPTER V

# Of Providence

---

## Part One: Of Providence in General
### CONFESSION OF FAITH V:1-7
### LARGER CATECHISM 18-19 · SHORTER CATECHISM 11

---

**THE WESTMINSTER**
### CONFESSION OF FAITH

God, the great Creator of all things, doth uphold, direct, dispose, and govern all creatures, actions, and things, from the greatest even to the least,[1] by his most wise and holy providence,[2] according to his infallible fore-knowledge,[3] and the free and immutable counsel of his own will,[4] to the praise of the glory of his wisdom, power, justice, goodness, and mercy.[5]

(1) Neh. 9:6; Heb. 1:3; Psa. 135:6; Matt. 10:29, 30, 31; Acts 17:25, 28; Matt. 6:26, 30; Job, chapters 38-41.
(2) Prov. 15:3; II Chron. 16:9; Psa. 145:17; 104:24.
(3) Acts 15:18.
(4) Eph. 1:11; Psa. 33:11.
(5) Eph. 3:10; Rom. 9:17; Psa. 145.

2. Although in relation to the fore-knowledge and decree of God, the first cause, all things come to pass immutably and infallibly,[6] yet, by the same providence, he ordereth them to fall out according to the nature of second causes, either necessarily,[7] freely, or contingently.[8]

(6) Acts 2:23; See under figures 3 and 4 above.
(7) Gen. 8:22; Jer. 31:35.
(8) Ex. 21:13; Gen. 50:19, 20; I Kings 22:34; Isa. 10:6, 7.

3. God, in his ordinary providence, maketh use of means,[9] yet is free to work without,[10] above,[11] and against them, at his pleasure.[12]

(9) Acts 27:24, 31, 44; Isa. 55:10, 11.
(10) Hos. 1:7.
(11) Rom. 4:19, 20, 21.
(12) II Kings 6:6; Dan. 3:27.

**THE WESTMINSTER**
### LARGER CATECHISM

Q. 18. *What are God's works of providence?*

A. God's works of providence are his most holy,[1] wise,[2] and powerful preserving,[3] and governing all his creatures;[4] ordering them, and all their actions,[5] to his own glory.[6]

(1) Psa. 145:17.
(2) Psa. 104:24; Isa. 28:29.
(3) Heb. 1:3.
(4) Psa. 103:19; Job, chapters 38-41.
(5) Matt. 10:29, 30; Gen. 45:7; Psa. 135:6.
(6) Rom. 11:36; Isa. 63:14.

**THE WESTMINSTER**
### SHORTER CATECHISM

Q. 11. *What are God's works of providence?*

A. God's works of providence are, his most holy,[1] wise,[2] and powerful preserving[3] and governing all his creatures, and all their actions.[4]

(1) Psa. 145:17.
(2) Psa. 104:24.
(3) Heb. 1:3.
(4) Psa.103:19; Matt. 10:29, 30; Job, chapters 38-41.

## THE WESTMINSTER CONFESSION OF FAITH

4. The almighty power, unseachable wisdom, and infinite goodness of God, so far manifest themselves in his providence, that it extendeth itself even to the first fall,[13] and all other sins of angels and men,[14] and that not by a bare permission, but such as hath joined with it a most wise and powerful bounding,[15] and otherwise ordering and governing of them, in a manifold dispensation, to his own holy ends;[16] yet so, as the sinfulness thereof proceedeth only from the creature, and not from God; who being most holy and righteous, neither is nor can be the author or approver of sin.[17]

(13) This statement is sustained by the doctrines of God's decrees and providence. See citations under Chapter III and Chapter V, Sections 1, 2, 3.
(14) Rom. 11:32, 33; II Sam. 24:1; Acts 4:27, 28. See citations under Chapter III and Chapter V, Sections 1, 2, 3.
(15) II Kings 19:28; Isa. 10:5, 6, 7, 12, 15.
(16) Gen. 50:20.
See under figure 15 above.
(17) I John 2:16; Psa. 50:21; James 1:13, 14.

5. The most wise, righteous, and gracious God, doth oftentimes leave for a season his own children to manifold temptations and the corruption of their own hearts, to chastise them for their former sins, or to discover unto them the hidden strength of corruption and deceitfulness of their hearts, that they may be humbled;[18] and to raise them to a more close and constant dependence for their support upon himself, and to make them more watchful against all future occasions of sin, and for sundry other just and holy ends.[19]

(18) Deut. 8:2; II Chron. 32:25, 26, 31.
(19) II Cor. 12:7, 8, 9; Psa. 73; Psa. 77:1-12; Mark 14:66-72; John 21:15, 16, 17.

6. As for those wicked and ungodly men whom God, as a right-

## THE WESTMINSTER LARGER CATECHISM

Q. 19. *What is God's providence toward the angels?*

A. God by his providence permitted some of the angels, willfully and irrecoverably, to fall into sin and damnation,[1] limiting and ordering that, and all their sins, to his own glory;[2] and established the rest in holiness and happiness;[3] employing them all, at his pleasure, in the administrations of his power, mercy, and justice.[4]

(1) Jude 6; II Pet. 2:4.
(2) Job 1:12; Luke 10:17; Matt. 8:31.
(3) I Tim. 5:21; Mark 8:38; Heb. 12:22.
(4) Psa. 104:4; Heb. 1:14.

## THE WESTMINSTER SHORTER CATECHISM

| THE WESTMINSTER CONFESSION OF FAITH | THE WESTMINSTER LARGER CATECHISM | THE WESTMINSTER SHORTER CATECHISM |
|---|---|---|

eous judge, for former sins, doth blind and harden;[20] from them he not only withholdeth his grace, whereby they might have been enlightened in their understandings, and wrought upon in their hearts;[21] but sometimes also withdraweth the gifts which they had;[22] and exposeth them to such objects as their corruption makes occasion of sin;[23] and withal, giveth them over to their own lusts, the temptations of the world, and the power of Satan;[24] whereby it cometh to pass that they harden themselves, even under those means which God useth for the softening of others.[25]

(20) Rom. 1:24, 26, 28; Rom. 11:7, 8; II Thess. 2:11, 12.
(21) Deut. 29:4; Mark 4:11, 12.
(22) Matt. 13:12; Matt. 25:29.
(23) II Kings 8:12, 13.
(24) Psa. 81:11, 12; II Thess. 2:10-12.
(25) Ex. 8:15, 32; II Cor. 2:15, 16; Isa. 8:14; Ex. 7:3; I Pet. 2:7, 8; Isa. 6:9, 10; Acts 28:26, 27.

7. As the providence of God doth, in general, reach to all creatures; so, after a most special manner, it taketh care of his church, and disposeth all things to the good thereof.[26]

(26) Amos 9:8-9; Rom. 8:28; Eph. 1:22.

# EXPLANATORY NOTES

THE student should not fail to notice the emphasis of the Confession on the subject of divine providence, devoting to it a chapter of seven sections. The importance of the subject justifies the emphasis.

## CONF. V:1; L.C. 18; S.C. 11

*The Fact and Features of Providence*

Analysis of these parts of the Standards yield answers to the following questions:

1. What are the branches of providence as indicated by the verbs?
2. What is the nature of providence as indicated by the adjectives?
3. What are the subjects of providence as indicated by certain nouns?
4. What are the grounds of providence as expressed in certain phrases?
5. What is the end or objective of providence as asserted in the final words of the Confession and Larger Catechism?

## L.C. 19

As the Larger Catechism is peculiar in devoting a question and answer to the creation of angels, so it is peculiar again in devoting a question and answer to God's providence over angels. This paragraph states:

1. God's relation to the fall of some of the angels and His purpose in it.
2. The nature of their sin and its consequence, namely, willfulness and hopeless perdition.
3. God's activity toward the angels who fell not.
4. His use of all angels, good and bad.

### CONF. V:2-3

*The Modes of Providence*

Though divine providence is certainly efficacious, yet the mode of it is consistent with the mode of action of every creature. The agency of the First Cause is concurrent with the agency of second causes. God respects the laws of all His creatures and realizes His purpose in conjunction with them and not in contravention of them. Would His providence be wise if He violated the laws which He Himself impressed upon His creation? God is not the God of confusion. So, the free act freely; the unfree necessarily; and the casual falls out by chance, so to speak.

Ordinarily, God works mediately; that is, makes use of means. Occasionally He works immediately; that is, without the use of means. Extraordinary providences are called miracles.

### CONF. V:4-6; L.C. 19

*The Relation of Providence to Moral Evil*

Section 4 defines God's relation to moral evil in general. Mark the words which express that relation: permission, bounding, ordering, and governing. This section not only defines God's connection with moral evil, but denies His complicity in it: it safeguards His character.

Section 5 defines God's providence toward His own people. It is His disciplinary providence that is described. Mark the word which expresses God's action: "doth . . . leave" — negative. Note the limiting phrase, "for a season." Now consider the infinitives (4) which express His purpose in thus dealing with His children.

Section 6 is occupied with God's providence toward those not His people. Above, it is His disciplinary, but here it is His punitive providence that is dealt with. These aspects of providence are explained because they trouble people. A question often asked is, Why does God deal thus and so with people? The aim of the Standards here is to justify the ways of God with men.

Now underscore the verbs which express divine action: "doth blind and harden," "withholdeth," "withdraweth," "exposeth," "giveth . . . over." A list of terrible words. Do they shock you? It will relieve you to observe in what capacity God does these things: "as a righteous judge." It will relieve you further to consider why God acts thus toward wicked and ungodly men: "for [their] former sins." The right of judgment belongs to God. If men abuse His gifts, He has the right to withhold them.

One thing more in this distressing section should be noticed. The result of God's actions toward the "wicked and ungodly" is that they sin yet further: "whereby it cometh to pass that they harden themselves," that is, they set, confirm, themselves in the way of evil. Men react differently, according to their natures, to divine providence. The same sun that softens wax hardens clay.

An illustration here will help. It troubles the student to read that God "exposeth [men] to such objects as their corruption makes occasion of sin." That seems to come perilously near to saying that God tempts men to sin. Yet the Scripture says "he himself tempteth no man." (James 1:13, A.S.V.)

Judas is a case in point. God's choice of him to membership in the apostolic band exposed him to temptations which his corruption made the occasion of sin. Judas' position in the college of apostles exposed him to influences which might have transformed him into a saint, but they actually changed him into "a devil."

The hard things of the Standards are the hard things of Scripture and of life.

### CONF. V:7

*Providence in Its Diversity and Unity*

Divine providence has its departments:
1. Over the material universe.
2. Over rational creation — intelligent beings.
3. Over mankind in general.
4. Over the elect in particular.

These departments are not independent and co-ordinate, each an end in itself; but there is a relation of subordination between them, and all converge upon the Church of the Redeemer. God's purpose of grace in His Son is the key to providence and history. This is the theistic view of God's relation to His world: it is more than theistic — it is Christian.

What is the deistic view of God's relation to His world? What is the pantheistic view of His relation to His world?

# Of Providence

## Part Two:
## Of Providence in Special . . . Of the Covenant of Works

CONFESSION OF FAITH VII:1-2
LARGER CATECHISM 20 · SHORTER CATECHISM 12

THE distance between God and the creature is so great, that although reasonable creatures do owe obedience unto him as their Creator, yet they could never have any fruition of him, as their blessedness and reward, but by some voluntary condescension on God's part, which he hath been pleased to express by way of covenant.[1] (*Conf. of Faith, VII:1.*)

2. The first covenant made with man was a covenant of works,[2] wherein life was promised to Adam, and in him to his posterity, upon condition of perfect and personal obedience.[3] (*Conf. of Faith, VII:2.*)

(1) See General Note, Confession of Faith, Chapter 1, Section 1.

(2) Gen. 2:16, 17; Gal. 3:10; Hosea 6:7; Rom. 5:12, 19; I Cor. 15:22, 47.

(3) Compare Gen. 2:16, 17 with Rom. 5:12-14; Rom. 10:5; Luke 10:25-28; and with the covenants made with Noah and Abraham.

Q. 20. *What was the providence of God toward man in the estate in which he was created?*

A. The providence of God toward man in the estate in which he was created was, the placing him in paradise, appointing him to dress it, giving him liberty to eat of the fruit of the earth,[1] putting the creatures under his dominion,[2] ordaining marriage for his help,[3] affording him communion with himself,[4] and instituting the Sabbath;[5] entering into a covenant of life with him, upon condition of personal, perfect, and perpetual obedience,[6] of which the tree of life was a pledge; and forbidding to eat of the tree of the knowledge of good and evil, upon pain of death.[7]

(1) Gen. 2:8; Gen. 2:15, 16.

(2) Gen. 1:28.

(3) Gen. 2:18.

(4) Gen. 1:27, 28.

(5) Gen. 2:3.

(6) Compare Gen. 2:16, 17 with Rom. 5:12-14; 10:5; Luke 10:25-28, and with the covenants made with Noah and Abraham.

(7) Gen. 2:17.

Q. 12. *What special act of providence did God exercise towards man, in the estate wherein he was created?*

A. When God had created man, he entered into a covenant of life with him, upon condition of perfect obedience;[1] forbidding him to eat of the tree of the knowledge of good and evil, upon pain of death.[2]

(1) Compare Gen. 2:16, 17 with Rom. 5:12-14; Rom. 10:5; Luke 10:25-28, and with the covenants made with Noah and Abraham.

(2) Gen. 2:17.

# EXPLANATORY NOTES

HERE the order of the Confession is departed from. For the Confession treats of the two covenants in one chapter, and that chapter is placed after the chapter on the Fall. The Catechisms follow the historic sequence, and treat first of the Covenant of Works; then of the Fall and Sin; and then of the Covenant of Grace.

The parallel arrangement of the Standards requires that Chapter VII of the Confession be divided: sections 1 and 2 are brought back into Chapter V, while sections 3-6 are carried forward to Chapter VII of the Harmony; the chapter on the Fall and Sin coming in between, as Chapter VI of the Harmony as well as of the Confession.

## CONF. VII:1-2; L.C. 20; S.C. 12

Name the features (7) of man's pre-covenant condition as given in the Larger Catechism. Which of the Standards assigns a reason for the covenant arrangement?

What is the title of the first covenant according to the Catechisms? According to the Confession? Why so styled in each case?

The elements of a covenant, deducible from the Standards, are four: parties, promise, condition, penalty. Are they deducible from the Scripture? Who were the parties to this first covenant? What was the promise? What was the condition? What was the penalty?

Read the condition of the covenant as given first in the Shorter Catechism, then in the Confession, and thirdly in the Larger Catechism, and mark the adjectives before obedience. What is named as the seal (pledge) of the covenant? Why is the other tree called the tree of the knowledge of good and evil?

What would have been the results if man had kept the covenant? May they be described as justification, confirmation, and adoption? Who could have enjoyed these blessings with the first man? Was the first covenant gracious then? Wherein?

If the covenant had issued favorably, everyone would have approved and praised the arrangement. Does the fact that the covenant issued unfavorably constitute a just ground for condemning the covenant as unfair to man and unworthy of God? We see the representative principle in operation here. It is emphasized throughout the Bible. The highest example of its use is in redemption. If it was right for the second man, the last Adam, to represent us without our consent, was it not right for the first man, the first Adam, so to represent us? If you will think the matter all the way round and all the way through, I think you will agree that the covenant arrangement for man's benefit was the fairest and most promising that divine wisdom could have devised; and if you had been given an option on the matter, you would have voted for it.

# CHAPTER VI

# Of the Fall of Man, of Sin, and of the Punishment Thereof

CONFESSION OF FAITH VI:1-6
LARGER CATECHISM 21-29 · SHORTER CATECHISM 13-19

Our first parents, being seduced by the subtilty and temptation of Satan, sinned in eating the forbidden fruit.[1] This their sin God was pleased, according to his wise and holy counsel, to permit, having purposed to order it to his own glory.[2]

(1) Gen. 3:13; II Cor. 11:3; Gen. 3:1-14.

(2) Rom. 5:19, 20, 21.

Q. 21. *Did man continue in that estate wherein God at first created him?*

A. Our first parents, being left to the freedom of their own will, through the temptation of Satan, transgressed the commandment of God, in eating the forbidden fruit, and thereby fell from the estate of innocency wherein they were created.[1]

(1) Gen. 3:6, 7, 8, 13; II Cor. 11:3.

Q. 24. *What is sin?*

A. Sin is any want of conformity unto, or transgression of, any law of God, given as a rule to the reasonable creature.[1]

(1) Rom. 3:23; I John 3:4; Jas. 4:17.

Q. 13. *Did our first parents continue in the estate wherein they were created?*

A. Our first parents, being left to the freedom of their own will, fell from the estate wherein they were created, by sinning against God.[1]

(1) Gen. 3:6, 7, 8, 13; II Cor. 11:3.

Q. 14. *What is sin?*

A. Sin is any want of conformity unto, or transgression of, the law of God.[1]

(1) I John 3:4; Jas. 4:17; Rom. 3:23.

Q. 15. *What was the sin whereby our first parents fell from the estate wherein they were created?*

A. The sin whereby our first parents fell from the estate wherein they were created, was their eating the forbidden fruit.[1]

(1) See proof to Answer 13. Gen. 3:6.

| THE WESTMINSTER CONFESSION OF FAITH | THE WESTMINSTER LARGER CATECHISM | THE WESTMINSTER SHORTER CATECHISM |
|---|---|---|
| 2. By this sin they fell from their original righteousness and communion with God,[3] and so became dead in sin,[4] and wholly defiled in all the faculties and parts of soul and body.[5] <br><br>(3) Gen. 3:7, 8; Gen. 2:17. <br>(4) Rom. 5:12; Eph. 2:3. <br>(5) Gen. 6:5; Jer. 17:9; Rom. 3:10-19; Rom. 8:6-8; Psa. 58:1-5. | | |
| 3. They being the root of all mankind, the guilt of this sin was imputed,[6] and the same death in sin and corrupted nature conveyed to all their posterity, descending from them by ordinary generation.[7] <br><br>(6) Acts 17:26. Compare Gen. 2:16, 17 with Rom. 5:12, 15-19; I Cor. 15:21, 22, 45, 49. <br>(7) Psa. 51:5; Gen. 5:3; John 3:6; Rom. 3:10-18. | Q. 22. *Did all mankind fall in that first transgression?* <br>A. The covenant being made with Adam, as a public person, not for himself only, but for his posterity, all mankind, descending from him by ordinary generation,[1] sinned in him, and fell with him in that first transgression.[2] <br>(1) Acts 17:26. See under figure 6 above. <br>(2) Gen. 2:17; compare with Rom. 5:12-20 and with I Cor. 15:21, 22. | Q. 16. *Did all mankind fall in Adam's first transgression?* <br>A. The covenant being made with Adam, not only for himself, but for his posterity,[1] all mankind, descending from him by ordinary generation, sinned in him, and fell with him in his first transgression.[2] <br>(1) Acts 17:26. See under Question 12. <br>(2) Gen. 2:17. Compared with Rom. 5:12-20; I Cor. 15:21, 22. |
| | Q. 23. *Into what estate did the fall bring mankind?* <br>A. The fall brought mankind into an estate of sin and misery.[1] <br>(1) Rom. 5:12; Gal. 3:10. | Q. 17. *Into what estate did the fall bring mankind?* <br>A. The fall brought mankind into an estate of sin and misery.[1] <br>(1) Rom. 5:12; Gal. 3:10. |
| 4. From this original corruption, whereby we are utterly indisposed, disabled, and made opposite to all good, and wholly inclined to all evil,[8] do proceed all actual transgressions.[9] <br><br>(8) Rom. 5:6; Rom. 8:7; John 3:6; Rom. 7:18; Gen. 8:21; Rom. 3:10, 11, 12. <br>(9) James 1:14, 15; Matt. 15:19. | Q. 25. *Wherein consists the sinfulness of that estate whereinto man fell?* <br>A. The sinfulness of that estate whereinto man fell, consisteth in the guilt of Adam's first sin,[1] the want of that righteousness wherein he was created, and the corruption of his nature, whereby he is utterly indisposed, disabled, and made opposite unto all that is spiritually good, and wholly inclined to all evil, and that continually;[2] which is commonly called original sin, and from which do proceed all actual transgressions.[3] <br>(1) Rom. 5:12, 19; I Cor. 15:22. <br>(2) Rom. 5:6; Eph. 2:1, 2, 3; Rom. 8:7, 8; Gen. 6:5; Rom. 3:10-20; Psa. 51:5; 58:3. <br>(3) James 1:14, 15; Matt. 15:19. | Q. 18. *Wherein consists the sinfulness of that estate whereinto man fell?* <br>A. The sinfulness of that estate whereinto man fell, consists in the guilt of Adam's first sin,[1] the want of original righteousness, and the corruption of his whole nature, which is commonly called original sin;[2] together with all actual transgressions which proceed from it.[3] <br>(1) Rom. 5:12, 19; I Cor. 15:22. <br>(2) Rom. 5:6; Eph. 2:1, 2, 3; Rom. 8:7, 8; Rom. 3:10-20; Psa. 51:5; 58:3. <br>(3) James 1:14-15; Matt. 15:19. |

| THE WESTMINSTER CONFESSION OF FAITH | THE WESTMINSTER LARGER CATECHISM | THE WESTMINSTER SHORTER CATECHISM |
|---|---|---|

5. This corruption of nature, during this life, doth remain in those that are regenerated:[10] and although it be through Christ pardoned and mortified, yet both itself, and all the motions thereof, are truly and properly sin.[11]

(10) Rom. 7:14, 17, 18, 23; James 3:2; I John 1:8, 10; Prov. 20:9.
(11) Rom. 7:5, 7, 8, 25.

Q. 26. *How is original sin conveyed from our first parents unto their posterity?*

A. Original sin is conveyed from our first parents unto their posterity by natural generation, so as all that proceed from them in that way, are conceived and born in sin.[1]

(1) Psa. 51:5; John 3:6.

6. Every sin, both original and actual, being a transgression of the righteous law of God, and contrary thereunto, doth, in its own nature, bring guilt upon the sinner,[12] whereby he is bound over to the wrath of God,[13] and curse of the law,[14] and so made subject to death,[15] with all miseries spiritual, temporal, and eternal.[16]

(12) Rom. 3:19; Rom. 2:15; I John 3:4.
(13) Eph. 2:3; Rom. 5:12.
(14) Gal. 3:10.
(15) Rom. 6:23; Gen. 2:17.
(16) Eph. 4:18; Matt. 25:41; II Thess. 1:9; Rom. 1:21-28; Lev. 26:14 ff; Deut. 28:15 ff.

Q. 27. *What misery did the fall bring upon mankind?*

A. The fall brought upon mankind the loss of communion with God,[1] his displeasure and curse; so as we are by nature children of wrath,[2] bondslaves to Satan,[3] and justly liable to all punishments in this world and that which is to come.[4]

(1) Gen. 3:8, 24.
(2) Eph. 2:2, 3.
(3) II Tim. 2:26; Luke 11:21, 22; Heb. 2:14.
(4) Rom. 6:23; Rom. 5:14.

Q. 28. *What are the punishments of sin in this world?*

A. The punishments of sin in this world, are either inward, as blindness of mind,[1] a reprobate sense,[2] strong delusions,[3] hardness of heart,[4] horror of conscience,[5] and vile affections: or outward, as the curse of God upon the creatures for our sake,[7] and all other evils that befall us in our bodies, names, estates, relations, and employments;[8] together with death itself.[9]

Q. 19. *What is the misery of that estate whereinto man fell?*

A. All mankind, by their fall, lost communion with God,[1] are under his wrath and curse,[2] and so made liable to all miseries in this life, to death itself, and to the pains of hell forever.[3]

(1) Gen. 3:8, 24.
(2) Eph. 2:3.
(3) Rom. 5:14; Rom. 6:23.

| THE WESTMINSTER CONFESSION OF FAITH | THE WESTMINSTER LARGER CATECHISM | THE WESTMINSTER SHORTER CATECHISM |
|---|---|---|
| | (1) Eph. 4:18.<br>(2) Rom. 1:28.<br>(3) II Thess. 2:11.<br>(4) Rom. 2:5.<br>(5) Isa. 33:14; Gen. 4:13, 14; Matt. 27:4; Heb. 10:27.<br>(6) Rom. 1:26.<br>(7) Gen. 3:17.<br>(8) Deut. 28:15-68.<br>(9) Rom. 6:21, 23. | |

Q. 29. *What are the punishments of sin in the world to come?*

A. The punishments of sin in the world to come are, everlasting separation from the comfortable presence of God, and most grievous torments in soul and body, without intermission, in hell-fire for ever.[1]

(1) II Thess. 1:9; Mark 9:43, 44; Luke 16:24,26; Matt. 25:41, 46; Rev. 14:11; John 3:36.

# EXPLANATORY NOTES

### CONF. VI:1; L.C. 21; S.C. 13

These words introduce us to a dark subject. This is the first tragedy in the tragic history of man. The Standards treat it with great fullness, and we should study it with great care. For according to our conception of sin will be our conception of grace. Grace is the remedy for the situation created by sin. If sin is a light matter, so is grace. No one ever thought much of grace who thought little of sin.

What account, explanation, of the fall of man do the Standards give?

The Shorter Catechism names one factor, the Larger Catechism two, while the Confession adds a third. The Confession in its first section affirms five things about the fall: the fact of the fall, the form of the sin, the source of the sin, God's relation to it, and His purpose in it.

### L.C. 24; S.C. 14-15

The subject is the Nature of Sin.

You will observe that the Confession contains no formal definition of sin and that the Catechisms treat the subject in different connections. The nature of sin as defined by the Catechisms is worthy of careful study. They define it in relation to the law or will of God. They present sin in its negative and positive aspects — in its inward and outward features.

Sin is an act and a state. It is not being and not doing what God requires. It is doing and being what God forbids. As omission it is a coming short. As transgression it is an overstepping.

Defect of being and behavior is as really sin as depravity of being and behavior. Want of conformity is as truly sin as criminality. Is hatred of

God and man sin? Yes, and so is lack of love toward them. Absence of right feeling as well as presence of wrong feeling is sin: disharmony of soul as well as disobedience of will.

The inward and the negative sides of sin are too much ignored, too little regarded.

## CONF. VI:2-6; L.C. 22-23, 25-26; S.C. 16-19

We have had the Fact of the Fall and the Nature of Sin. The third phase of the subject is the Effect of Sin, a subject large and difficult.

Section 2 of the Confession sets forth the effects in the *parents* of the race. They are:

1. Loss: of what?
2. Death: in what sense?
3. Defilement or depravity: in what part? in what measure? The depravity is described as total in degree: "wholly defiled." If wholly defiled, it cannot be more so. It is further described as total in extent: "in all the faculties and parts of soul and body."

"Total depravity" is one of the Calvinistic doctrines. As commonly explained, the doctrine is reasonable and Scriptural, but as defined by the Confession, it seems extreme and indefensible. As commonly defined, depravity is "total" in extent. That is, it affects every part of man's dual being — soul and body — the whole area of his life. When man fell, he fell all over, the resulting corruption reaches from the center to the circumference of his being. But as commonly explained by orthodox theologians, depravity is not "total" also in degree. That is, fallen men are not as bad as they can be, nor are they equally bad. There are degrees of badness in bad men, and kinds and measures of goodness in good men. Jesus said, "If ye then, being evil, know how to give *good* gifts unto your children, how much more shall the heavenly Father give the Holy Spirit to them that ask him?" (Luke 11:13, A.S.V.)

If "evil" men are capable of "good" deeds, then they ought not to be regarded as "wholly" evil.

Neither Catechism supports the Confession here. The Shorter Catechism in defining the sinfulness of that estate into which man fell uses the phrase "the corruption of his whole nature"; but it does not say the *entire* corruption of *his whole* nature. The Larger Catechism says that fallen man is "utterly indisposed, disabled, and made opposite unto all that is *spiritually* good." Thus the Larger Catechism limits the statement to that which is spiritually good. There is no limitation in the Confession; its statement is unqualified and absolute.

Some think that the Confession should be made to conform to the Catechisms and to the commonly accepted definitions of total depravity.

## CONF. VI:3-4; L.C. 22-23, 25-26; S.C. 16-18

Sections 3 and 4 of the Confession, the answers of the Larger Catechism under questions 22, 23, 25, and 26, and the answers of the Shorter Catechism under questions 16, 17, and 18 are practically parallel, and are engaged in explaining the sinfulness of sin as it affects the *descendants* of the first pair of sinners.

The Catechisms (L.C. 22; S.C. 16) declare that all mankind, descending from the first man by ordinary generation, sinned in him, and fell with him in the first transgression.

These parts of the Catechisms together with the Confession, section 3, tell why all mankind, with one exception, fell in the first man. The Confession says it so happened because the first man was "the root of all mankind." The Catechisms say that it happened so because the first man was the representative of all mankind. Adam was "a public person"; the covenant was made with him for himself and all in him. The threefold Standard gives the full explanation of our sharing in the consequences of Adam's first transgression. The Confession explains it naturally: we were in him seminally, as a son is in the loins of his father. The Catechisms explain it federally: we were in him legally, by covenant arrangement. First the natural, then the federal. Adam could become the federal (or covenant) head because he was the natural head of the race.

## L.C. 26

Having learned why we participate in Adam's sin, let us learn how. There are two elements in sin: guilt and corruption. These elements come to us by different modes: guilt is "imputed" — a divine act; corruption is "conveyed" by generation, a human act. That is, transmission of depravity is bound up with the natural law of heredity. Yet the two elements come down together. The relation of God's agency to the parents' agency may not be exactly stated.

Our inheritance from Adam's first sin is called "original sin." Original sin is the sin we were born to, and it is commonly regarded as including both guilt and corruption. The corruption becomes ours in virtue of our natural connection with Adam. The guilt becomes ours in consequence of our federal connection with Adam.

This explains why we inherit only from Adam's first sin. When he sinned, he ceased to be our representative, for the covenant was broken.

### CONF. VI:3-4; L.C. 25

Two other effects of Adam's sin in his posterity remain to be mentioned. They are death and inability. The words are "death in sin and corrupted nature," and "utterly . . . disabled." Death and disability equal inability.

From Genesis 2 onward the Bible warns men that sin means death. "The day thou eatest thereof thou shalt surely die." Death instantaneous and entire, *i.e.*, complete, separation from God, from whom alone is ability to anything. To be wholly dead toward God is "surely" to be disabled toward Him. To deny the disability is to deny the death, and to deny the death is to deny the declaration of Scripture, which we have received to hold as the inspired word of God.

According to the Standards, sin has a twofold classification: original and actual. Original sin is the root or spring of all actual transgression. Original sin is a state of being from which proceed acts of life. The reader of the Standards cannot fail to note the frequent use of the word "state" or "estate": "state of innocency," "an estate of sin and misery," "the state of grace," "the state of glory." Back of acts of life lie states of being.

### CONF. VI:5

The fifth section of the Confession completes the Standards' treatment of the state of sin. The subject of this section is the continuing effect of the fall in the regenerate.

Two points are to be noted:

1. The fact or reality of this remaining effect.

2. The nature of it as sin, really and properly sin.

The first of these points is made versus perfectionists; the second versus Catholics.

### CONF. VI:6; L.C. 27-29; S.C. 19

The subject of the sixth chapter of the Confession is threefold: the Fall, Sin, and the Punishment of Sin. We now come to the third division of the subject: the punishment of sin. The punishment of sin is an "estate of misery." The misery follows the sin naturally, yet by judicial act of God.

The Larger Catechism amplifies and particularizes more than do the Confession and the Shorter Catechism. The misery of sin as described here is not single, but manifold. Do not read these terrific statements from the Balcony, to use a figure of Dr. MacKay of Princeton Seminary; but take them down onto the Road of Life where the miseries of sin are real and threatening to grow to more and more. Make a list of the ingredients of human misery, actual and potential, and mark their varied character: physical and spiritual, inward and outward, personal and social, particular and universal, temporal and eternal.

Reading these terrible words and phrases of the Standards, the sensitive soul becomes conscious of the weight of bonds and chains, and hears the hiss and feels the heat of flames intolerable even to thought. It would not be strange if the reader should feel impelled to cry out against the harsh language of the creed offered for his acceptance.

I would not repress criticism, but I would suggest that one's time and energy might be more profitably employed in considering whether the language of the Standards is harsher than the language of Scripture and the facts of life.

This chapter of the creed is dark; is there no light? The punishments of sin seem insufferable; is there no escape? Yes, thank God! Turn a page, and behold, light and an open road!

# CHAPTER VII

# Of God's Covenant with Man

CONFESSION OF FAITH VII:(1-2), 3-6
LARGER CATECHISM 30-35 · SHORTER CATECHISM 20

| THE WESTMINSTER CONFESSION OF FAITH | THE WESTMINSTER LARGER CATECHISM | THE WESTMINSTER SHORTER CATECHISM |
|---|---|---|

(THE distance between God and the creature is so great, that although reasonable creatures do owe obedience unto him as their Creator, yet they could never have any fruition of him, as their blessedness and reward, but by some voluntary condescension on God's part, which he hath been pleased to express by way of covenant.[1]

(2. The first covenant made with man was a covenant of works,[2] wherein life was promised to Adam, and in him to his posterity, upon condition of perfect and personal obedience.[3]

(1) See General Note, Confession of Faith, Chapter 1, Section 1.

(2) Gen. 2:16, 17; Gal. 3:10; Hosea 6:7; Rom. 5:12, 19; I Cor. 15:22, 47.

(3) Compare Gen. 2:16, 17 with Rom. 5:12-14; Rom. 10:5; Luke 10:25-28; and with the covenants made with Noah and Abraham.)

3. Man, by his fall, having made himself incapable of life by that covenant, the Lord was pleased to make a second, commonly called the covenant of grace:[4] wherein he freely offered unto sinners life and salvation by Jesus Christ, requiring of them faith in him, that they may be saved,[5] and promising to give unto all those that are ordained unto

Q. 30. *Doth God leave all mankind to perish in the estate of sin and misery?*

A. God doth not leave all men to perish in the estate of sin and misery, into which they fell by the breach of the first covenant, commonly called the covenant of works;[1] but of his mere love and mercy de-

Q. 20. *Did God leave all mankind to perish in the estate of sin and misery?*

A. God having, out of his mere good pleasure, from all eternity, elected some to everlasting life,[1] did enter into a covenant of grace, to deliver them out of the estate of sin and misery, and to bring them

life, his Holy Spirit, to make them willing and able to believe.[6]

(4) Matt. 26:28; Gal. 3:21; Rom 8:3; Isa. 42:6; Gen. 3:15; Heb. 10:5-10.
(5) John 3:16; Acts 16:30, 31.
(6) John 3:5, 6, 7, 8; John 6:37, 44; Ezek. 36:26, 27.

4. This covenant of grace is frequently set forth in the Scripture by the name of a testament, in reference to the death of Jesus Christ, the testator, and to the everlasting inheritance, with all things belonging to it, therein bequeathed.

livereth his elect out of it, and bringeth them into an estate of salvation by the second covenant, commonly called the covenant of grace.[2]

(1) I Thess. 5:9.
(2) Tit. 3:4-7; Tit. 1:2; Gal. 3:21; Rom. 3:20-22.

Q. 31. *With whom was the covenant of grace made?*

A. The covenant of grace was made with Christ as the second Adam, and in him with all the elect as his seed.[1]

(1) I Cor. 15:22, 45; Eph. 1:4; II Tim. 1:9; Isa. 53:10, 11; Heb. 2:10, 11, 14.

Q. 32. *How is the grace of God manifested in the second covenant?*

A. The grace of God is manifested in the second covenant, in that he freely provideth and offereth to sinners a mediator,[1] and life and salvation by him;[2] and requiring faith as the condition to interest them in him,[3] promiseth and giveth his Holy Spirit to all his elect, to work in them that faith, with all other saving graces;[4] and to enable them unto all holy obedience,[5] as the evidence of the truth of their faith[6] and of their thankfulness to God,[7] and as the way which he hath appointed them to salvation.[8]

(1) I Tim. 2:5.
(2) I John 5:11, 12.
(3) John 3:16; John 1:12; John 3:36.
(4) John 1:12, 13; John 3:5, 6, 8; Gal. 5:22, 23.
(5) Ezek. 36:27.
(6) James 2:18, 22.
(7) II Cor. 5:14, 15.
(8) Eph. 2:10; Tit. 2:14; 3:8.

into an estate of salvation, by a Redeemer.[2]

(1) Eph. 1:4, 5, 6, 7.
(2) Titus 3:4, 5, 6, 7; Titus 1:2; Gal. 3:21; Rom. 3:20-22.

THE WESTMINSTER
## CONFESSION OF FAITH

THE WESTMINSTER
## LARGER CATECHISM

THE WESTMINSTER
## SHORTER CATECHISM

5. This covenant was differently administered in the time of the law, and in the time of the gospel:[7] under the law it was administered by promises, prophecies, sacrifices, circumcision, the paschal lamb, and other types and ordinances delivered to the people of the Jews, all fore-signifying Christ to come,[8] which were for that time sufficient and efficacious, through the operation of the Spirit, to instruct and build up the elect in faith in the promised Messiah,[9] by whom they had full remission of sins, and eternal salvation; and is called the Old Testament.[10]

(7) Heb. 1:1, 2; II Cor. 3:6, 7, 8, 9.
(8) Rom. 4:11; Heb., chapters 8, 9, 10.
(9) Heb. 11:13; John 8:56; Gal. 3:6, 7, 8.
(10) Acts 15:11; Rom. 3:30; Gal. 3:8, 9, 14.

6. Under the gospel, when Christ the substance was exhibited, the ordinances in which this covenant is dispensed, are the preaching of the word, and the administration of the sacraments of baptism and the Lord's supper;[11] which, though fewer in number, and administered with more simplicity and less outward glory, yet in them it is held forth in more fullness, evidence, and spiritual efficacy,[12] to all nations, both Jews and Gentiles;[13] and is called the New Testament. There are not, therefore, two covenants of grace differing in substance, but one

Q. 33. *Was the covenant of grace always administered after one and the same manner?*

A. The covenant of grace was not always administered after the same manner, but the administrations of it under the Old Testament were different from those under the New.[1]

(1) II Cor. 3:6; Heb. 1:1, 2; 8:7, 8 ff.

Q. 34. *How was the covenant of grace administered under the Old Testament?*

A. The covenant of grace was administered under the Old Testament, by promises,[1] prophecies,[2] sacrifices,[3] circumcision,[4] the passover,[5] and other types and ordinances; which did all fore-signify Christ then to come, and were for that time sufficient to build up the elect in faith in the promised Messiah,[6] by whom they then had full remission of sin and eternal salvation.[7]

(1) Rom. 15:8; Acts 3:20.
(2) Acts 3:20, 24.
(3) Heb. 10:1.
(4) Rom. 4:11.
(5) I Cor. 5:7; Ex. 12:14, 17, 24.
(6) Heb. 11:13.
(7) Gal. 3:7, 8, 9; Heb. 11.

Q. 35. *How is the covenant of grace administered under the New Testament?*

A. Under the New Testament, when Christ the substance was exhibited, the same covenant of grace was, and still is to be, administered in the preaching of the word,[1] and the administration of the sacraments of baptism,[2] and the Lord's supper;[3] in which grace and salvation are held forth in more fullness, evidence, and efficacy to all nations.[4]

(1) Matt. 28:19, 20.
(2) Matt. 28:19.
(3) I Cor. 11:23, 24, 25, 26.
(4) Heb. 8:6, 7.

| THE WESTMINSTER CONFESSION OF FAITH | THE WESTMINSTER LARGER CATECHISM | THE WESTMINSTER SHORTER CATECHISM |
| --- | --- | --- |

and the same under various dispensations.[14]

(11) Matt. 28:19, 20; I Cor. 11:23, 24, 25.

(12) Heb. 8:6-13; II Cor. 3:9-11.

(13) Eph. 2:15-19.
See under figure 11 above.

(14) Gal. 3:17, 29.
See context and citations under figure 10 above.

## EXPLANATORY NOTES

THE caption of Chapter VII in the Confession is "Of God's Covenant with Man." Should not the word covenant be plural? For the chapter treats of two covenants.

### CONF. VII:3; L.C. 30; S.C. 20

"First Covenant," "Second Covenant"; there is no third. One was legal; the other, evangelical. The legal covenant or the covenant of works has been treated in Chapter V. The evangelical covenant or the covenant of grace is the subject of this chapter.

From Genesis 3 onward men have been under the second covenant as means of grace, but still under the first as means of punishment and discipline.

The other covenants of which we read in Scripture — the covenants with Noah, with Abraham, with David — are comprehended under the second covenant, and were means of carrying it into effect. The "new covenant" spoken of in Jeremiah 31 and in the New Testament is not new as compared with the covenant of grace but only with reference to the covenant with Israel at Sinai which was a re-enactment of the covenant of works for educational and disciplinary purposes. "New covenant" in Scripture signifies new dispensation of the covenant of grace.

The Catechisms speak in different tenses of God's action in the matter of the covenant: "Doth God," "Did God." The Shorter Catechism, having in mind the institution of the covenant which was an act done once for all, uses the past tense; while the Larger Catechism, thinking of the execution of the covenant, which is a process still going on, employs the present tense.

The Confession gives the reason for a second covenant.

To what in God do the Confession and the Shorter Catechism attribute the new covenant? To what does the Larger Catechism attribute it? Since they mean practically the same thing, we learn that God's "good pleasure" is merciful and gracious.

### CONF. VII:3; L.C. 31; S.C. 20

With whom was the covenant of grace made? Primarily with Christ, secondarily with the elect; directly with the Saviour, mediately with those ordained unto salvation.

How are the beneficiaries designated in the Catechisms? "Some," "all the elect." How, in the Confession? "Sinners," without limitation. This differing phraseology means that the covenant has a general reference and also a special reference. There is no harmonizing of all Scripture except on. that supposition.

**L.C. 32**

Wherein is the second covenant gracious?

1. In its offer — "life and salvation" to "sinners": that is, to rebels.

2. In its requirements — "faith [only] as the condition to interest them in" the Saviour.

3. In its promise — the Holy Spirit "to work in them that faith"; that is, God requires faith, and gives what He requires.

   One is reminded of the prayer of Augustine: "Give what Thou bidst and bid what Thou wilt."

God's grace in its sum:

1. The gift of His Son to provide salvation.

2. The gift of His Spirit to apply salvation.

or

1. The gift of His Son to work salvation out.

2. The gift of His Spirit to work salvation in.

The last lines of Larger Catechism 32 express the value of obedience. Obedience has, first, the value of evidence. The evidence of what? "Of the truth of their faith and of their thankfulness to God." It has, secondly, the value of a "way." "The way which He hath appointed them to salvation." Does this imply salvation by obedience? No; not salvation *by* obedience, but salvation *in* or *with* obedience.

## CONF. VII:4

Is it true that "this covenant of grace is *frequently* set forth in the Scripture by the name of a testament"? Not according to the American Standard Version, nor hardly according to the King James Version, though it *is* there several times so designated. The American Standard Version uses testament only twice, in a single passage, Hebrews 9:16-17. Some Bible scholars contend against the use of that term even in this passage. In the Revised Standard Version it is translated "will." One wonders why no Scriptures are cited in support of this section.

In the covenant idea, promise is prominent; in the testamentary idea, heirship is emphasized. Combining the two ideas we learn that the end of the covenant arrangement is salvation plus inheritance

## CONF. VII:5-6; L.C. 33-35

These statements relate to the administration of the covenant. The Standards recognize two dispensations: that "under the law" and that "under the gospel." The dispensation under the law is called the Old Testament, and the dispensation under the gospel is called the New Testament. So, "Old Testament" and "New Testament" here do not mean the major divisions of the Bible; but they mean eras or dispensations. It would make for clearness if dispensation were substituted for testament.

The important truth under this head is stated in the end of section 6 of the Confession: "There are not, therefore, two covenants of grace differing in substance, but one and the same under various dispensations."

## CONF. VII:5; L.C. 34

Why did the framers of the Confession and the Larger Catechism think it necessary to affirm that the people under this old dispensation "had full remission of sins, and eternal salvation"? Because the Catholics deny that this is so.

# CHAPTER VIII

# Of Christ the Mediator

CONFESSION OF FAITH VIII:1-8
LARGER CATECHISM 36-56, (57) · SHORTER CATECHISM 21-28

IT pleased God, in his eternal purpose, to choose and ordain the Lord Jesus, his only begotten Son, to be the mediator between God and man,[1] the prophet,[2] priest,[3] and king;[4] the head and saviour of his church,[5] the heir of all things,[6] and judge of the world;[7] unto whom he did, from all eternity, give a people to be his seed,[8] and to be by him in time redeemed, called, justified, sanctified, and glorified.[9]

(1) Isa. 42:1; I Pet. 1:19, 20; I Tim. 2:5; John 3:16.
(2) Acts 3:22; Deut. 18:15.
(3) Heb. 5:5, 6.
(4) Psa. 2:6; Luke 1:33; Isa. 9:6, 7.
(5) Eph. 5:23.
(6) Heb. 1:2.
(7) Acts 17:31; II Cor. 5:10.
(8) John 17:6; Eph. 1:4; John 6:37, 39; Isa. 53:10.
(9) I Tim. 2:5, 6; Mark 10:45; I Cor. 1:30; Rom. 8:30.

2. The Son of God, the second person in the Trinity, being very and eternal God, of one substance, and equal with the Father, did, when the fullness of time was come, take upon him man's nature,[10] with all the essential properties and common infirmities thereof; yet without sin:[11] being conceived by the power of the Holy Ghost, in the womb of the Virgin Mary, of her substance.[12] So that two whole, perfect, and distinct natures, the Godhead and the manhood, were inseparably joined together in one person, without conversion, composition, or confusion.[13]

Q. 36. *Who is the Mediator of the covenant of grace?*

A. The only Mediator of the covenant of grace is the Lord Jesus Christ,[1] who being the eternal Son of God, of one substance and equal with the Father, in the fullness of time became man, and so was, and continues to be, God and man, in two entire distinct natures, and one person forever.[2]

(1) I Tim. 2:5.
(2) John 1:1; John 10:30; Phil. 2:6; Gal. 4:4; Col. 2:9; Phil. 2:5-11.

Q. 21. *Who is the Redeemer of God's elect?*

A. The only Redeemer of God's elect is the Lord Jesus Christ,[1] who, being the eternal Son of God, became man,[2] and so was, and continueth to be, God and man, in two distinct natures, and one person, forever.[3]

(1) I Tim. 2:5.
(2) John 1:1, 14; John 10:30; Phil. 2:6; Gal. 4:4.
(3) See texts just cited; also Phil. 2:5-11.

| THE WESTMINSTER CONFESSION OF FAITH | THE WESTMINSTER LARGER CATECHISM | THE WESTMINSTER SHORTER CATECHISM |
|---|---|---|

Which person is very God and very man, yet one Christ, the only mediator between God and man.[14]

(10) John 1:1, 14; I John 5:20; Phil. 2:6; Gal. 4:4; Heb. 2:14.
(11) Heb. 2:17; Heb. 4:15.
(12) Luke 1:27, 31, 35; Gal. 4:4.
    See under figure 10 above.
(13) Col. 2:9; Rom. 9:5.
    See under figure 12 above.
(14) Rom. 1:3, 4; I Tim. 2:5.

**Q. 37.** *How did Christ, being the Son of God, become man?*

A. Christ, the Son of God, became man by taking to himself a true body, and a reasonable soul,[1] being conceived by the power of the Holy Ghost, in the womb of the Virgin Mary, of her substance, and born of her,[2] yet without sin.[3]

(1) John 1:14; Matt. 26:38.
(2) Luke 1:31, 35, 42; Gal. 4:4.
(3) Heb. 4:15.

**Q. 38.** *Why was it requisite that the Mediator should be God?*

A. It was requisite that the Mediator should be God; that he might sustain and keep the human nature from sinking under the infinite wrath of God, and the power of death; give worth and efficacy to his sufferings, obedience, and intercession; and to satisfy God's justice, procure his favor, purchase a peculiar people, give his Spirit to them, conquer all their enemies, and bring them to everlasting salvation.[1]

(1) See General Note, question 1 of Larger Catechism.

**Q. 39.** *Why was it requisite that the Mediator should be man?*

A. It was requisite that the Mediator should be man; that he might advance our nature, perform obedience to the law,[1] suffer and make intercession for us in our nature,[2] have a fellow-feeling of our infirmities;[3] that we might receive the adoption of sons,[4] and have comfort and access with boldness unto the throne of grace.[5]

(1) Rom. 5:19; Gal. 4:4, 5.
(2) Heb. 2:14; Heb. 7:24, 25.
(3) Heb. 4:15.
(4) Gal. 4:5.
(5) Heb. 4:14, 15, 16.

**Q. 22.** *How did Christ, being the Son of God, become man?*

A. Christ, the Son of God, became man, by taking to himself a true body and a reasonable soul,[1] being conceived by the power of the Holy Ghost, in the womb of the Virgin Mary, and born of her,[2] yet without sin.[3]

(1) John 1:14; Heb. 2:14; Matt. 26:38.
(2) Luke 1:31, 35, 41, 42; Gal. 4:4.
(3) Heb. 4:15; Heb. 7:26.

| THE WESTMINSTER CONFESSION OF FAITH | THE WESTMINSTER LARGER CATECHISM | THE WESTMINSTER SHORTER CATECHISM |
|---|---|---|
| | Q. 40. *Why was it requisite that the Mediator should be God and man in one person?* | |
| | A. It was requisite that the Mediator who was to reconcile God and man, should himself be both God and man, and this in one person; that the proper works of each nature might be accepted of God for us, and relied on by us, as the works of the whole person.[1] | |
| | (1) See General Note, question 1 of Larger Catechism. | |
| | Q. 41. *Why was our Mediator called Jesus?* | |
| | A. Our Mediator was called Jesus, because he saveth his people from their sins.[1] | |
| | (1) Matt. 1:21. | |
| 3. The Lord Jesus in his human nature thus united to the divine, was sanctified and anointed with the Holy Spirit above measure;[15] having in him all the treasures of wisdom and knowledge,[16] in whom it pleased the Father that all fullness should dwell:[17] to the end that being holy, harmless, undefiled, and full of grace and truth, he might be thoroughly furnished to execute the office of a mediator and surety.[18] Which office he took not unto himself, but was thereunto called by his Father;[19] who put all power and judgment into his hand, and gave him commandment to execute the same.[20] | Q. 42. *Why was our Mediator called Christ?* | Q. 23. *What offices doth Christ execute as our Redeemer?* |
| | A. Our Mediator was called Christ, because he was anointed with the Holy Ghost above measure;[1] and so set apart, and fully furnished with all authority and ability,[2] to execute the office of prophet,[3] priest,[4] and king of his church, in the estate both of his humiliation and exaltation.[5] | A. Christ, as our Redeemer, executeth the offices of a prophet,[1] of a priest,[2] and of a king, both in his estate of humiliation and exaltation.[3] |
| | (1) John 3:34; Luke 4:18-21. | (1) Acts 3:22; Luke 4:18, 21. |
| | (2) Luke 4:14; Heb. 9:14; Matt. 28:18, 19, 20. | (2) Heb. 5:5, 6; Heb. 4:14, 15. |
| (15) Luke 4:18, 19, 21; Acts 10:38. | (3) Acts 3:22; Luke 4:18, 21. | (3) Rev. 19:16; Isa. 9:6, 7; Psa. 2:6. |
| (16) Col. 2:3. | (4) Heb. 5:5, 6; Heb. 4:14, 15. | |
| (17) Col. 1:19. | (5) Rev. 19:16; Isa. 9:6, 7; Psa. 2:6. | |
| (18) Heb. 7:26; John 1:14; Luke 4:18-21. | | |
| (19) Heb. 5:4, 5. | | |
| (20) John 5:22, 27; Matt. 28:18. | Q. 43. *How doth Christ execute the office of a prophet?* | Q. 24. *How doth Christ execute the office of a prophet?* |
| | A. Christ executeth the office of a prophet, in his revealing to the church in all ages,[1] by his Spirit and word,[2] in divers ways of admin- | A. Christ executeth the office of a prophet, in revealing to us,[1] by his word and Spirit, the will of God for our salvation.[2] |

| THE WESTMINSTER CONFESSION OF FAITH | THE WESTMINSTER LARGER CATECHISM | THE WESTMINSTER SHORTER CATECHISM |
|---|---|---|

**THE WESTMINSTER LARGER CATECHISM** (continued)

istration, the whole will of God, in all things concerning their edification and salvation.[3]

(1) John 1:1, 4.
(2) II Pet. 1:21; II Cor. 2:9, 10.
(3) Eph. 4:11, 12, 13; John 20:31.

**THE WESTMINSTER SHORTER CATECHISM** (continued)

(1) John 1:1, 4.
(2) John 15:15; John 20:31; II Pet. 1:21; John 14:26.

---

**THE WESTMINSTER CONFESSION OF FAITH** (continued)

5. The Lord Jesus, by his perfect obedience and sacrifice of himself, which he through the eternal Spirit once offered up unto God, hath fully satisfied the justice of his Father;[33] and purchased not only reconciliation, but an everlasting inheritance in the kingdom of heaven, for all those whom the Father hath given unto him.[34]

(33) Rom. 5:19; Heb. 9:14; Rom. 3:25, 26; Heb. 10:14; Eph. 5:2.
(34) Eph. 1:11, 14; John 17:2; Rom. 5:10, 11; Heb. 9:12, 15.

---

**THE WESTMINSTER LARGER CATECHISM** (continued)

Q. 44. *How doth Christ execute the office of a priest?*

A. Christ executeth the office of a priest, in his once offering himself a sacrifice without spot to God,[1] to be a reconciliation for the sins of his people;[2] and in making continual intercession for them.[3]

(1) Heb. 9:14, 28.
(2) Heb. 2:17.
(3) Heb. 7:25.

Q. 45. *How doth Christ execute the office of a king?*

A. Christ executeth the office of a king, in calling out of the world a people to himself;[1] and giving them officers,[2] laws,[3] and censures, by which he visibly governs them;[4] in bestowing saving grace upon his elect,[5] rewarding their obedience,[6] and correcting them for their sins,[7] preserving and supporting them under all their temptations and sufferings;[8] restraining and overcoming all their enemies,[9] and powerfully ordering all things for his own glory,[10] and their good;[11] and also in taking vengeance on the rest, who know not God, and obey not the gospel.[12]

(1) John 10:16, 27; Isa. 55:5.
(2) I Cor. 12:28; Eph. 4:11, 12.
(3) Matt. 28:19, 20.
(4) Matt. 18:17, 18; I Cor. 5:4, 5; I Tim. 5:20; Tit. 3:10.
(5) Acts 5:31.
(6) Rev. 22:12; Matt. 25:34-36; Rom. 2:7.
(7) Rev. 3:19; Heb. 12:6, 7.
(8) II Cor. 12:9, 10; Rom. 8:35-39.
(9) I Cor. 15:25; Acts 12:17; Acts 18:9, 10.
(10) Rom. 14:11; Col. 1:18; Matt. 28:19, 20.
(11) Rom. 8:28.
(12) II Thess. 1:8; Psa. 2:9.

---

**THE WESTMINSTER SHORTER CATECHISM** (continued)

Q. 25. *How doth Christ execute the office of a priest?*

A. Christ executeth the office of a priest, in his once offering up of himself a sacrifice to satisfy divine justice,[1] and reconcile us to God,[2] and in making continual intercession for us.[3]

(1) Heb. 9:14, 28; Rom. 3:26; Rom. 10:4.
(2) Heb. 2:17.
(3) Heb. 7:25.

Q. 26. *How doth Christ execute the office of a king?*

A. Christ executeth the office of a king, in subduing us to himself,[1] in ruling and defending us,[2] and in restraining and conquering all his and our enemies.[3]

(1) Psa. 110:3.
(2) Isa. 33:22.
(3) I Cor. 15:25; Acts 12:17; 18:9, 10.

THE WESTMINSTER
## CONFESSION OF FAITH

THE WESTMINSTER
## LARGER CATECHISM

THE WESTMINSTER
## SHORTER CATECHISM

7. Christ, in the work of mediation, acteth according to both natures; by each nature doing that which is proper to itself;[36] yet by reason of the unity of the person, that which is proper to one nature is sometimes, in Scripture, attributed to the person denominated by the other nature.[37]

(36) I Pet. 3:18; Heb. 9:14; John 10:17, 18.
(37) Acts 20:28; John 3:13; I John 3:16.

4. This office the Lord Jesus did most willingly undertake,[21] which, that he might discharge, he was made under the law,[22] and did perfectly fulfill it;[23] endured most grievous torments immediately in his soul,[24] and most painful sufferings in his body;[25] was crucified and died;[26] was buried, and remained under the power of death, yet saw no corruption.[27] On the third day he arose from the dead,[28] with the same body in which he suffered;[29] with which also he ascended into heaven, and there sitteth at the right hand of his Father,[30] making intercession;[31] and shall return to judge men and angels, at the end of the world.[32]

(21) Psa. 40:7, 8; Phil. 2:5, 6, 7, 8.
(22) Gal. 4:4.
(23) Matt. 3:15; John 17:4.
(24) Matt. 26:37, 38; Luke 22:44; Matt. 27:46.
(25) Matt., chapters 26 and 27.
(26) Phil. 2:8.
(27) Acts 2:24, 27; Acts 13:37.
(28) I Cor. 15:4.
(29) John 20:25, 27.
(30) Luke 24:50, 51; Acts 1:9; Acts 2:33, 34, 35, 36.
(31) Rom. 8:34; Heb. 7:25.
(32) Acts 10:42; Matt. 13:40-42; Matt. 16:27; Matt. 25:31, 32, 33; II Tim. 4:1.

**Q. 46. *What was the estate of Christ's humiliation?***

A. The estate of Christ's humiliation was that low condition, wherein he, for our sakes, emptying himself of his glory, took upon him the form of a servant, in his conception and birth, life, death, and after his death until his resurrection.[1]

(1) Phil. 2:6, 7, 8; II Cor. 8:9; Gal. 4:4.

**Q. 47. *How did Christ humble himself in his conception and birth?***

A. Christ humbled himself in his conception and birth, in that, being from all eternity the Son of God in the bosom of the Father, he was pleased in the fullness of time to become the son of man, made of a woman of low estate, and to be born of her, with divers circumstances of more than ordinary abasement.[1]

(1) John 1:18.
 See citations under Q. 46 above.

**Q. 48. *How did Christ humble himself in his life?***

A. Christ humbled himself in his life, by subjecting himself to the law,[1] which he perfectly fulfilled,[2] and by conflicting with the indignities of the world,[3] temptations of Satan,[4] and infirmities in his flesh; whether common to the nature of

**Q. 27. *Wherein did Christ's humiliation consist?***

A. Christ's humiliation consisted in his being born, and that in a low condition,[1] made under the law,[2] undergoing the miseries of this life,[3] the wrath of God,[4] and the cursed death of the cross,[5] in being buried and continuing under the power of death for a time.[6]

(1) Luke 2:7; Phil. 2:6-8; II Cor. 8:9.
(2) Gal. 4:4.
(3) Isa. 53:3.
(4) Matt. 27:46; Luke 22:41-44.
(5) Gal. 3:13; Phil. 2:8.
(6) I Cor. 15:3, 4.

| THE WESTMINSTER CONFESSION OF FAITH | THE WESTMINSTER LARGER CATECHISM | THE WESTMINSTER SHORTER CATECHISM |
|---|---|---|
| | man, or particularly accompanying that his low condition.[5] | |

(1) Gal. 4:4.
(2) Matt. 3:15; John 19:30; Rom. 5:19.
(3) Heb. 12:2, 3; Isa. 53:2, 3; Psa. 22:6.
(4) Matt. 4:1. See verses 2-12; Luke 4:1-14.
(5) Heb. 2:17, 18; Heb. 4:15; Isa. 52:13, 14.

Q. 49. *How did Christ humble himself in his death?*

A. Christ humbled himself in his death, in that having been betrayed by Judas,[1] forsaken by his disciples,[2] scorned and rejected by the world,[3] condemned by Pilate, and tormented by his persecutors;[4] having also conflicted with the terrors of death and the powers of darkness, felt and borne the weight of God's wrath,[5] he laid down his life an offering for sin,[6] enduring the painful, shameful, and cursed death of the cross.[7]

(1) Matt. 27:4.
(2) Matt. 26:56.
(3) Luke 18:32, 33; Isa. 53:3.
(4) Matt. 27:26; John 19:34; Luke 22:63, 64.
(5) Luke 22:44; Matt. 27:46; Rom. 8:32.
(6) Rom. 4:25; I Cor. 15:3, 4; Isa. 53:10.
(7) Phil. 2:8; Heb. 12:2; Gal. 3:13.

Q. 50. *Wherein consisted Christ's humiliation after his death?*

A. Christ's humiliation after his death consisted in his being buried,[1] and continuing in the state of the dead, and under the power of death till the third day,[2] which hath been otherwise expressed in these words, He descended into hell.

(1) I Cor. 15:3, 4.
(2) Matt. 12:40; Luke 18:33.

(4. This office the Lord Jesus did most willingly undertake,[21] which, that he might discharge, he was made under the law,[22] and did perfectly fulfill it;[23] endured most grievous torments immediately in his soul,[24] and most painful sufferings

in his body;[25] was crucified and died;[26] was buried, and remained under the power of death, yet saw no corruption.[27]) On the third day he arose from the dead,[28] with the same body in which he suffered;[29] with which also he ascended into heaven, and there sitteth at the right hand of his Father,[30] making intercession;[31] and shall return to judge men and angels, at the end of the world.[32]

(21) Psa. 40:7, 8; Phil. 2:5, 6, 7, 8.
(22) Gal. 4:4.
(23) Matt. 3:15; John 17:4.
(24) Matt. 26:37, 38; Luke 22:44; Matt. 27:46.
(25) Matt., chapters 26 and 27.
(26) Phil. 2:8.
(27) Acts 2:24, 27; Acts 13:37.
(28) I Cor. 15:4.
(29) John 20:25, 27.
(30) Luke 24:50, 51; Acts 1:9; Acts 2:33, 34, 35, 36.
(31) Rom. 8:34; Heb. 7:25.
(32) Acts 10:42; Matt. 13:40-42; Matt. 16:27; Matt. 25:31, 32, 33; II Tim. 4:1.

Q. 51. *What was the estate of Christ's exaltation?*

A. The estate of Christ's exaltation comprehendeth his resurrection,[1] ascension,[2] sitting at the right hand of the Father,[3] and his coming again to judge the world.[4]

(1) I Cor. 15:4.
(2) Luke 24:51; Acts 1:9-11.
(3) Eph. 1:20.
(4) Acts 1:11; Acts 17:31.

Q. 52. *How was Christ exalted in his resurrection?*

A. Christ was exalted in his resurrection, in that, not having seen corruption in death (of which it was not possible for him to be held),[1] and having the very same body in which he suffered, with the essential properties thereof[2] (but without mortality and other common infirmities belonging to this life), really united to his soul,[3] he rose again from the dead the third day by his own power;[4] whereby he declared himself to be the Son of God,[5] to have satisfied divine justice,[6] to have vanquished death and him that had the power of it,[7] and to be Lord of quick and dead.[8] All which he did as a public person,[9] the head of his church,[10] for their justification,[11] quickening in grace,[12] support against enemies,[13] and to assure them of their resurrection from the dead at the last day.[14]

(1) Acts 2:24; Psa. 16:10.
(2) Luke 24:39.
(3) Rev. 1:18.
(4) John 10:18.
(5) Rom. 1:4.
(6) Rom. 4:25; I Cor. 15:17.

Q. 28. *Wherein consisteth Christ's exaltation?*

A. Christ's exaltation consisteth in his rising again from the dead on the third day,[1] in ascending up into heaven, in sitting at the right hand of God the Father,[2] and in coming to judge the world at the last day.[3]

(1) I Cor. 15:3, 4.
(2) Acts 1:9; Eph. 1:19, 20.
(3) Acts 1:11; Acts 17:31.

| THE WESTMINSTER CONFESSION OF FAITH | THE WESTMINSTER LARGER CATECHISM | THE WESTMINSTER SHORTER CATECHISM |
|---|---|---|
| | (7) Heb. 2:14; Rev. 1:18.<br>(8) Rom. 14:9.<br>(9) I Cor. 15:21, 22.<br>(10) Eph. 1:22, 23; Col. 1:18.<br>(11) Rom. 4:25.<br>(12) Eph. 2:5, 6; Col. 2:12.<br>(13) I Cor. 15:25, 26; Acts 12:17; Acts 18:9, 10.<br>(14) I Cor. 15: 20; I Thess. 4:13-18. | |

Q. 53. *How was Christ exalted in his ascension?*

A. Christ was exalted in his ascension, in that having, after his resurrection, often appeared unto, and conversed with his apostles, speaking to them of the things pertaining to the kingdom of God,[1] and giving them commission to preach the gospel to all nations;[2] forty days after his resurrection, he, in our nature, and as our head, triumphing over enemies, visibly went up into the highest heavens,[3] there to receive gifts for men,[4] to raise up our affections thither,[5] and to prepare a place for us,[6] where himself is, and shall continue till his second coming at the end of the world.[7]

(1) Acts 1:2, 3.
(2) Matt. 28:19, 20; Acts 1:8.
(3) Heb. 6:20; Eph. 4:8; Acts 1:9.
(4) Psa. 68:18.
(5) Col. 3:1, 2.
(6) John 14:2.
(7) Acts 3:21.

Q. 54. *How is Christ exalted in his sitting at the right hand of God?*

A. Christ is exalted in his sitting at the right hand of God, in that as God-man he is advanced to the highest favor with God the Father,[1] with all fullness of joy,[2] glory,[3] and power over all things in heaven and earth;[4] and doth gather and defend his church, and subdue their enemies; furnisheth his ministers and people with gifts and graces,[5] and maketh intercession for them.[6]

(1) Phil. 2:9.
(2) Acts 2:28. Compared with Psa. 16:11.
(3) John 17:5.

| THE WESTMINSTER CONFESSION OF FAITH | THE WESTMINSTER LARGER CATECHISM | THE WESTMINSTER SHORTER CATECHISM |
|---|---|---|

(4) Eph. 1:22; I Pet. 3:22.
(5) Eph. 4:11, 12.
    See citations under Q. 45.
(6) Rom. 8:34.
  • See citations under Q. 44.

Q. 55. *How doth Christ make intercession?*

A. Christ maketh intercession, by his appearing in our nature continually before the Father in heaven,[1] in the merit of his obedience and sacrifice on earth;[2] declaring his will to have it applied to all believers;[3] answering all accusations against them;[4] and procuring for them quiet of conscience, notwithstanding daily failings,[5] access with boldness to the throne of grace,[6] and acceptance of their persons[7] and services.[8]
(1) Heb. 9:24.
(2) Heb. 1:3.
(3) John 17:9, 20, 24.
(4) Rom. 8:33, 34.
(5) Rom. 5:1, 2.
(6) Heb. 4:16.
(7) Eph. 1:6.
(8) I Pet. 2:5; Rev. 8:3, 4.

Q. 56. *How is Christ to be exalted in his coming again to judge the world?*

A. Christ is to be exalted in his coming again to judge the world, in that he, who was unjustly judged and condemned by wicked men, shall come again at the last day in great power, and in the full manifestation of his own glory, and of his Father's, with all his holy angels, with a shout, with the voice of the archangel, and with the trumpet of God, to judge the world in righteousness.[1]
(1) Matt. 24:30; Luke 9:26; I Thess. 4:16; Acts 17:31; Matt. 25:31.

6. Although the work of redemption was not actually wrought by Christ till after his incarnation, yet the virtue, efficacy, and benefits thereof were communicated unto the elect, in all ages sucessively from the beginning of the world, in and

| THE WESTMINSTER CONFESSION OF FAITH | THE WESTMINSTER LARGER CATECHISM | THE WESTMINSTER SHORTER CATECHISM |
|---|---|---|

by those promises, types, and sacrifices wherein he was revealed, and signified to be the seed of the woman, which should bruise the serpent's head, and the lamb slain from the beginning of the world, being yesterday and today the same and for ever.[35]

(35) Gen. 3:15; Rev. 13:8; Heb. 13:8. See citations under chapter 7, section 5, figures 9 and 10.

8. To all those for whom Christ hath purchased redemption, he doth certainly and effectually apply and communicate the same;[38] making intercession for them,[39] and revealing unto them, in and by the word, the mysteries of salvation;[40] effectually persuading them by his Spirit to believe and obey; and governing their hearts by his word and Spirit;[41] overcoming all their enemies by his almighty power and wisdom, in such manner and ways as are most consonant to his wonderful and unsearchable dispensation.[42]

(38) John 6:37, 39; John 10:16.
(39) I John 2:1; Rom. 8:34.
(40) John 15:15; John 17:6; Gal. 1:11, 12; Eph. 1:7-9.
(41) Rom. 8:9, 14; Titus 3:4, 5; Rom. 15:18, 19; John 17:17.
(42) Psa. 110:1; I Cor. 15:25, 26; Mal. 4:2, 3; Col. 2:15.

(Q. 57. *What benefits hath Christ procured by his mediation?*

(A. Christ by his mediation hath procured redemption, with all other benefits of the covenant of grace.)

# EXPLANATORY NOTES

THE Confession and Catechisms differ in their emphases. The Confession stresses the general idea of mediation. The Catechisms stress the functions and estates of the Mediator. The Confession treats of the person, office, and work of Christ in one chapter. This suggests that they are so closely connected as to be fittingly combined in one discussion.

The contents of this chapter are so full and varied that it seems to be wise to present them under several heads.

### I. THE PERSON OF THE MEDIATOR

CONF. VIII:1-2; L.C. 36-37; S.C. 21-22

The first section of the Confession is a general statement. There are embraced in it two main points with subdivisions under the first.

1. God's appointment of His Son to the mediatorial office.

   a. The functions of the office.

   b. The prerogatives of the office.

2. God's gift to His Son of a people, and the Son's task in relation to His people.

The general subject of Confession .VIII:2, of Larger Catechism 36-37, and of Shorter Catechism 21-22 is the constitution of the Redeemer's person; the special subject is the incarnation. It was by the incarnation that He was constituted the divine-human person.

Of the incarnation two things are affirmed and a third thing is implied.

1. The fact of it: "the eternal Son of God . . . became man."

2. The method of it: "by taking to Himself" — "being conceived."

3. The purpose of it: the purpose is implied in the names or titles: Mediator, Redeemer, Jesus, Christ.

The factors of correct Christology are in these compact statements:

1. The reality of the two natures.

2. The integrity of the two natures.

3. The distinctness of the two natures after the union.

4. The oneness of the personality.

The phrasing of the statements was determined by the several errors which they oppose. These errors were:

1. Ebionitism, which denied the reality of the divine nature.

2. Gnosticism, which denied the reality of the human nature.

3. Arianism, which denied the integrity of the divine nature.

4. Apollinarianism, which denied the integrity of the human nature.

5. Nestorianism, which overemphasized the distinctness of the natures after their union, endangering the unity of the person.

6. Eutychianism, which so fused the natures in the union as to sacrifice the human nature. This last was a reaction to the fifth in the interest of the unipersonality of the Redeemer.

These false views exhaust the possibilities of Christological error. Later errors are only variations of the earlier ones. Thus early did human ingenuity exhaust itself in efforts to rationalize or explain the union of two distinct natures in one person in Christ.

A summary statement will be interesting and perhaps helpful. These six erroneous views together with the true view teach:

1. That Jesus Christ is only man; or

2. That Jesus Christ is only God; or

3. That Jesus Christ is neither God nor man; or

4. That Jesus Christ is both God and man.

What is the meaning of these phrases in the Confession: "essential properties and common infirmities thereof"? Do they not mean the same as the Catechisms' phrases, "true body" and "reasonable soul"?

The Standards teach that Jesus Christ was of "one [numerical] substance . . . with the Father," *i.e.,* consubstantial with God; that He was of one (specific) substance with Mary, *i.e.,* consubstantial with man.

## II. QUALIFICATIONS FOR THE OFFICE OF MEDIATOR

### CONF. VIII:3-4; L.C. 38-42

How was Jesus "thoroughly furnished to execute the office of a mediator and surety"?

Regarding the order of logic and disregarding the order of the Standards, I list His qualifications thus:

1. That He should have divine appointment, affirmed in section 1 and reaffirmed in section 3.

2. That He should be God.

3. That He should be man.

4. That He should be one person. (L.C. 40.)

5. That He should be sinless.

6. That He should be anointed with the Holy Spirit above measure. This anointing equipped

Him with fullness of grace and wisdom and power.

7. That He should be willing to undertake the office.

Can you show from the Standards that each of these elements of His fitness was required by the work He had to do?

### III. THE WORK OF THE REDEEMER, THE FUNCTIONS OF HIS OFFICE

#### CONF. VIII:1, 5, 7; L.C. 42-45; S.C. 23-26

The office of the Redeemer was one, but the functions of His office were three; and He did the work of His office in filling the three functions of prophet, priest, and king.

As prophet His mediatorship is downward from God to man. As priest His mediatorship is upward from man to God. As king His mediatorial activity is performed in both directions. Upward in intercession, which has a royal aspect (see last clause, L.C. 54). Downward in applying the benefits of redemption and administering the affairs of His church.

#### L.C. 43; S.C. 24

1. To whom is the prophet's message?

   The church is the recipient, and therefore the custodian, exponent, and herald of the message. The prophet's mission is to the church, and the church's mission is to the whole world. This is the Confessional basis ·for world-wide missions

2. Name the agent and instrument of Christ as prophet. (L.C. indicates correct order.)

3. Consider the modes of His prophetic work.

4. What is said about the extent of His prophetic work?

5. What is said about the period of His prophetic work?

6. What is said about the end in view?

#### CONF. VIII:5; L.C. 44; S.C. 25

1. What are the branches or parts of Christ's work as priest?
   Sacrifice and intercession.

2. What is said about His sacrificial work?
   a. That He made an offering.
   b. That the offering He made was Himself. Both priest and victim, perfect in each.
   c. That He offered Himself, not only in His death, but also in His life. His obedient life and sacrificial death made the perfect offering. (Conf. VIII:5.)
   d. That the object and effect of His priestly work were satisfaction, reconciliation, inheritance.
   e. That the nature of His sufferings was penal and vicarious. These words are not in the Standards, but the ideas are.
   f. That the beneficiaries of His sacrificial ministry are all those whom the Father hath given Him.

Christ's intercession, the second part of His priestly work, is not elaborated here. For that, see L.C. 55.

#### L.C. 45; S.C. 26

Compare the Larger Catechism with the Shorter here and consider whether it contains additions or only amplifications.

Observe how the King is represented as identifying Himself with His people; His enemies are their enemies, and their enemies are His enemies.

Mark the participles which express the King's actions. Which are directed toward His people? Which toward His and their enemies?

What means of conquest does the Larger Catechism indicate? "Calling out" by the gospel, and "bestowing saving grace."

What means of government are specified?

The immediate end of Christ's activities as king is the good of His people; the ultimate end is His own glory. (L.C. 45.)

Why does Christ as mediator execute these three offices — no less and no more? Because in performing these offices He fulfills all the needs of men.

As prophet He meets the problem of man's ignorance, supplying him with knowledge. As priest He meets the problem of man's guilt, supplying him with righteousness. As king He meets the problem of man's weakness and dependence, supplying him with power and protection.

"Of him [God] are ye in Christ Jesus, who was made unto us wisdom [prophet] . . . and righteousness and sanctification [priest], and redemption [king]." (I Cor. 1:30, A.S.V.) Verily in Him we are complete. (Col. 2:10.)

We have been to Calvary in exposition of the Standards. Have we been to Calvary in experience?

As James Stalker says, "This is the centre of all things. Here two eternities meet. The streams of ancient history converge here, and here the river of modern history takes its rise. This is the end of all roads. The seeker after truth, who has explored the realm of knowledge, comes to Calvary and finds there that at last he has reached the centre. Lord, to whom can we go? Thou hast the words of eternal life." (*The Trial and Death of Jesus*, p. 157.)

## CONF. VIII:7

This section teaches that Christ's work of mediation whereby He effected atonement, purchased salvation, was performed in both His natures. If He could have achieved our redemption in one nature alone, it would not have been necessary for Him to have two natures.

Since His incarnation the Mediator acts as God-man, and the works of each nature are ascribed to the one person, in which both natures are united. That is, all the acts of the two natures are the acts of the one person.

So that we can designate Christ by a divine title, and ascribe to Him a human act; for example, one of our hymns says (Presbyterian Hymnal 101), "God, the mighty Maker, died for man the creature's sin." Or, we can call Christ by a human name, and attribute to Him a divine act. After the miracle of stilling the storm, the disciples said one to another: "What manner of man is this, that even the wind and the sea obey him?" (Mark 4:41.)

If the Christian doctrine of Christ's person is true, this language makes sense. But if the Christian doctrine of Christ's person is not true, said language makes nonsense.

The teaching of this section is important; for upon the communion of the one person of Christ in

the acts of the two natures the inherent value of His work depends.

## IV. The Estates of Christ

### CONF. VIII:4; L.C. 46-56; S.C. 27-28

Of the three Standards the Larger Catechism gives the estates of Christ most ample treatment.

The Shorter Catechism devotes two questions to the estates, while the Confession describes in one section the experience of the Redeemer in both estates, but does not name the estates. The Larger Catechism devotes eleven questions to the elucidation of this subject.

### *Humiliation*

### CONF. VIII:4; L.C. 46-50; S.C. 27

In regard to Christ's humiliation, the first thing to note is that it was voluntary. It was not forced upon Him. It is His self-humiliation we are to study. Note the active form of the verbs used to express His humiliation: "humbled Himself," "emptying Himself," "took upon Him," "subjecting Himself." The next thing to observe is that His humiliation consisted not in a single act, but in a series of acts. Beginning in heaven's height, it ended in the depth of death and the grave. (Phil. 2:5 ff.) The phrase "the cursed death of the cross" means that His death was penal.

Name and study the stages of His humiliation as they are designated and depicted in the Standards.

Down, down He went till He reached the lowest level of man's fall. Only the plummet of the cross can measure the depth of that descent. Having struck bottom the return movement began, which is called His exaltation.

Before passing to the consideration of Christ's exaltation, the student should notice the explanation the Larger Catechism gives, under question 50, of the famous phrase in the Apostles' Creed, "He descended into hell." There are other explanations, but Dr. Charles Hodge in his theology accepts the Larger Catechism's construction as the correct one. This commentator would like to see the words in question omitted from the Creed.

## Exaltation

**CONF. VIII:4; L.C. 51-56; S.C. 28**

The exaltation of Christ like His humiliation is in several stages, and is yet to be completed. The movement began in the Resurrection and is to end in the Return. Christ's humiliation belongs to the past, and was of short duration. His exaltation belongs to the present and the future, and is to be everlasting. The several stages are given in both Catechisms. The accounts of the several stages are given under questions 52-56 in the Larger Catechism.

### Exaltation in Resurrection

Five things should be noted in this statement.

1. How Christ was exalted in His resurrection. "He rose . . . from the dead . . . by His own power." As He humbled Himself so He exalted Himself. The Scriptures teach both that Christ raised Himself and that He was raised. He was both the agent and the object of resurrective power. After the event the deed is uniformly referred by Scripture to God, as proof of God's approval of Christ and acceptance of His work.
2. What the resurrection consisted in: "Having the very same body in which He suffered . . . really united to His soul."
3. The meaning of the resurrection: "Whereby He declared . . . [four things]."
4. The character in which Christ acted: as a public person, the head of the church.
5. The end for which He acted.

### Exaltation in Ascension

The ascension is a neglected fact and truth of Scripture. The resurrection has occupied the place of pre-eminence in the thought of ministers of the church, because it validates the death. The comparative neglect of the ascension is due perhaps to the fact that it is regarded (and rightly regarded) as a stage of the resurrection, being a continuation and consummation of the same.

Yet the ascension has independent significance. There are twenty clear references to it in the New Testament. Griffith Thomas points out that in the Epistle to the Hebrews no reference to the resurrection is found, while the ascension is the main spiritual truth. (*The Principles of Theology*, p. 82.) The Larger Catechism correctly represents New Testament teaching in presenting the ascension with its complementary truths of the session of Christ (at the right hand of the Father) and His intercession for His people as the continuation of the first stage of His redemptive work and the inauguration of the second. Ascension and session mean consummation and new commencement.

While the Scripture and the Catechisms represent Christ as sitting, they do not represent Him as idle. "Sitting" is the symbol of rest, rest from work finished. But atonement accomplished must be applied. Christ must reign, administering the affairs of His church and kingdom till the restitution of all things.

Now what is the central proposition in the answer to question 53?

"Christ was exalted in His ascension, in that . . . He . . . went up into the highest heavens." All the rest of the statement is built around this nucleus.

What does this whole statement teach: (1) About the nature of the ascension? It was the local transfer of Christ's humanity from earth to heaven. (2) About the significance of the ascension? To Christ it meant triumph over enemies and investiture with rights and gifts for men. To His disciples it meant the exaltation of their nature and their affections, and the preparation of a dwelling place over there where He is. (3) About the time of His return?

### Exaltation in Intercession

**L.C. 55**

While the fact of Christ's intercession is one of the certainties of our faith, little can be said with confidence about the nature of it, because little has been revealed. What is the Spirit's intercession like? What is Christ's intercession like? We cannot form a mental image of it.

Intercession is commonly thought of as prayer or supplication. In hymn and sermon Christ is represented as pleading in heaven His sacrifice, exhibiting His wounds and appealing to God to have mercy upon those for whom He has suffered.

> "Five bleeding wounds He bears,
> Received on Calvary;
> They pour effectual prayers,
> They strongly speak for me:
> Forgive him, O forgive, they cry,
> Nor let that ransomed sinner die."

Is the poet's conception wrong? Not necessarily. But the reader should beware of conceiving of Christ as a suppliant with outstretched arms, pleading our cause before a reluctant God. Christ is not a suppliant *before* the throne. As we have just seen, He is a king-priest on the throne, "asking what He will from the Father, who always hears and grants His requests."

"Our Lord's life in heaven is His prayer." His presence is His perpetual and prevailing intercession with God in behalf of His people, and secures for them all the benefits of redemption.

1. Read the answers to questions 54 and 55 in the Larger Catechism. In the former of these statements the fact of Christ's intercession is asserted; in the latter, the truth or doctrine of Christ's intercession is explained.

2. Mark the phrases which describe the nature of His intercession: "appearing in our nature," etc.; "declaring His will . . ."; "answering all accusations . . ."

3. Note the ground of His intercession: the merit of His obedience and sacrifice.

4. Consider the fruits of His intercession: quiet of conscience; access with boldness . . . ; and acceptance. . . .

Here is the framework of a sermon that would prove informing and edifying.

Praise His Name! For "he is able to save to the uttermost them that draw near unto God through him, seeing he ever liveth to make intercession for them." (Heb. 7:25.)

### Exaltation in His Coming Again

**L.C. 56**

Contrast Christ's first coming and His second coming:

1. As to manner.

   At first He came as it were in disguise; the world did not recognize Him for what He was. In apparent weakness He endured the hardships of this life and underwent the unjust judgments of an unbelieving and hostile world. At His second coming He will be seen and acknowledged for what He is, the Lord of Glory, the King and Judge of men and angels.

2. As to purpose.

   His first coming was for salvation. "Faithful is the saying, and worthy of all acceptation, that Christ Jesus came into the world to save sinners." (I Tim. 1:15; Matt. 1:21.)

   His second coming will be for judgment. "For the Son of man shall come in the glory of his Father with his angels; and then shall he render unto every man according to his deeds." (Matt. 16:27.) "And just as it is appointed for men to die once and after that to be judged, so Christ, after being once sacrificed to bear the sins of many, will appear again, not to deal with sin but for the saving of those who are on the outlook for him." (Heb. 9:27-28, Moffatt.)

   Those who have rejected or neglected His first coming, and have not been looking out for His coming again, will they be saved? No — judged! Can you say, "Amen: come, Lord Jesus"?

### V. The Application of Redemption

**CONF. VIII:6, 8; (L.C. 57)**

The final section of this long, not too long, eighth chapter of the Confession together with the sixth section relates to the application of redemption. This chapter is perhaps the most important in the Confession, for it treats of the person of the Saviour; then of His work in providing salvation; and then of His work in applying the same.

The sixth section points out the important fact that the benefits of redemption were applied before redemption was actually accomplished. That is to say, the work of Christ was retroactive. Since He as the Lamb of God was virtually slain before the foundation of the world, the benefits of His death were available from paradise lost to paradise regained.

Milton evinced true spiritual insight in closing his great poem "Paradise Regained" with Christ's victory over Satan in the wilderness temptation.

So this commentator will not be surprised to learn in the day of the manifestation of the Son of God that the first sinners became the first saints through faith in the promise that the Seed of the woman would bruise the head of the serpent.

The teaching of the final paragraph of the Confession may be comprehended under two heads:

1. The certainty of the application of redemption to all those for whom it hath been purchased. This inference is inescapable, *viz.,* that Christ did not come to make the salvation of all men possible, but to make the salvation of some men certain. For the mere possibility of salvation of all means of course the possibility of the damnation of all. Certainty is a characteristic note of Calvinism, while contingency or uncertainty is a characteristic note of other systems of theology.

2. The means and manner of the application. Salvation is applied in the exercise of the same offices by which it was provided. Which words of this eighth paragraph describe the activity Christ as prophet? His activity as priest? and His activity as king?

This completes what the Standards have to say about salvation in its outward or objective aspect. Up to this point, through Chapter VIII of the Confession, question 56 of the Larger Catechism, and question 28 of the Shorter Catechism, the Standards run parallel, and are occupied with the same grand subject: Salvation in its provision. From this point onward they are concerned with salvation in its application and experience, and follow a different order, which makes the task of the harmonist more difficult.

# CHAPTER IX
# Of the Holy Spirit
## CONFESSION OF FAITH IX:1-4

| THE WESTMINSTER CONFESSION OF FAITH | THE WESTMINSTER LARGER CATECHISM | THE WESTMINSTER SHORTER CATECHISM |
| --- | --- | --- |

THE Holy Spirit, the third person in the Trinity, proceeding from the Father and the Son, of the same substance and equal in power and glory, is, together with the Father and the Son, to be believed in, loved, obeyed, and worshipped throughout all ages.[1]

(1) II Cor. 13:14; John 15:26; Matt. 28:19; Matt. 3:16, 17; Luke 1:35; Eph. 4:30; Heb. 10:29; I Cor. 10:10, 11; Rev. 22:17; Eph. 2:18-22; John 14:26; John 16:7; Gal. 4:6; Acts 5:3, 4; Acts 16:6, 7; Mark 3:29; Rom. 8:26, 27; I John 2:20-27.

2. He is the Lord and Giver of life, everywhere present, and is the source of all good thoughts, pure desires, and holy counsels in men. By him the prophets were moved to speak the word of God, and all the writers of the Holy Scriptures inspired to record infallibly the mind and will of God. The dispensation of the gospel is especially committed to him. He prepares the way for it, accompanies it with his persuasive power, and urges its message upon the reason and conscience of men, so that they who reject its merciful offer are not only without excuse, but are also guilty of resisting the Holy Spirit.[2]

(2) Eph. 4:30; Eph. 5:9; Gen. 1:2; John 3:5, 6, 8; Acts 2:1-21; Gal. 5:22-25; John 16:8-11; II Pet. 1:21; II Tim. 3:16; I Cor. 2:10-14; I Pet. 1:11; John 16:13-15; I Cor. 2:10-14; Acts 7:51; I Thess. 5:19; Eph. 4:30; Psa. 104:30.

3. The Holy Spirit, whom the Father is ever willing to give to all

| THE WESTMINSTER CONFESSION OF FAITH | THE WESTMINSTER LARGER CATECHISM | THE WESTMINSTER SHORTER CATECHISM |
|---|---|---|

who ask him, is the only efficient agent in the application of redemption. He regenerates men by his grace, convicts them of sin, moves them to repentance, and persuades and enables them to embrace Jesus Christ by faith. He unites all believers to Christ, dwells in them as their Comforter and Sanctifier, gives to them the spirit of Adoption and Prayer, and performs all those gracious offices by which they are sanctified and sealed unto the day of redemption.[3]

(3) John 3:1-8; Acts 2:38; Luke 11:13; I Cor. 12:3; John 7:37-39; John 16:13; John 16:7-11; Rev. 22:17; Titus 3:5-7; II Thess. 2:13; Gal. 4:6; I John 4:2; Rom. 8:14, 17, 26, 27; Eph. 4:30; I Cor. 2:13-16.

4. By the indwelling of the Holy Spirit all believers being vitally united to Christ, who is the Head, are thus united one to another in the church, which is his body. He calls and anoints ministers for their holy office, qualifies all other officers in the church for their special work, and imparts various gifts and graces to its members. He gives efficacy to the word and to the ordinances of the gospel. By him the church will be preserved, increased, purified, and at last made perfectly holy in the presence of God.[4]

(4) Eph. 2:14-18; Eph. 4:1-6; Eph. 5:18; Acts 2:4; Acts 13:2; I Cor. 12; II Pet. 1:19-21; I Thess. 1:5, 6; John 20:22, 23; Matt. 28:19, 20.

THE 1942 General Assembly added two chapters to the Confession of Faith. These chapters contain nothing altogether new. The chapter on the Holy Spirit merely gathers together the teachings on that subject scattered throughout the Confession and Catechisms. This is a real service to the student, who unaided might never assemble into one comprehensive statement all aspects of the Confessional doctrine of the Holy Spirit and His work.

The chapter on the Gospel is meant to make explicit what is only implicit in the Westminster Standards. The Westminster Assembly emphasized the love of God for the elect. This chapter was not designed to correct that emphasis but to supplement it. The fact of the love of God for all mankind underlies the whole statement of the Calvinistic creed. The revisers thought that this general love of God and His call to all men should have clear recognition. Hence this chapter.

# EXPLANATORY NOTES

THE sections of this chapter follow each other logically and develop the doctrine of the Holy Spirit in orderly sequence. The first section sets forth the nature of the Spirit as revealed in His relation to the Godhead and to all rational creatures.

The second section sets forth the work of the Spirit in relation to the cosmos, to character, to revelation, and to the dispensation of the Gospel.

The third section describes the activities of the Spirit in the application of redemption, while the last section expounds His work in the edification and administration of the church.

# CHAPTER X

# Of the Gospel

## CONFESSION OF FAITH X:1-4

GOD in infinite and perfect love, having provided in the covenant of grace, through the mediation and sacrifice of the Lord Jesus Christ, a way of life and salvation, sufficient for and adapted to the whole lost race of man, doth freely offer this salvation to all men in the gospel.[1]

(1) Rev. 22:17; John 3:16; I John 2:1, 2; Acts 2:38, 39; Matt. 11:28-30; II Cor. 5:14-19; Tit. 2:11; Heb. 2:9; Luke 24:46, 47.

2. In the gospel God declares his love for the world and his desire that all men should be saved; reveals fully and clearly the only way of salvation; promises eternal life to all who truly repent and believe in Christ; invites and commands all to embrace the offered mercy; and by his Spirit accompanying the word pleads with men to accept his gracious invitation.[2]

(2) Matt. 28:19, 20; Acts 4:12; John 6:37-40; John 17:3; Acts 16:31; Acts 2:38; Gal. 2:16-20; Rom. 1:16, 17; Rom. 4:5; Acts 13:38, 39, 48; II Pet. 3:9; Matt. 11:28-30; Mark 1:14, 15; Acts 17:30; Rev. 22:17; Ezek. 33:11; Isa. 1:18; Luke 13:34.

3. It is the duty and privilege of everyone who hears the gospel immediately to accept its merciful provisions; and they who continue in impenitence and unbelief incur aggravated guilt and perish by their own fault.[3]

(3) Heb. 2:3; Heb. 12:25; Acts 13:46; Matt. 10:32, 33; Luke 12:47, 48; Heb. 10:29.

| THE WESTMINSTER **CONFESSION OF FAITH** | THE WESTMINSTER **LARGER CATECHISM** | THE WESTMINSTER **SHORTER CATECHISM** |
|---|---|---|

4. Since there is no other way of salvation than that revealed in the gospel, and since in the divinely established and ordinary method of grace faith cometh by hearing the word of God, Christ hath commissioned his church to go into all the world and to make disciples of all nations. All believers are, therefore, under obligation to sustain the ordinances of the Christian religion where they are already established, and to contribute by their prayers, gifts, and personal efforts to the extension of the kingdom of Christ throughout the whole earth.[4]

(4) Acts 4:12; Matt. 28:19, 20; Acts 1:8; Rom. 10:13-15; Heb. 10:19-25; Gal. 3:28; I Cor. 16:1, 2; Matt. 9:36-38; Acts 13:2-4; Col. 3:16; Rev. 22:17; Col. 1:28, 29.

# EXPLANATORY NOTES

THE first section of the chapter on the Gospel states the fact and the ground of the offer of salvation to all men. The ground of that offer is the suitability and sufficiency of the atoning work of Christ for the whole lost race of man. This general offer is known as the external call.

The second section sets forth the content of the external call. (See Charles Hodge's *Systematic Theology*, Vol. 11, pp. 641-2.)

The third section teaches that it is the duty and privilege of all who hear the gospel to accept its overtures. of mercy, and warns the disobedient of the consequences of continued unbelief.

The last section asserts and explains the obligation of all believers to assist in the support and spread of the kingdom of Christ throughout the whole earth.

# CHAPTER XI

# Of Free Will

CONFESSION OF FAITH XI:1-5
(See also LARGER CATECHISM 149-152) · (See also SHORTER CATECHISM 82-84)

| THE WESTMINSTER CONFESSION OF FAITH | THE WESTMINSTER LARGER CATECHISM | THE WESTMINSTER SHORTER CATECHISM |
|---|---|---|

GOD hath endued the will of man with that natural liberty, that it is neither forced, nor by any absolute necessity of nature determined to good or evil.[1]
(1) Deut. 30:19; John 7:17; Rev. 22:17; James 1:14; John 5:40.

2. Man, in his state of innocency, had freedom and power to will and to do that which is good and well-pleasing to God;[2] but yet mutably, so that he might fall from it.[3]
(2) Gen. 1:26.
(3) Gen. 2:16, 17; Gen. 3:6.

3. Man, by his fall into a state of sin, hath wholly lost all ability of will to any spiritual good accompanying salvation;[4] so as a natural man, being altogether averse from that good,[5] and dead in sin,[6] is not able, by his own strength, to convert himself, or to prepare himself thereunto.[7]
(4) Rom. 5:6; Rom. 8:7; John 15:5.
(5) Rom. 3:10, 12; Rom. 8:7.
(6) Eph. 2:1, 5; Col. 2:13.
(7) John 6:44, 65; I Cor. 2:14; Rom. 8:8; Eph. 2:2-5; Tit. 3:3-5.

(Q. 149. *Is any man able perfectly to keep the commandments of God?*

(A. No man is able, either of himself, or by any grace received in this life, perfectly to keep the commandments of God; but doth daily break them in thought, word, and deed.)

(Q. 150. *Are all transgressions of the law of God equally heinous in themselves, and in the sight of God?*

(Q. 82. *Is any man able perfectly to keep the commandments of God?*

(A. No mere man, since the fall, is able, in this life, perfectly to keep the commandments of God; but doth daily break them, in thought, word, and deed.)

(Q. 83. *Are all transgressions of the law equally heinous?*

(A. Some sins in themselves, and by reason of several aggravations, are more heinous in the sight of God than others.)

(Q. 84. *What doth every sin deserve?*

(A. Every sin deserveth God's wrath and curse, both in this life, and that which is to come.)

| THE WESTMINSTER CONFESSION OF FAITH | THE WESTMINSTER LARGER CATECHISM | THE WESTMINSTER SHORTER CATECHISM |
|---|---|---|
| | (A. All transgressions of the law of God are not equally heinous; but some sins in themselves, and by reason of several aggravations, are more heinous in the sight of God than others.) | |

(Q. 151. *What are those aggravations that make some sins more heinous than others?*

(A. Sins receive their aggravations,

1. From the persons offending: If they be of riper age, greater experience, or grace; eminent for profession, gifts, place, office, guides to others, and whose example is likely to be followed by others.

2. From the parties offended: If immediately against God, his attributes, and worship; against Christ, and his grace; the Holy Spirit, his witness, and workings; against superiors, men of eminency, and such as we stand especially related and engaged unto; against any of the saints, particularly weak brethren, the souls of them or any other; and the common good of all or many.

3. From the nature and quality of the offense: if it be against the express letter of the law, break many commandments, contain in it many sins: if not only conceived in the heart, but break forth in words and actions, scandalize others, and admit of no reparation: if against means, mercies, judgments, light of nature, conviction of conscience, public or private admonition, censures of the church, civil punishments; and our prayers, purposes, promises, vows, covenants, and engagements to God or men: if done deliberately, willfully, presumptuously, impudently, boastingly, maliciously, frequently, obstinately, with light, continuance, or relapsing after repentance.

4. From circumstances of time, and place: if on the Lord's day, or

| THE WESTMINSTER CONFESSION OF FAITH | THE WESTMINSTER LARGER CATECHISM | THE WESTMINSTER SHORTER CATECHISM |
|---|---|---|
| | other times of divine worship; or immediately before, or after these, or other helps to prevent or remedy such miscarriages: if in public, or in the presence of others, who are thereby likely to be provoked or defiled.) | |

(Q. 152. *What doth every sin deserve at the hands of God?*

(A. Every sin, even the least, being against the sovereignty, goodness, and holiness of God, and against his righteous law, deserveth his wrath and curse, both in this life, and that which is to come; and cannot be expiated but by the blood of Christ.)

4. When God converteth a sinner and translateth him into the state of grace, he freeth him from his natural bondage under sin, and by his grace alone, enableth him freely to will and to do that which is spiritually good;[8] yet so as that, by reason of his remaining corruption, he doth not perfectly, nor only, will that which is good, but doth also will that which is evil.[9]

(8) Col. 1:13; John 8:34, 36; Phil. 2:13; Rom. 6:18, 22.
(9) Gal. 5:17; Rom. 7:15. See context.

5. The will of man is made perfectly and immutably free to good alone, in the state of glory[10] only.[11]

(10) I John 3:2; Rev. 22:3, 4.
(11) II Chron. 6:36.

# EXPLANATORY NOTES

A CHAPTER on freedom in a severely Calvinistic Confession; and a chapter that affirms freedom, not denies it. This may surprise not a few. For it seems to be a common opinion that there is no room for freedom in a system built on Divine Sovereignty and Predestination. Yet here it is, a whole chapter of five sections on freedom, and a noble chapter it is.

The title of the chapter is perhaps not the best. I suggest "Of Free Agency" instead of "Of Free Will." Or, "Of Freedom of the Soul."

This subject is one of the most difficult in philosophy and theology. Men have never held, and probably will never hold, the same opinion in regard to freedom. Though realizing this to be so, I yet venture to set down the following propositions as all but self-evidently true.

Freedom is properly predicated only of a moral agent. The will is not a distinct agent and therefore should not be regarded as possessing the attributes of freedom. As Dabney rightly says, freedom is the property not of a faculty, but of a person. The acts of the will are conditioned by the character of the person whose the will is. Otherwise the acts of the will would not represent and reveal the character of the person, and the saying of Jesus, "The tree is known by its fruit," would be false.

God acts invariably and necessarily according to His character.

So do angels.

So does the devil.

And so do men.

What God does is determined by what God is. It is true of every moral agent, when left free from outward constraint, that his acts are determined by what he is. There is no escape from determinism. The determinism here intended is consistent with free agency and responsibility. For it is moral determinism — a determinism in which the self has part. An undetermined will has no existence except in the imagination of the proponent. Even the will of God is determined in its activity.

This eleventh chapter is a comprehensive statement on human freedom.

The first section affirms the fact of liberty, and states the origin and nature of it. The next four sections present a fourfold view of man's moral agency in his fourfold state. Read Boston's *Fourfold State*.

In his state of innocence man's will was inclined only to the good; but he was so constituted that he could do evil. He had the power of alternative choice; he thus had a power which God has not — the ability to sin. In the state of sin, man is still a free agent, though destitute of ability of will to any spiritual good. Sin disqualifies for righteousness, but leaves the sinner free in respect of evil.

The state of grace is a mixed state, wherein a man is both a saint and a sinner, with ability both to the good and to the bad.

The final state of the believer in Christ is a state of glory, in which the soul is wholly inclined to the good alone, with immunity from temptation. He has transcended the probationary stage. He no longer has the power of contrary choice. Only when goodness is done by inward necessity is one perfectly free.

To put it differently and more briefly: In the original state the will was determined to the good, yet mutably. In the state resulting from the fall, the will was determined to the evil, with no possibility of self-recovery. In the state resulting from regeneration, the will is determined now to the good and now to the evil. In the final state the will is immutably determined to the good. This is the state of glory, the state of God.

I say again, there is no escape from determinacy. Neither is there any escape from indeterminacy. We must do as the Bible does, affirm both divine determination and human free agency. These two doctrines, sovereignty and human freedom, as one of the Princeton Alexanders said, are like the two sides of a roof which meet at a ridgepole (somewhere) above the clouds; and he who accepts only one has only half a roof over his head.

# CHAPTER XII

# Of Effectual Calling

CONFESSION OF FAITH XII:1-4
LARGER CATECHISM 57-60, (66), 67-68 · SHORTER CATECHISM 29-32

| THE WESTMINSTER CONFESSION OF FAITH | THE WESTMINSTER LARGER CATECHISM | THE WESTMINSTER SHORTER CATECHISM |
|---|---|---|
| | Q. 57. *What benefits hath Christ procured by his mediation?*<br><br>A. Christ by his mediation hath procured redemption, with all other benefits of the covenant of grace.[1]<br>(1) Heb. 9:12; I Cor. 1:30; Rom. 8:32; II Cor. 1:20. | |
| | Q. 58. *How do we come to be made partakers of the benefits which Christ hath procured?*<br><br>A. We are made partakers of the benefits which Christ hath procured, by the application of them unto us, which is the work especially of God the Holy Ghost.[1]<br>(1) John 1:12, 13; John 3:5, 6; Tit. 3:5, 6. | Q. 29. *How are we made partakers of the redemption purchased by Christ?*<br><br>A. We are made partakers of the redemption purchased by Christ, by the effectual application of it to us by his Holy Spirit.[1]<br>(1) John 1:12, 13; John 3:5, 6; Tit. 3:5, 6. |
| | Q. 59. *Who are made partakers of redemption through Christ?*<br><br>A. Redemption is certainly applied, and effectually communicated, to all those for whom Christ hath purchased it;[1] who are in time by the Holy Ghost enabled to believe in Christ, according to the gospel.[2]<br>(1) John 6:37, 39; John 10:15, 16; Rom. 8:29, 30.<br>(2) I Pet. 1:2; II Thess. 2:13. | Q. 30. *How doth the Spirit apply to us the redemption purchased by Christ?*<br><br>A. The Spirit applieth to us the redemption purchased by Christ, by working faith in us,[1] and thereby uniting us to Christ in our effectual calling.[2]<br>(1) Eph. 2:8.<br>(2) John 15:5; I Cor. 6:17; I Cor. 1:9; I Pet. 5:10. |
| | (Q. 66. *What is that union which the elect have with Christ?*<br><br>(A. The union which the elect have with Christ is the work of God's grace, whereby they are spiritually and mystically, yet really and inseparably, joined to Christ as their head and husband; which is done in their effectual calling.) | |

## THE WESTMINSTER
## CONFESSION OF FAITH

ALL those whom God hath predestinated unto life, and those only, he is pleased, in his appointed and accepted time, effectually to call, by his word and Spirit, out of that state of sin and death in which they are by nature, to grace and salvation by Jesus Christ:[1] enlightening their minds, spiritually and savingly, to understand the things of God,[2] taking away their heart of stone, and giving unto them an heart of flesh;[3] renewing their wills, and by his almighty power determining them to that which is good;[4] and effectually drawing them to Jesus Christ;[5] yet so as they come most freely, being made willing by his grace.[6]

(1) Rom. 11:7; Rom. 8:30; II Thess. 2:13, 14; Rom. 8:2; II Tim. 1:9, 10.
(2) Acts 26:18; I Cor. 2:10, 12.
(3) Ezek. 36:26.
(4) Ezek. 11:19; Ezek. 36:27; Phil. 2:13; Phil. 4:13; Deut. 30:6.
(5) John 6:44, 45.
(6) John 6:37.
See under figure 5 above.

2. This effectual call is of God's free and special grace alone, not from anything at all foreseen in man,[7] who is altogether passive therein, until, being quickened and

## THE WESTMINSTER
## LARGER CATECHISM

Q. 67. *What is effectual calling?*

A. Effectual calling is the work of God's almighty power and grace,[1] whereby (out of his free and especial love to his elect, and from nothing in them moving him thereunto)[2] he doth in his accepted time invite and draw them to Jesus Christ, by his word and Spirit;[3] savingly enlightening their minds,[4] renewing and powerfully determining their wills,[5] so as they (although in themselves dead in sin) are hereby made willing and able, freely to answer his call, and to accept and embrace the grace offered and conveyed therein.[6]

(1) Eph. 1:18, 19, 20; II Tim. 1:9.
(2) Tit. 3:4, 5; Rom. 9:11; Eph. 2:4-10.
(3) II Cor. 5:20; John 6:44; II Thess. 2:13, 14.
(4) Acts 26:18.
(5) Ezek. 11:19; Ezek. 36:26, 27.
(6) John 6:45; Phil. 2:13; Deut. 30:6; Eph. 2:5.

Q. 68. *Are the elect only effectually called?*

A. All the elect, and they only, are effectually called;[1] although others may be, and often are, outwardly called by the ministry of the word,[2] and have some common operations of the Spirit,[3] who, for their willful neglect and contempt of the grace offered to them, being justly left in their unbelief, do never truly come to Jesus Christ.[4]

(1) Acts 13:48; John. 6:39, 44; John 17:9.
(2) Matt. 22:14.
(3) Matt. 13:20, 21; Heb. 6:4-6.
(4) Psa. 81:11, 12; John 12:38, 39, 40; Acts 28:25-27; John 6:64, 65; Prov. 1:24-32; Psa. 95:9-11.

## THE WESTMINSTER
## SHORTER CATECHISM

Q. 31. *What is effectual calling?*

A. Effectual calling is the work of God's Spirit,[1] whereby, convincing us of our sin and misery,[2] enlightening our minds in the knowledge of Christ,[3] and renewing our wills,[4] he doth persuade and enable us to embrace Jesus Christ freely offered to us in the gospel.[5]

(1) II Tim. 1:8, 9; Eph. 1:18, 19, 20.
(2) Acts 2:37.
(3) Acts 26:18.
(4) Ezek. 11:19; Ezek. 36:26, 27.
(5) John 6:44, 45; Phil. 2:13; Deut. 30:6; Eph. 2:5.

| THE WESTMINSTER CONFESSION OF FAITH | THE WESTMINSTER LARGER CATECHISM | THE WESTMINSTER SHORTER CATECHISM |
|---|---|---|

renewed by the Holy Spirit,[8] he is thereby enabled to answer this call, and to embrace the grace offered and conveyed in it.[9]

(7) II Tim. 1:9; Tit. 3:4, 5; Rom. 9:11; Eph. 2:4, 5, 8, 9.
(8) I Cor. 2:14; Rom. 8:7; Eph. 2:5.
(9) John 6:37; Ezek. 36:27; John 5:25.

3. Elect infants, dying in infancy, are regenerated and saved by Christ through the Spirit, who worketh when, and where, and how he pleaseth. So also are all other elect persons who are incapable of being outwardly called by the ministry of the word.[10]

(10) Acts 4:12; John 3:8.

4. Others, not elected, although they may be called by the ministry of the word, and may have some common operations of the Spirit, yet they never truly come to Christ, and therefore cannot be saved:[11] much less can men, not professing the Christian religion, be saved in any other way whatsoever,[12] be they never so diligent to frame their lives according to the light of nature, and the law of that religion they do profess; and to assert and maintain that they may is without warrant of the word of God.[13]

(11) Matt. 22:14; Matt. 13:20, 24; John 6:64, 65, 66; John 8:24; I John 2:19; Heb. 6:4-6.
(12) Acts 4:12; John 14:6; John 17:3.
(13) II John 9, 10, 11; Gal. 1:8.

Q. 60. *Can they who have never heard the gospel, and so know not Jesus Christ, nor believe in him, be saved by their living according to the light of nature?*

A. They who having never heard the gospel, know not Jesus Christ, and believe not in him, cannot be saved,[1] be they never so diligent to frame their lives according to the light of nature,[2] or the laws of that religion which they profess;[3] neither is there salvation in any other, but in Christ alone,[4] who is the Saviour only of his body the church.[5]

(1) Rom. 10:14; II Thess. 1:8, 9; Acts 4:12; Rom. 1:18-32.
(2) I Cor. 1:21; Rom. 1:18-32; Rom. 3:9-19.
(3) John 4:22; Phil. 3:4-10.
(4) Acts 4:12.
(5) John 6:39, 44; John 17:9.

Q. 32. *What benefits do they that are effectually called partake of in this life?*

A. They that are effectually called do in this life partake of justification,[1] adoption,[2] sanctification, and the several benefits which, in this life, do either accompany or flow from them.[3]

(1) Rom. 8:30.
(2) Eph. 1:5.
(3) I Cor. 1:30.

## EXPLANATORY NOTES

REDEMPTION is applied by the Holy Spirit, the third person in the blessed Trinity. This He does by "calling." Hence the technical name for His work is vocation. "Calling" (from the Greek) and "vocation" (from the Latin) are two names for the same activity of the Spirit.

### L.C. 57-59; S.C. 29-30

The Catechisms have certain preliminary questions which lead up to Effectual Calling. They direct attention to the limits and certainty of the application of redemption, points already emphasized by the Confession, III:6; VIII:8.

### CONF. XII:1; L.C. 67-68; S.C. 31

Analyze these statements to find the following points of teaching:

1. The subjects of the call.
2. The agent and instrumentality of the call.
3. The effects of the call.
4. The sovereignty of the call. (See parentheses in L.C.)
5. The safeguarding of the free agency of man.

### CONF. XII:2

This section denies human co-operation in regeneration, but affirms such co-operation in conversion and sanctification. In the first, man is passive, acted on. Being quickened he becomes active. To use technical terms, regeneration is monergistic; conversion and sanctification are synergistic.

### CONF. XII:3

This section has perhaps been the occasion of more debate than any other article of the Creed. It was not a part of the original draft of this chapter, and one could almost wish that it had never been added.

The bone of contention has been the clause, "elect infants, dying in infancy." The interpreters have not been content to confine themselves to what the statement says, but insist on bringing into the discussion what they think the statement implies. There are two possible implications. One makes the antithesis to be "non-elect infants dying in infancy." This view gives occasion for the slander sometimes heard that Presbyterians teach or have taught infant damnation.

The other possible implication makes the antithesis to be "elect infants *not* dying in infancy." This is the proper way to fill out the meaning, according to the defenders of the Confession. But that this is a legitimate construction of the passage may be doubted. For infants not dying in infancy, but growing to years of accountability, are classed with adults, with "capables," who are saved as indicated in sections 1 and 2. This class of infants therefore are not in the purview of this section at all. (But see Shedd: *Calvinism, Pure and Mixed*, p. 118.)

To obviate misunderstanding and controversy it was suggested at a class discussion in Columbia Seminary that the language be changed to read: "Infants dying in infancy, being elect, are regenerated and saved," etc. That would not go beyond what the church believes, but it would go beyond what the Scriptures definitely authorize.

The committee on the revision of the Standards recommended that the division of "incapables" into two classes, "infants" and "others," be eliminated, and the section in question be altered to read as follows: "All elect persons, who are incapable of being outwardly called by the ministry of the word, are regenerated and saved by Christ through the Spirit, who worketh when, and where, and how He pleaseth."

But someone will rise up to ask, Are there non-elect persons among the incapables? The Confession makes no deliverance on that question. Let the silence of the Confession be respected. It has the right to be judged by what it says and not by what it omits to say.

### CONF. XII:4; L.C. 60

Larger Catechism question 60 is parallel with the second half of section 4 of the Confession. Sections 1-3 of this chapter relate to the elect and tell how they are saved; section 4 relates to "others, not elect," and teaches that they cannot be saved. Why? Because they never came to Christ.

Now there are two classes of these non-elect. First, those who hear the word but "never truly come to Christ" (though they may profess to come). Second, those who never hear the word, and therefore of course do not come to Christ, being ignorant of Him. These latter "be they never so diligent to frame their lives according to the light of nature, and the law of that religion they do profess" cannot be saved; for there is no salvation by works of law for the elect, and of course none for the non-elect.

The Standards teach that all the elect, and only the elect, will be saved. But they do not teach that in order to be saved the elect must profess the Christian religion. It is not only conceivable but believable that there are elect souls among those who never hear of Christ. If so they will be saved as children and incapables are saved, by Christ through the Spirit who worketh when, and where, and how, He pleaseth.

## S.C. 32

The Shorter Catechism closes this chapter with a question and answer which look backward and forward and so is a means of transition to succeeding chapters.

# CHAPTER XIII

# Of Justification

CONFESSION OF FAITH XIII:1-6
LARGER CATECHISM 70-71 · SHORTER CATECHISM 33

---

**THE WESTMINSTER
CONFESSION OF FAITH**

THOSE whom God effectually call-eth, he also freely justifieth:[14] not by infusing righteousness into them, but by pardoning their sins, and by accounting and accepting their persons as righteous; not for anything wrought in them, or done by them, but for Christ's sake alone; not by imputing faith itself, the act of be-lieving, or any other evangelical obedience to them, as their right-eousness; but by imputing the obedi-ence and satisfaction of Christ unto them,[15] they receiving and resting on him and his righteousness by faith; which faith they have not of themselves, it is the gift of God.[16]

(14) Rom. 8:30; Rom. 3:24.
(15) Rom. 4:5-8; II Cor. 5:19, 21; Tit. 3:5, 7; Eph. 1:7; Jer. 23:6; Rom. 3:22, 24, 25, 27, 28; I Cor. 1:30, 31; Rom. 5:17-19.
(16) Phil. 3:9; Eph. 2:8; Acts 13:38, 39.

2. Faith, thus receiving and rest-ing on Christ and his righteousness, is the alone instrument of justifica-tion;[17] yet is it not alone in the per-son justified, but is ever accom-panied with all other saving graces, and is no dead faith, but worketh by love.[18]

(17) John 1:12; Rom. 3:28; Rom. 5:1.
(18) James 2:17, 22, 26; Gal. 5:6.

3. Christ, by his obedience and death, did fully discharge the debt of all those that are thus justified, and did make a proper, real, and full satisfaction to his Father's jus-

---

**THE WESTMINSTER
LARGER CATECHISM**

Q. 70. *What is justification?*

A. Justification is an act of God's free grace unto sinners, in which he pardoneth all their sin, accepteth and accounteth their persons right-eous in his sight;[1] not for anything wrought in them, or done by them,[2] but only for the perfect obedience and full satisfaction of Christ, by God imputed to them,[3] and received by faith alone.[4]

(1) II Cor. 5:19, 21; Rom. 3:22, 24, 25; Rom. 4:5.
(2) Eph. 1:6, 7; Rom. 3:28.
(3) Rom. 3:24, 25; Rom. 5:17, 18, 19; Rom. 4:6, 7, 8.
(4) Rom. 5:1; Acts 10:43; Gal. 2:16; Phil. 3:9; Rom. 3:25, 26.

Q. 71. *How is justification an act of God's free grace?*

A. Although Christ by his obedi-ence and death, did make a proper,

---

**THE WESTMINSTER
SHORTER CATECHISM**

Q. 33. *What is justification?*

A. Justification is an act of God's free grace, wherein he pardoneth all our sins,[1] and accepteth us as righteous in his sight,[2] only for the righteousness of Christ, imputed to us,[3] and received by faith alone.[4]

(1) Eph. 1:7.
(2) II Cor. 5:19, 21; Rom. 4:5; Rom. 3:22, 24, 25.
(3) Rom. 5:17, 18, 19; Rom. 4:6-8.
(4) Rom. 5:1; Acts 10:43; Gal. 2:16; Phil. 3:9.

---

tice in their behalf.[19] Yet inasmuch as he was given by the Father for them, [20] and his obedience and satisfaction accepted in their stead,[21] and both freely, not for anything in them, their justification is only of free grace;[22] that both the exact justice and rich grace of God might be glorified in the justification of sinners.[23]

(19) Rom. 5:8-10, 19; I Cor. 15:3; II Cor. 5:21; I Pet. 2:24; I Pet. 3:18; Heb. 10:10, 14; Isa. 53.
(20) Rom. 8:32; John 3:16.
(21) II Cor. 5:21; Isa. 53:6.
(22) Rom. 3:24; Rom. 6:23; Eph. 1:7; Eph. 2:6-9.
(23) Rom. 3:26; Eph. 2:7.

4. God did, from all eternity, decree to justify all the elect;[24] and Christ did, in the fullness of time, die for their sins and rise again for their justification:[25] nevertheless they are not justified until the Holy Spirit doth, in due time, actually apply Christ unto them.[26]

(24) I Pet. 1:2, 19, 20; Rom. 8:30.
(25) Gal. 4:4; I Tim. 2:6; Rom. 4:25.
(26) John 3:5, 18, 36; Gal. 2:16; Titus 3:4-7.

5. God doth continue to forgive the sins of those that are justified;[27] and although they can never fall from the state of justification,[28] yet they may by their sins fall under God's fatherly displeasure, and not have the light of his countenance restored unto them, until they humble themselves, confess their sins, beg pardon, and renew their faith and repentance.[29]

(27) Matt. 6:12; I John 1:9; I John 2:1.
(28) Luke 22:32; John 10:28; Heb. 10:14; Phil. 1:6; I John 2:19.
(29) Psa. 89:31-33; Psa. 32:5; Matt. 26:75; Psa. 51:7-12; I Cor. 11:30, 32.

6. The justification of believers under the Old Testament was, in all these respects, one and the same

real, and full satisfaction to God's justice in the behalf of them that are justified: yet inasmuch as God accepteth the satisfaction from a surety, which he might have demanded of them; and did provide this surety, his only Son, imputing his righteousness to them, and requiring nothing of them for their justification, but faith, which also is his gift, their justification is to them of free grace.[1]

(1) See citations under Question 70.

THE WESTMINSTER
CONFESSION OF FAITH

THE WESTMINSTER
LARGER CATECHISM

THE WESTMINSTER
SHORTER CATECHISM

with the justification of believers under the New Testament.[30]

(30) Heb. 11:13; John 8:56; Gal. 3-6, 7, 8; Acts 15:11; Rom. 3:30; Gal. 3:8, 9, 14.

## EXPLANATORY NOTES

THE subject of this chapter is a doctrine precious beyond all describing. Luther says it is the test of a standing or falling church. This truth was lost once. When? By whom and when was it discovered and restored?

What followed its loss? Darkness! What followed its recovery? Light! The preaching of this primitive truth by Luther shook a continent and started and shaped an era.

### CONF. XIII:1; L.C. 70; S.C. 33

Note the first personal pronouns in the Shorter Catechism: "us," "our." The statement reads as if we had written it. The statement is brief because it is only meant to include the truth; the Confession and Larger Catechism are longer because they aim not only to include truth but to exclude error. An analysis of the Shorter Catechism yields the following points:

1. The origin of justification: it is of God.
2. The nature of justification: it is an act, a gracious act.
3. The elements of justification: pardon and acceptance.
4. The completeness and comprehensiveness of the act: "all our sins."
5. The ground of justification: the imputed righteousness of Christ.
6. The condition of justification: "faith alone."

Now consider the Larger Catechism and the Confession, and note how they expand the Shorter Catechism. Mark the denial by the Larger Catechism that justification is "for anything wrought in them, or done by them." Who say that it *is*? All but Calvinists. The phrase "for the perfect obedience and full satisfaction of Christ" is the equivalent of what phrase in the Shorter Catechism? "For the righteousness of Christ."

The Confession not only describes the method of justification, negatively and positively, but also the subjects of justification: the "effectually called," and adds that justifying faith is not of man but of God.

### CONF. XIII:2

This section is meant to safeguard the doctrine of salvation by faith alone. While faith alone justifies, justifying faith does not remain alone in the person justified. It is the parent of other graces. It is an active principle and produces fruit. It works by or through love.

### CONF. XIII:3; L.C. 71

These paragraphs meet an objection or solve a difficulty. How is justification an act of free grace on the part of God, since Christ paid the price of justification? How can that be free which is fully paid for? The answer is that justification is indeed free to man but not to God or Christ. God in Christ met all the demands of the case, purchasing salvation and inclining and enabling man to accept it.

Since God only requires faith for justification and gives the faith He requires, surely justification is without price to man.

## CONF. XIII:4

This section also is meant to meet an objection or a difficulty.

In the business world, if a man's debt is paid by another, he is at once discharged from all obligation in the matter. Reasoning from this commercial transaction some men say, Since God has taken the obligation of all the elect and discharged it, why are not all the elect at once set free?

The trouble arises from supposing that the commercial transaction is a perfect analogue of what takes place in justification.

In the business transaction interest centers in the payment of the debt; the payment of the debt is an end in itself. In the religious sphere, the interest centers in the moral condition of the debtor; the payment of the debt is the means to an end, the sanctification of the debtor. God's main concern is character, holiness, so that justification is never actually given apart from sanctification. The elect are all now virtually justified and will in the course of time be actually justified. Virtual justification is eternal; actual justification is temporal. The elect are objectively justified as a class, they are subjectively justified as individuals, as they one by one appropriate Christ by faith.

## CONF. XIII:5

Justification though temporal is not temporary. The justified are never afterwards condemned, though they may be chastised. Once justified, always justified. Though the justified may fall under the Father's displeasure, they never fall out of His purpose of grace. Justification on the divine side is complete from the beginning; on the human side it is progressively realized.

## CONF. XIII:6

The way of salvation has ever been the same. The method of justification has not varied with the changing dispensations.

# CHAPTER XIV

# Of Adoption

CONFESSION OF FAITH XIV:1
LARGER CATECHISM 74 · SHORTER CATECHISM 34

| THE WESTMINSTER **CONFESSION OF FAITH** | THE WESTMINSTER **LARGER CATECHISM** | THE WESTMINSTER **SHORTER CATECHISM** |
|---|---|---|
| ALL those that are justified, God vouchsafeth, in and for his only Son Jesus Christ, to make partakers of the grace of adoption:[1] by which they are taken into the number, and enjoy the liberties and privileges of the children of God;[2] have his name put upon them;[3] receive the Spirit of adoption;[4] have access to the throne of grace with boldness;[5] are enabled to cry, Abba, Father;[6] are pitied,[7] protected,[8] provided for,[9] and chastened by him as by a father;[10] yet never cast off,[11] but sealed to the day of redemption,[12] and inherit the promises,[13] as heirs of everlasting salvation.[14] | Q. 74. *What is adoption?*  A. Adoption is an act of the free grace of God,[1] in and for his only Son Jesus Christ,[2] whereby all those that are justified are received into the number of his children,[3] have his name put upon them,[4] the Spirit of his Son given to them,[5] are under his fatherly care and dispensations,[6] admitted to all the liberties and privileges of the sons of God, made heirs of all the promises, and fellow-heirs with Christ in glory.[7] | Q. 34. *What is adoption?*  A. Adoption is an act of God's free grace,[1] whereby we are received into the number, and have a right to all the privileges, of the sons of God.[2]  (1) I John 3:1.  (2) John 1:12; Rom. 8:17. |
| (1) Eph. 1:5; Gal. 4:4, 5.  (2) John 1:12; Rom. 8:17.  (3) Rev. 3:12.  (4) Rom. 8:15.  (5) Eph. 3:12; Heb. 4:16; Rom. 5:2.  (6) Gal. 4:6.  (7) Psa. 103:13.  (8) Prov. 14:26; Psa. 27:1, 2, 3.  (9) Matt. 6:30, 32; I Pet. 5:7.  (10) Heb. 12:6.  (11) Lam. 3:31; Heb. 13:5.  (12) Eph. 4:30.  (13) Heb. 6:12.  (14) I Pet. 1:4; Heb. 1:14. | (1) I John 3:1.  (2) Eph. 1:5; Gal. 4:4, 5.  (3) John 1:12.  (4) Rev. 3:12; II Cor. 6:18.  (5) Gal. 4:6.  (6) Psa. 103:13; Prov. 14:26; Matt. 6:32.  (7) Rom. 8:17; Heb. 6:12. | |

# EXPLANATORY NOTES

THE doctrine of adoption has received scant recognition in theological discussions and pulpit dissertations. Some great treatises omit it altogether, others devote to it a few remarks, while scarcely one of them articulates it as a separate head in divinity. Emphasis on adoption is a peculiarity of Columbia Seminary. Two of its men, Dr. James L. Girardeau and Dr. R. A. Webb, teacher and pupil respectively, signalized and developed this truth as a distinctive and precious article of the Christian Faith. Girardeau devotes a long chapter to the elucidation of the subject in his *Discussions of Theological Questions,* while Webb in his published lectures on *Christian Salvation — Its Doctrine and Experience,* develops and articulates this neglected doctrine of divine grace.

Of the great creeds of Christendom, not one contains a formal article on adoption except the Westminster Standards. Adoption has a place in the Confession of Faith and in both Catechisms.

### CONF. XIV:1; L.C. 74; S.C. 34

The Shorter Catechism speaks of the nature of adoption and of the right of the adopted.

The Larger Catechism amplifies the Shorter Catechism statement, speaking of the subjects of adoption, the sphere and ground of adoption, and the liberties and privileges of the adopted. The Confession gives an admirable enumeration of the liberties and privileges of the children of God.

For sermonic treatment, the Scriptures on adoption may be arranged as follows:

1. Ephesians 1:5: The End of Foreordination Is Adoption.
2. Galatians 4:4-5: The End of Incarnation and Redemption Is Adoption.
3. Romans 8:23: The Object of Christian Hope Is Adoption.
4. Romans 8:15: The Filial Spirit Is the Evidence of Adoption.
5. Galatians 4:7: Inheritance Is the Privilege of Adoption (of the Adopted).

# CHAPTER XV

# Of Sanctification

CONFESSION OF FAITH XV:1-3
LARGER CATECHISM 75, 77-78 · SHORTER CATECHISM 35-36

THEY who are effectually called and regenerated, having a new heart and a new spirit created in them, are further sanctified, really and personally, through the virtue of Christ's death and resurrection, by his word and Spirit dwelling in them;[1] the dominion of the whole body of sin is destroyed,[2] and the several lusts thereof are more and more weakened and mortified,[3] and they more and more quickened and strengthened, in all saving graces,[4] to the practice of true holiness, without which no man shall see the Lord.[5]

(1) Acts 20:32; Rom. 6:5, 6; John 17:17; Eph. 5:26; II Thess. 2:13.
(2) Rom. 6:6, 14.
(3) Rom. 8:13; Gal. 5:24; Col. 3:5.
(4) Col. 1:11; II Pet. 3:13, 14; Eph. 3:16-19.
(5) II Cor. 7:1; Heb. 12:14.

2. This sanctification is throughout in the whole man,[6] yet imperfect in this life: there abideth still some remnants of corruption in every part, whence ariseth a continual and irreconcilable war, the flesh lusting against the Spirit, and the Spirit against the flesh.[7]

(6) I Thess. 5:23.
(7) I John 1:10; Phil. 3:12; Gal. 5:17; Rom. 7:18, 23.

3. In which war, although the remaining corruption for a time may much prevail,[8] yet, through the continual supply of strength from the sanctifying Spirit of Christ, the

Q. 75. *What is sanctification?*

A. Sanctification is a work of God's grace, whereby they, whom God hath, before the foundation of the world, chosen to be holy, are, in time, through the powerful operation of his Spirit, applying the death and resurrection of Christ unto them, renewed in their whole man after the image of God;[1] having the seeds of repentance unto life, and all other saving graces, put into their hearts,[2] and those graces so stirred up, increased and strengthened,[3] as that they more and more die unto sin, and rise into newness of life.[4]

(1) Eph. 1:4; I Cor. 6:11; II Thess. 2:13; Rom. 6:4, 5, 6; Eph. 4:23, 24; Phil. 3:10.
(2) Acts 11:18; I John 3:9.
(3) Jude 20; Eph. 3:16, 17, 18; Col. 1:10, 11.
(4) Rom. 6:4, 6, 14.

Q. 78. *Whence ariseth the imperfection of sanctification in believers?*

A. The imperfection of sanctification in believers ariseth from the remnants of sin abiding in every part of them, and the perpetual lusting of the flesh against the Spirit; whereby they are often foiled with temptations, and fall into many sins,[1] are hindered in all their spiritual services,[2] and their best works are imperfect and defiled in the sight of God.[3]

(1) Rom. 7:18, 23.
(2) Gal. 5:17; Heb. 12:1.
(3) Ex. 28:38; Rom. 7:18, 23.

Q. 35. *What is sanctification?*

A. Sanctification is the work of God's free grace,[1] whereby we are renewed in the whole man after the image of God,[2] and are enabled more and more to die unto sin, and live unto righteousness.[3]

(1) II Thess. 2:13.
(2) Eph. 4:23, 24.
(3) Rom. 6:4, 6, 14; Rom. 8:4.

| THE WESTMINSTER CONFESSION OF FAITH | THE WESTMINSTER LARGER CATECHISM | THE WESTMINSTER SHORTER CATECHISM |
|---|---|---|

**THE WESTMINSTER CONFESSION OF FAITH**

regenerate part doth overcome:[9] and so the saints grow in grace,[10] perfecting holiness in the fear of God.[11]

(8) Rom. 7:23.
(9) Rom: 6:14; I John 5:4; Eph. 4:16.
(10) II Pet. 3:18; II Cor. 3:18.
(11) II Cor. 7:1.

**THE WESTMINSTER LARGER CATECHISM**

Q. 77. *Wherein do justification and sanctification differ?*

A. Although sanctification be inseparably joined with justification,[1] yet they differ in that God, in justification, imputeth the righteousness of Christ;[2] in sanctification, his Spirit infuseth grace, and enableth to the exercise thereof;[3] in the former, sin is pardoned;[4] in the other, it is subdued;[5] the one doth equally free all believers from the revenging wrath of God, and that perfectly in this life, that they never fall into condemnation;[6] the other is neither equal in all,[7] nor in this life perfect in any,[8] but growing up to perfection.[9]

(1) I Cor. 6:11; I Cor. 1:30; Rom. 8:30.
(2) Rom. 4:6, 8; Phil. 3:8, 9; II Cor. 5:21.
(3) Ezek. 36:27.
(4) Rom. 3:24, 25.
(5) Rom. 6:6, 14.
(6) Rom. 8:1, 33, 34.
(7) I Cor. 3:1, 2; Mark 4:8, 28.
(8) I John 1:8, 10.
(9) II Cor. 7:1; Phil. 3:12, 13, 14; Eph. 4:11-15.

**THE WESTMINSTER SHORTER CATECHISM**

Q. 36. *What are the benefits which in this life do accompany or flow from justification, adoption, and sanctification?*

A. The benefits which in this life do accompany or flow from justification, adoption, and sanctification, are: assurance of God's love, peace of conscience, joy in the Holy Ghost,[1] increase of grace,[2] and perseverance therein to the end.[3]

(1) Rom. 5:1, 2, 5; Rom. 14:17.
(2) Col. 1:10, 11; Prov. 4:18; Eph. 3:16-18; 11 Pet. 3:18.
(3) Jer. 32:40; I John 2:19, 27; Rev. 14:12; I Pet. 1:5; I John 5:13.

# EXPLANATORY NOTES

CHRIST was a sanctificationist; the Apostles were sanctificationists. They (Christ and His disciples) both practiced and preached sanctification. We must be as they were and do as they did. "Sanctification is the Christianizing of the Christian."

## S.C. 35

The answer to this question contains three points of teaching.

1. The nature of sanctification.

    It is a "work," as distinguished from an "act."

    It is a work of God (note the passive voice of the verbs): a gracious work gradually, progressively accomplished: "more and more"; a work with two aspects: "a dying" and "a living."

2. The sphere and extent of sanctification.
    Sphere: "In the whole man."

    Extent: "Throughout in the whole man." (Conf. 15:2.)

    Sanctification like depravity is "total" *in extent*, though partial in degree. Do not hesitate to say that you believe in entire sanctification in this life. Say it, and then explain that sanctification is entire in the sense that it affects every part of man's being, soul and body, and influences in some measure his whole life.

3. The end and issue of sanctification.
    "The image of God," renewal unto righteousness.

    How does "righteousness" in this answer differ from "righteousness" in answer 33?

    How many righteousnesses are there? The righteousness of God, which is an attribute; the righteousness of Christ, which is an achievement; the righteousness of man, which is an attainment.

## CONF. XV:1-3; L.C. 75, 78

What do the Confession and the Larger Catechism add to the statement of the Shorter Catechism?

1. They tell who are the subjects of sanctification — the "chosen," the "effectually called and regenerated."

    Why are the sanctified not described as "the justified"? Because while the sanctified are "the justified," justification is not the beginning of sanctification. Sanctification begins in effectual calling and regeneration, the latter being here defined. In what words in the Confession? This is the only definition of regeneration given in the Standards.

2. They name the meritorious ground of sanctification. What is the ground according to the Confession? What, according to the Larger Catechism?

3. They name the agent and instruments in sanctification; that is, tell how sanctification is accomplished.

4. They describe the effects of the destruction of sin: the development of graces, the practice of holiness, newness of life.

5. They state not only the fact of imperfect sanctification in this life: "some remnants of corruption in every part"; but the effect of the fact, *viz.*, continual conflict, "irreconcilable war," between the Spirit and the flesh.

6. The third section of the Confession affirms the final victory of the saints through growth in grace and "perfecting holiness in the fear of God."

    "This day the noise of battle,
    The next the victor's song."

Before leaving this subject attention should be directed to the suggestive words in the Larger Catechism: "having the seeds of repentance unto life, and all the other saving graces, put into their hearts." When were those seeds planted? In regeneration, which is the beginning of sanctification.

### L.C. 77

The answer to this question presents an interesting and important comparison between justification and sanctification. The comparison is threefold.

1. In one righteousness is imputed, in the other righteousness is imparted.
2. In one guilt is dealt with (pardoned); in the other defilement of sin is dealt with (its power subdued).
3. One is complete and equal in all, while the other is incomplete and unequal in all.

### S.C. 36

This is a summary statement. The subject is the Benefits of Redemption. The grand inclusive benefits are justification, adoption, and sanctification. Flowing from these three are five other precious benefits. Name them.

"What more can He say than to you He hath said,
You who unto Jesus for refuge have fled?"

# CHAPTER XVI

# Of Saving Faith

CONFESSION OF FAITH XVI:1-3
LARGER CATECHISM 153, 72-73 · SHORTER CATECHISM 85-86

## THE WESTMINSTER CONFESSION OF FAITH

THE grace of faith, whereby the elect are enabled to believe to the saving of their souls, is the work of the Spirit of Christ in their hearts;[1] and is ordinarily wrought by the ministry of the word:[2] by which also, and by the administration of the sacraments, and prayer, it is increased and strengthened.[3]

(1) I Cor. 12:3; Eph. 2:8; Heb. 12:2.
(2) Rom. 10:14, 17.
(3) I Pet. 2:2; Acts 20:32; Matt. 28:19; I Cor. 11:23-29; II Cor. 12:8-10.

2. By this faith, a Christian believeth to be true whatsoever is revealed in the word, for the authority of God himself speaking therein;[4] and acteth differently, upon that which each particular passage thereof containeth; yielding obedience to the commands, trembling at the threatenings, and embracing the promises of God for this life, and

## THE WESTMINSTER LARGER CATECHISM

Q. 153. *What doth God require of us, that we may escape his wrath and curse due to us by reason of the transgression of the law?*

A. That we may escape the wrath and curse of God due to us by reason of the transgression of the law, he requireth of us repentance towards God, and faith towards our Lord Jesus Christ,[1] and the diligent use of the outward means whereby Christ communicates to us the benefits of his mediation.[2]

(1) Acts 20:21; Mark 1:15; John 3:18.
(2) See texts cited under Q. 154.

Q. 72. *What is justifying faith?*

A. Justifying faith is a saving grace,[1] wrought in the heart of a sinner, by the Spirit and word of God;[2] whereby he, being convinced of his sin and misery, and of the disability in himself and all other creatures to recover him out of his lost condition,[3] not only assenteth to the truth of the promise of the gospel,[4] but receiveth and resteth upon Christ and his righteousness therein held forth, for pardon of sin,[5] and for the accepting and accounting of his person righteous in the sight of God for salvation.[6]

(1) Heb. 10:39.
(2) Rom. 10:14, 17; II Thess. 2:13.
(3) John 16:8, 9; Acts 16:30; Acts 2:37; Eph. 2:1; Acts 4:12; Rom. 7:9.
(4) Rom. 10:8, 9, 10.
(5) Acts 10:43; Gal. 2:15, 16; Acts 16:31.
(6) Phil. 3:9; Acts 15:11.

## THE WESTMINSTER SHORTER CATECHISM

Q. 85. *What doth God require of us, that we may escape his wrath and curse, due to us for sin?*

A. To escape the wrath and curse of God, due to us for sin, God requireth of us faith in Jesus Christ, repentance unto life,[1] with the diligent use of all the outward means whereby Christ communicateth to us the benefits of redemption.[2]

(1) Acts 20:21; Mark 1:15; John 3:18.
(2) See under Question 88 below.

Q. 86. *What is faith in Jesus Christ?*

A. Faith in Jesus Christ is a saving grace,[1] whereby we receive[2] and rest upon him alone for salvation,[3] as he is offered to us in the gospel.[4]

(1) Heb. 10:39.
(2) John 1:12.
(3) Phil. 3:9.
(4) John 6:40.

| THE WESTMINSTER CONFESSION OF FAITH | THE WESTMINSTER LARGER CATECHISM | THE WESTMINSTER SHORTER CATECHISM |
|---|---|---|

**CONFESSION OF FAITH**

that which is to come. But the principal acts of saving faith are, accepting, receiving, and resting upon Christ alone for justification, sanctification, and eternal life, by virtue of the covenant of grace.

(4) I Thess. 2:13; I John 5:10; Acts 24:14.

**LARGER CATECHISM**

Q. 73. *How doth faith justify a sinner in the sight of God?*

A. Faith justifies a sinner in the sight of God, not because of those other graces which do always accompany it, or of good works that are the fruits of it;[1] nor as if the grace of faith, or any act thereof, were imputed to him for justification;[2] but only as it is an instrument, by which he receiveth and applieth Christ and his righteousness.[3]

(1) Gal. 3:11; Rom. 3:28.
(2) Titus 3:5, 6, 7; Rom. 4:5-8.
(3) Phil. 3:9

**CONFESSION OF FAITH**

3. This faith is different in degrees, weak or strong;[5] may be often and many ways assailed and weakened, but gets the victory;[6] growing up in many to the attainment of a full assurance through Christ,[7] who is both the author and finisher of our faith.[8]

(5) Matt. 6:30; Matt. 8:10; Rom. 4:19, 20.
(6) Luke 22:31, 32; I Cor. 10:13.
(7) Heb. 6:11, 12; Heb. 10:22; II Tim. 1:12.
(8) Heb. 12:2.

# EXPLANATORY NOTES

**L.C. 153; S.C. 85**

This chapter and the next, which treat of faith and repentance, are prefaced by a question and answer in each of the Catechisms. These statements show the relation of faith and repentance to the will of God and our salvation.

The Confession speaks of saving faith; the Larger Catechism of justifying faith; and the Shorter Catechism of faith in Jesus Christ. Read these subjects forward thus: Saving faith is justifying faith, and justifying faith is faith in Jesus Christ.

Read them backward: Faith in Jesus Christ is justifying faith, and justifying faith is saving faith.

### CONF. XVI:1-2; L.C. 72; S.C. 86

What is said in the Shorter Catechism is amplified and enlarged upon in the Larger Catechism and the Confession. Compare and combine these statements and find the answers to these questions concerning saving faith:

1. Its origin and nature?
2. Its seat?
3. Its author and instrumental agent?
4. Its acts?
5. Its objects? That is, what faith takes hold upon. Mark the little word "alone." The general object: the word; the special object: Christ.
6. Its effects or fruits? Pardon and acceptance.
7. Its ultimate end?

There is a clause in the Shorter Catechism which should not be passed over lightly: "as He is offered to us in the gospel." How is He offered in the gospel? As Son of God and Son of Man; as Mediator and Redeemer; as Prophet, Priest, and King. Saving faith *accepts* Him not under one of these titles only nor in one of these offices only, but in all of them! What wealth of material here for preaching and teaching!

### L.C. 73

Larger Catechism question 73 is an inquiry concerning the mode or way in which faith justifies. Faith justifies not meritoriously nor efficaciously but instrumentally. That is, faith justifies not because of anything in it, but because it is the means whereby a sinner appropriates Christ and His righteousness. It is Christ that justifies, and faith is the hand which receives Him.

### CONF. XVI:3

Section 3 of the Confession relates to degrees of faith.

1. Faith differs in different individuals and in the same individual at different times.
2. The degree of faith affects sanctification and assurance, not justification.
3. Weak faith, if only it is real, as certainly secures pardon as does strong faith.
4. True faith never fails; it may be often weakened and worsted, but never wrecked. This is due to the prayer of Christ. (Luke 22:32.)

# CHAPTER XVII

# Of Repentance Unto Life

CONFESSION OF FAITH XVII:1-6
LARGER CATECHISM 76 · SHORTER CATECHISM 87

---

| THE WESTMINSTER CONFESSION OF FAITH | THE WESTMINSTER LARGER CATECHISM | THE WESTMINSTER SHORTER CATECHISM |

REPENTANCE unto life is an evangelical grace,[1] the doctrine whereof is to be preached by every minister of the gospel, as well as that of faith in Christ.[2]

(1) Acts 11:18.
(2) Luke 24:47; Mark 1:15; Acts 20:21.

2. By it a sinner, out of the sight and sense, not only of the danger, but also of the filthiness and odiousness of his sins, as contrary to the holy nature and righteous law of God, and upon the apprehension of his mercy in Christ to such as are penitent, so grieves for, and hates his sins, as to turn from them all unto God,[3] purposing and endeavoring to walk with him in all the ways of his commandments.[4]

(3) Ezek. 18:30, 31; Ezek. 36:31; Psa. 51:4; Jer. 31:18, 19; II Cor. 7:11.
(4) Psa. 119:59, 106; John 14:23.

3. Although repentance be not to be rested in as any satisfaction for sin, or any cause of the pardon thereof,[5] which is the act of God's free grace in Christ;[6] yet is it of such

Q. 76. *What is repentance unto life?*

A. Repentance unto life is a saving grace,[1] wrought in the heart of a sinner by the Spirit and word of God,[2] whereby out of the sight and sense, not only of the danger,[3] but also of the filthiness and odiousness of his sins,[4] and upon the apprehension of God's mercy in Christ to such as are penitent,[5] he so grieves for, and hates his sins,[6] as that he turns from them all to God,[7] purposing and endeavoring constantly to walk with him in all the ways of new obedience.[8]

(1) II Tim. 2:25; Luke 24:47.
(2) Acts 11:18, 20, 21; Zech. 12:10; Acts 2:37.
(3) Ezek. 18:30, 32; Luke 15:17, 18; Hos. 2:6, 7.
(4) Ezek. 36:31; Ezek. 16:61, 63; Isa. 30:22.
(5) Luke 22:61, 62; Zech. 12:10.
(6) II Cor. 7:11; Acts 2:37.
(7) Acts 26:18; Ezek. 14:6; I Kings 8:47, 48; I Sam. 7:3.
(8) Psa. 119:59, 128.

Q. 87. *What is repentance unto life?*

A. Repentance unto life is a saving grace,[1] whereby a sinner, out of a true sense of his sin,[2] and apprehension of the mercy of God in Christ,[3] doth, with grief and hatred of his sin, turn from it unto God,[4] with full purpose of, and endeavor after, new obedience.[5]

(1) Acts 11:18.
(2) Acts 2:37.
(3) Joel 2:13.
(4) II Cor. 7:11; Jer. 31:18, 19; Acts 26:18.
(5) Psa. 119:59.

| THE WESTMINSTER CONFESSION OF FAITH | THE WESTMINSTER LARGER CATECHISM | THE WESTMINSTER SHORTER CATECHISM |
|---|---|---|

necessity to all sinners, that none may expect pardon without it.[7]

(5) Titus 3:5; Acts 5:31.
(6) Rom. 3:24; Eph. 1:7.
(7) Luke 13:3, 5; Acts 17:30.

4. As there is no sin so small but it deserves damnation;[8] so there is no sin so great that it can bring damnation upon those who truly repent.[9]

(8) Rom. 6:23; Matt. 12:36; James 2:10.
(9) Isa. 55:7; Rom. 8:1; Isa. 1:18.

5. Men ought not to content themselves with a general repentance, but it is every man's duty to endeavor to repent of his particular sins, particularly.[10]

(10) Psa. 19:13; Luke 19:8; I Tim. 1:13, 15; Dan. 9; Neh. 9.

6. As every man is bound to make private confession of his sins to God, praying for the pardon thereof,[11] upon which, and the forsaking of them, he shall find mercy:[12] so he that scandalizeth his brother, or the church of Christ, ought to be willing, by a private or public confession and sorrow for his sin, to declare his repentance to those that are offended;[13] who are thereupon to be reconciled to him, and in love to receive him.[14]

(11) Psa. 32:5, 6; Psa. 51:4, 5, 7, 9, 14.
(12) Prov. 28:13; I John 1:9.
(13) James 5:16; Luke 17:3, 4; Josh. 7:19; Psa. 51.
(14) II Cor. 2:7, 8; Gal. 6:1, 2.

# EXPLANATORY NOTES

THAT we may escape the wrath and curse of God due to us for sin, God requireth of us not only faith in Jesus Christ, but repentance toward God. Faith and repentance are twin graces, and they may be said to be born simultaneously. They may be separated in thought, but not in experience; in logic, but not in life. Faith of a kind precedes and produces repentance, and faith of another kind or degree follows and is the effect of repentance. So it may be truly said that each is in a sense prior and in a sense posterior to the other. In favor of the priority of faith is the fact that faith has primary reference to justification, while repentance has primary reference to sanctification. Still it is perhaps better to think of these graces as coeval and co-ordinate, though most would assign to faith the place of primacy.

The two Catechisms devote one question each to repentance, while the Confession dwells upon this element of Christian experience, devoting six sections to its elucidation and enforcement.

## CONF. XVII:1

The first section of the Confession is concerned with the nature of repentance and the obligation of the ministry to preach it.

## CONF. XVII:2; L.C. 76; S.C. 87

The second section is for the most part parallel with the Catechetical statements. They severally set forth the grounds and ingredients of repentance. The grounds out of which repentance springs are two kinds of new knowledge: knowledge of sin and knowledge of God's mercy in Christ.

Of the two grand ingredients of repentance the first is compounded of grief and hatred for sin, and the second, which is an effect of the first, is a turning from it unto God, with full purpose of, and endeavor after, new obedience. True repentance doesn't spend itself in emotion; it issues in action.

So genuine repentance involves the whole man, the intellect, the feelings, and the will.

## CONF. XVII:3

The third section of the Confession asserts the necessity of repentance, and tells why it is necessary. The statement is aimed at the error of Socinians and Rationalists, who hold that repentance is the only satisfaction God requires for sin. Repentance is not an atonement for sin, lays no basis for pardon; yet in the nature of the case there can be no pardon without it. For the purpose of God in re-

demption is to save men, not *in* sin but *from* sin. To pardon an impenitent would be to release him from the consequences of sin while leaving him in sin. So there must be a change of mind toward sin before there can be a cancellation of the penalty of sin. The man who persists in his impenitence must necessarily perish.

## CONF. XVII:4

The next section re-enforces the preceding. It teaches that no sin is so small that it may be forgiven without repentance; and that no sin is so great that it cannot be forgiven if repented of. Herein is a warning to those who are tempted to think that their sins are too little to receive divine notice, and encouragement to those whose sins seem too great for divine pardon: His grace is greater than all our sins.

## CONF. XVII:5

The fifth section of the Confession directs attention to a much neglected aspect of repentance. General repentance is common enough, but particular repentance, in which sins are named before the Lord, is rare. Jesus had little to say about sin in general, but much to say about sins in particular. General repentance may be without significance, for it may be attended with no pain of conscience and no purpose of improvement. Paul called his sins by name before the Lord. (I Tim. 1:13-15.)

## CONF. XVII:6

The last section teaches the duty of confession, both private and public, to both God and man. Confession attests the sincerity of the repentance. Repentance is not complete until it utters — outers — itself. This section teaches also that the offended party should receive the penitent confession of the offender and be reconciled to him.

Who can imagine the change that would come over the church and over society in general if all men should repent and confess their sins in detail before God and one another? The church and the world are much in arrears in this matter of repentance.

# CHAPTER XVIII

# Of Good Works

## CONFESSION OF FAITH XVIII:1-7
(See also LARGER CATECHISM 78)

| THE WESTMINSTER CONFESSION OF FAITH | THE WESTMINSTER LARGER CATECHISM | THE WESTMINSTER SHORTER CATECHISM |
|---|---|---|

GOOD works are only such as God hath commanded in his holy word,[1] and not such as, without the warrant thereof, are devised by men out of blind zeal, or upon any pretense of good intention.[2]

(1) Deut. 12:32; Psa. 119:9; Matt. 28:20; Luke 10:25, 26; II Pet. 1:19.
(2) Matt. 15:9; Isa. 29:13; John 16:2; I Sam. 15:22, 23; Col. 2:20-23.

2. These good works, done in obedience to God's commandments, are the fruits and evidences of a true and lively faith:[3] and by them believers manifest their thankfulness,[4] strengthen their assurance,[5] edify their brethren,[6] adorn the profession of the gospel,[7] stop the mouths of the adversaries,[8] and glorify God,[9] whose workmanship they are, created in Christ Jesus thereunto,[10] that, having their fruit unto holiness, they may have the end, eternal life.[11]

(3) James 2:18, 22.
(4) Psa. 116:12, 13; Col. 3:17; I Chron. 29:6-9.
(5) I John 2:3, 5; II Pet. 1:5-10.
(6) II Cor. 9:2; Matt. 5:16.
(7) Tit. 2:5; I Tim. 6:1; Tit. 2:9-12.
(8) I Pet. 2:15.
(9) I Pet. 2:12; Phil. 1:11; John 15:8.
(10) Eph. 2:10.
(11) Rom. 6:22.

3. Their ability to do good works is not at all of themselves, but wholly from the Spirit of Christ.[12] And that they may be enabled there-

THE WESTMINSTER
## CONFESSION OF FAITH

THE WESTMINSTER
## LARGER CATECHISM

THE WESTMINSTER
## SHORTER CATECHISM

unto, besides the graces they have already received, there is required an actual influence of the same Holy Spirit to work in them to will and to do of his good pleasure;[13] yet are they not hereupon to grow negligent, as if they were not bound to perform any duty unless upon a special motion of the Spirit; but they ought to be diligent in stirring up the grace of God that is in them.[14]

(12) John 15:5, 6; Ezek. 36:26, 27.
(13) Phil. 2:13; Phil. 4:13; II Cor. 3:5.
(14) Phil. 2:12; Heb. 6:11, 12; Isa. 64:7; II Pet. 1:3, 5, 10, 11; II Tim. 1:6; Jude 20, 21.

4. They, who in their obedience, attain to the greatest height which is possible in this life, are so far from being able to supererogate and to do more than God requires, that they fall short of much which in duty they are bound to do.[15]

(15) Luke 17:10; Gal. 5:17.

5. We cannot, by our best works, merit pardon of sin, or eternal life, at the hand of God, because of the great disproportion that is between them and the glory to come, and the infinite distance that is between us and God, whom by them we can neither profit, nor satisfy for the debt of our former sins;[16] but when we have done all we can, we have done but our duty, and are unprofitable servants:[17] and because, as they are good, they proceed from his Spirit;[18] and as they are wrought by us, they are defiled and mixed with so much weakness and imperfection that they cannot endure the severity of God's judgment.[19]

(16) Rom. 3:20; Rom. 4:2, 4, 6; Eph. 2:8, 9; Titus 3:5-7; Rom. 8:18.
(17) See citations under 15 above.
(18) Gal. 5:22, 23.
(19) Isa. 64:6; Psa. 143:2; Psa. 130:3; Gal. 5:17; Rom. 7:15, 18.

(Q. 78. *Whence ariseth the imperfection of sanctification in believers?*

(A. The imperfection of sanctification in believers ariseth from the remnants of sin abiding in every part of them, and the perpetual lusting of the flesh against the Spirit; whereby they are often foiled with temptations, and fall into many sins, are hindered in all their spiritual services, and their best works are imperfect and defiled in the sight of God.)

| THE WESTMINSTER CONFESSION OF FAITH | THE WESTMINSTER LARGER CATECHISM | THE WESTMINSTER SHORTER CATECHISM |
|---|---|---|

6. Yet notwithstanding, the persons of believers being accepted through Christ, their good works also are accepted in him,[20] not as though they were in this life wholly unblamable and unreprovable in God's sight;[21] but that he, looking upon them in his Son, is pleased to accept and reward that which is sincere, although accompanied with many weaknesses and imperfections.[22]

(20) Eph. 1:6; I Pet. 2:5; Gen. 4:4; Heb. 11:4.
(21) I Cor. 4:3, 4; Psa. 143:2.
(22) II Cor. 8:12; Heb. 6:10.

7. Works done by unregenerate men, although for the matter of them they may be things which God commands, and of good use both to themselves and others;[23] yet because they proceed not from a heart purified by faith;[24] nor are done in a right manner, according to the word;[25] nor to a right end, the glory of God;[26] they are therefore sinful, and cannot please God, or make a man meet to receive grace from God.[27] And yet their neglect of them is more sinful, and displeasing unto God.[28]

(23) II Kings 10:30, 31; Phil. 1:15, 16, 18.
(24) Heb. 11:4, 6; Gen. 4:3-5.
(25) I Cor. 13:3; Isa. 1:12.
(26) Matt. 6:2, 5, 16; Rom. 14:23.
(27) Tit. 1:15; Prov. 15:8; Prov. 28:9.
(28) Matt. 25:24, 25, 26, 27, 28, 41, 42, 43, 45; Matt. 23:23.

# EXPLANATORY NOTES

THIS chapter is profitable for instruction in the right view of works, and for correction or prevention of wrong views of works. It has importance for all who would know the place of works in a scheme of grace.

## CONF. XVIII:1

The first section defines good works. They are works done in obedience to God's Word. Neither the zeal nor the intention of the doer can make the work good if it lacks the warrant of the word. Saul

of the Old Testament, upon pretense of good intention, disobeyed the injunction of the Lord, and
the prophet said unto him: "Because thou hast rejected the word of the Lord, he hath also rejected
thee." (I Samuel 15:23.)

And Saul of the New Testament out of blind
zeal persecuted the Christians, thinking that he was
doing God service; but afterwards he confessed himself the chief of sinners. (I Tim. 1:13, 15.)

## CONF. XVIII:2

The second section is occupied with the value of
good works. A proper caption for this section is,
The Uses of Good Works.

1. They have evidential value; they accredit the
   believer, attest the reality of his faith.

2. They express, "manifest," gratitude.

3. They strengthen assurance.

4. They edify the brethren.

5. They adorn, render beautiful and attractive,
   the profession of the gospel.

6. They stop the mouths of adversaries. They are
   the best apologetic.

7. They glorify God.

8. They have as their end and issue holiness, and
   life everlasting. Good works are profitable to
   the doer and to others. Their value extends
   from earth to heaven, from time to eternity.
   Hence Paul's injunction to Titus. (Titus 3:8.)

## CONF. XVIII:3

The subject of the next section is the ability to do
good works. The chief concern of the authors of
this section is to define the source of that ability.
It is "wholly from the Spirit of Christ." He it is
that worketh in us both to will and to do. This
teaching is meant to correct the natural tendency
of the human heart to think of itself as sufficient
to live a life well-pleasing to God. This section
warns us against falling into the opposite error of
supposing that we are bound to do nothing except

upon a special motion of the Spirit. Sloth tempts
us to wait for a new supply of grace, while diligence
prompts us to stir up the grace already bestowed.
A correct balance may be maintained by looking to
Christ as if all depended upon Him, and laying
ourselves out as if all depended upon us.

## CONF. XVIII:4

The fourth section is pointed against the Catholic
doctrine of works. Rome teaches that good works
done after baptism have merit, and that a man may
do more than enough for himself, and may accumu-
late a surplus of merit which may be dispensed for
the benefit of others. This section teaches that
none can exceed duty, that all come short of it; that
none can do more than is required, that all actually do less.

## CONF. XVIII:5

The next section explains why our good works cannot merit pardon or eternal life. The reasons are
four. Two are introduced by the words, "because
of," and the other two by the words, "and because."
Two reasons are sufficient to prove the point:

1. Our works, even if perfect, could not merit
   eternal life, because of the vast disproportion
   between them and that glorious blessing. Let
   it be added that our works, if perfect, would
   not merit *anything* of the Lord; for they are all
   owed.

2. As a matter of fact our works are so far from
   being perfect that our best works are defiled,
   being "mixed with . . . much weakness and
   imperfection."

## CONF. XVIII:6

"Yet notwithstanding." Thus begins the next section, which is added to complete the Protestant doctrine of good works. It teaches that such works as
believers are capable of are accepted and rewarded.
This is not of justice but of grace. For let it be
carefully observed that the persons of believers are
accepted not because their works are accepted, but

their works are accepted because their persons are accepted, and both their persons and their works are accepted through Christ, God "looking upon them in His Son."

## CONF. XVIII:7

The final section is about the works of the unregenerate. It teaches that the works of such men are sinful, even those that are as to the matter of them such as God commands. Some object to this view as extreme and unfair. The objectors should consider that this doctrine is stated from God's standpoint. The unregenerate and unbelieving are rebels against God's authority. All acts of rebels are evil in the eyes of the ruler against whose government the rebels are in revolt. Some acts of rebels in some relations of life may as to the matter of them be good, but the spirit of them in relation to their rightful sovereign is bad. These Standards teach that the works, even the best works, of *saints* are defiled, and acceptable with God only because He looks upon them through His Son. Of course, then, the best works of *sinners* are sinful, and wholly without acceptance or reward, because they are not viewed through the mediation of Christ.

Let not saint or sinner complain that his works are judged severely, but let them both rejoice that there is escape from the severity of God through the goodness of God in Christ.

Be it remembered that you are bound to bring forth good works, though you have no ability to produce them. Good works are indispensable. You cannot be saved by them, yet you are not saved without them, if you have opportunity to do them. If the righteous is scarcely saved, where shall the ungodly and sinner appear! (I Peter 4:18.)

# CHAPTER XIX

# Of the Perseverance of the Saints

CONFESSION OF FAITH XIX:1-3
LARGER CATECHISM 79

---

### THE WESTMINSTER
## CONFESSION OF FAITH

---

### THE WESTMINSTER
## LARGER CATECHISM

---

### THE WESTMINSTER
## SHORTER CATECHISM

---

THEY whom God hath accepted in his Beloved, effectually called and sanctified by his Spirit, can neither totally nor finally fall away from the state of grace: but shall certainly persevere therein to the end, and be eternally saved.[1]

(1) Phil. 1:6; John 10:28, 29; Jer. 32:40; I John 3:9; I Pet. 1:5, 9.

2. This perseverance of the saints depends, not upon their own free-will, but upon the immutability of the decree of election, flowing from the free and unchangeable love of God the Father;[2] upon the efficacy of the merit and intercession of Jesus Christ;[3] the abiding of the Spirit and of the seed of God within them;[4] and the nature of the covenant of grace;[5] from all which ariseth also the certainty and infallibility thereof.[6]

(2) II Tim. 2:19; Jer. 31:3; Eph. 1:4, 5; John 13:1; Rom. 8:35-39.
(3) Heb. 10:10, 14; John 17:11, 24; Heb. 7:25; Heb. 9:12-15; Rom. 8:32-39; Luke 22:32.
(4) John 14:16, 17; I John 2:27; I John 3:9.
(5) Jer. 32:40; Heb. 8:10-12.
(6) II Thess. 3:3; I John 2:19; John 10:28; I Thess. 5:23, 24; Heb. 6:17-20.

3. Nevertheless they may, through the temptations of Satan and of the world, the prevalency of corruption remaining in them, and the neglect of the means of their preservation, fall into grievous sins;

Q. 79. *May not true believers, by reason of their imperfections, and the many temptations and sins they are overtaken with, fall away from the state of grace?*

A. True believers, by reason of the unchangeable love of God,[1] and his decree and covenant to give them perseverance,[2] their inseparable union with Christ,[3] his continual intercession for them,[4] and the Spirit and seed of God abiding in them,[5] can neither totally nor finally fall away from the state of grace, but are kept by the power of God through faith unto salvation.[6]

(1) Jer. 31:3; John 13:1.
(2) I Cor. 1:8; Heb. 6:17; Heb. 13:20, 21; Isa. 54:10.
(3) I Cor. 12:27. Compare with Rom. 8:35-39.
(4) Heb. 7:25; Luke 22:32.
(5) I John 3:9; I John 2:27.
(6) Jer. 32:40; John 10:28; I Pet. 1:5; Phil. 1:6.

Chap er XIX · Of the Perseverance of the Saints

| THE WESTMINSTER CONFESSION OF FAITH | THE WESTMINSTER LARGER CATECHISM | THE WESTMINSTER SHORTER CATECHISM |
|---|---|---|

and for a time continue therein:[7] whereby they incur God's displeasure,[8] and grieve his Holy Spirit;[9] come to be deprived of some measure of their graces and comforts;[10] have their hearts hardened,[11] and their consciences wounded;[12] hurt and scandalize others,[13] and bring temporal judgments upon themselves.[14]

(7)  Matt. 26:70, 72, 74; II Sam. 12:9, 13.
(8)  Isa. 64:7, 9; II Sam. 11:27.
(9)  Eph. 4:30.
(10) Psa. 51:8, 10, 12; Rev. 2:4.
(11) Mark 6:52; Psa. 95:8.
(12) Psa. 32:3, 4; Psa. 51:8.
(13) II Sam. 12:14; Ezek. 16:54.
(14) II Sam. 12:10; Psa. 89:31, 32; I Cor. 11:32.

# EXPLANATORY NOTES

THE doctrine of the perseverance of saints is peculiar to Calvinists. It is the logical implicate of the other points of Calvinism. The Cumberland Presbyterians illogically retain the last of the five points of Calvinism while rejecting the other four. All five points are true, or none of them is true.

This point of our creed would be less opposed if it were rightly understood. The first section states the doctrine. Consider how it describes the subjects of perseverance. They are the accepted in Christ, the effectually called and sanctified by His Spirit. Next observe just exactly what is said about them. Leaving out the adverbs concentrate attention on the bare statement: "they cannot fall from the *state* of grace." It is not said that they cannot fall from grace. Calvinists admit that saints may and do fall from attainments in grace, but they deny that saints fall out of the *state of grace*. The

doctrine of perseverance is not a denial of backsliding (see section 3), but of total and final apostasy. David in the affair of Bathsheba and Uriah fell from the experience of grace, and Peter likewise fell from the experience of grace when he denied his Lord with oaths, yet the faith of neither failed. Faith is the tie that binds to the Saviour, and so long as faith remains, the believer continues in the state of grace and salvation. The saint may fall *down*, but he does not fall *out*.

## CONF. XIX:1-2; L.C. 79

The first section asserts the fact of perseverance, and the second section states the reasons for the fact. The reasons are not found in man but in God. The reasons are five, and they are perhaps better stated by the Larger Catechism. Enumerate and estimate them.

## CONF. XIX:3

"Nevertheless." So begins the third and last section. The subject of the paragraph is the possibility and peril of falling. "They may!" Mark the reasons why they may fall: temptations from without, corruption within, and the neglect of the means of steadfastness.

Now search out the results, if they do fall. First result: sins, grievous sins, and continuance therein for a season. Second result: a series of consequences which pertain to God, the Holy Spirit, themselves, and others.

Are you interested in personal sanctification? in soul security? Then beware lest the terrible possibilities of evil in yourself and in your surroundings develop into more terrible actualities.

The grace of perseverance should be preached to encourage saints. The duty of perseverance should be preached to stir them out of their sloth into a living sense of their responsibility.

# CHAPTER XX

# Of the Assurance of Grace and Salvation

CONFESSION OF FAITH XX:1-4
LARGER CATECHISM 80-81

## THE WESTMINSTER CONFESSION OF FAITH

ALTHOUGH hypocrites, and other unregenerate men, may vainly deceive themselves with false hopes and carnal presumptions of being in the favor of God and estate of salvation;[1] which hope of theirs shall perish:[2] yet such as truly believe in the Lord Jesus, and love him in sincerity, endeavoring to walk in all good conscience before him, may in this life be certainly assured that they are in a state of grace,[3] and may rejoice in the hope of the glory of God: which hope shall never make them ashamed.[4]

(1) Deut. 29:19; John 8:41.
(2) Matt. 7:22, 23.
(3) II Tim. 1:12; I John 2:3; I John 5:13; I John 3:14, 18, 19, 21, 24.
(4) Rom. 5:2, 5.

2. This certainty is not a bare conjectural and probable persuasion, grounded upon a fallible hope; but an infallible assurance of faith,[5] founded upon the divine truth of the promises of salvation,[6] the inward evidence of those graces unto which these promises are made,[7] the testimony of the Spirit of adoption witnessing with our spirits that we are the children of God;[8] which Spirit is the earnest of our inheritance, whereby we are sealed to the day of redemption.[9]

(5) Heb. 6:11, 12.
(6) Heb. 6:17, 18; II Pet. 1:4, 5.
(7) II Pet. 1:10, 11; I John 3:14.
(8) Rom. 8:15, 16.
(9) Eph. 1:13, 14; II Cor. 1:21, 22.

## THE WESTMINSTER LARGER CATECHISM

Q. 80. *Can true believers be infallibly assured that they are in the estate of grace, and that they shall persevere therein unto salvation?*

A. Such as truly believe in Christ, and endeavor to walk in all good conscience before him, may, without extraordinary revelation, by faith grounded upon the truth of God's promises, and by the Spirit enabling them to discern in themselves those graces to which the promises of life are made, and bearing witness with their spirits that they are the children of God, be infallibly assured that they are in the estate of grace, and shall persevere therein unto salvation.[1]

(1) I John 2:3; I Cor. 2:12; I John 4:13, 16; I John 3:14, 18, 19, 21, 24; Rom. 8:16; I John 5:13.

## THE WESTMINSTER SHORTER CATECHISM

3. This infallible assurance doth not so belong to the essence of faith but that a true believer may wait long and conflict with many difficulties before he be partaker of it:[10] yet, being enabled by the Spirit to know the things which are freely given him of God, he may, without extraordinary revelation, in the right use of ordinary means, attain thereunto.[11] And therefore it is the duty of everyone to give all diligence to make his calling and election sure; that thereby his heart may be enlarged in peace and joy in the Holy Ghost, in love and thankfulness to God, and in strength and cheerfulness in the duties of obedience, the proper fruits of this assurance: so far is it from inclining men to looseness.[12]

(10) Isa. 50:10; I John 5:13; Psa. 73, 77, 88.

(11) I Cor. 2:12; I John 4:13; Psa. 77:10-20; Psa. 73.

See citations under Section 2 above.

(12) II Pet. I:10; Rom. 6:1, 2; Tit. 2:11, 12, 14.


4. True believers may have the assurance of their salvation divers ways shaken, diminished, and intermitted; as, by negligence in preserving of it; by falling into some special sin, which woundeth the conscience, and grieveth the Spirit; by some sudden or vehement temptation; by God's withdrawing the light of his countenance, and suffering even such as fear him to walk in darkness and to have no light:[13] yet are they never utterly destitute of that seed of God, and life of faith, that love of Christ and the brethren, that sincerity of heart and conscience of duty, out of which, by the operation of the Spirit, this assurance may in due time be revived,[14] and by the which, in the meantime,

Q. 81. *Are all true believers at all times assured of their present being in the estate of grace, and that they shall be saved?*

A. Assurance of grace and salvation not being of the essence of faith, true believers may wait long before they obtain it;[1] and, after the enjoyment thereof, may have it weakened and intermitted, through manifold distempers, sins, temptations, and desertions;[2] yet are they never left without such a presence and support of the Spirit of God, as keeps them from sinking into utter despair.[3]

(1) Isa. 50:10; Psa. 88.

(2) Psa. 31:22; Psa. 77:1-12; Psa. 30:6, 7; Psa. 51:8, 12.

(3) Job 13:15; Psa. 73:13, 14, 15, 23; I John 3:9; Isa. 54:7-11.

| THE WESTMINSTER CONFESSION OF FAITH | THE WESTMINSTER LARGER CATECHISM | THE WESTMINSTER SHORTER CATECHISM |
|---|---|---|

they are supported from utter despair.[15]

(13) Psa. 51:8, 12, 14; Eph. 4:30; Psa. 77:1-10; Matt. 26:69-72; Psa. 31:22; Psa. 88; Isa. 50:10.
(14) I John 3:9; Luke 22:32; Psa. 73:15; Psa. 51:8, 12; Isa. 50:10.
(15) Micah 7:7, 8, 9.

# EXPLANATORY NOTES

NOTE the emphasis on assurance. The Larger Catechism devotes two questions and the Confession four full sections to the subject. This is in sharp contrast to the absence of assurance from pulpit and pew today. Is not the absence of assurance a weakness in the Christian ministry and in the Christian life? How is this lack of assurance to be accounted for? And how is assurance to be attained unto? For answer read and analyze the statements before us.

## CONF. XX:1a

The Confession contains a warning not found in the Catechism. The warning is that a kind of assurance is possible even to hypocrites and other unregenerate. Let men look well to the foundations of their hope.

## CONF. XX:1b, 2-4; L.C. 80-81

With the exception of this warning the Confession and Catechism are parallel in their teaching here. Analysis yields the following points:

1. The possibility or privilege of true assurance. To whom? Section 1; Larger Catechism 80.

2. The nature of true assurance. Section 2. This point is maintained against Romanists and Arminians, who deny the kind and degree of assurance here affirmed.

3. The grounds of such assurance. Section 2; Larger Catechism 80.

4. Assurance is not an essential element of saving faith; yet it is more than a privilege: it is a duty. Section 3.

5. The proper fruits of assurance. Assurance itself is a fruit of faith and love and obedience; and the proper fruits of assurance are not carelessness and looseness of living, as some allege, but enlargement of heart "in peace and joy in the Holy Ghost, in love and thankfulness to God, and in strength and cheerfulness in the duties of obedience."

6. Assurance once possessed may in divers ways be lost, and if lost, may be recovered. In the meantime, the true believer is kept from utter despair. Hope, then, and not assurance, is the mark of the Christian life. Section 4.

In the New Testament we read of assurance of understanding, Colossians 2:2; of assurance of faith, Hebrews 10:22; of assurance of hope, Hebrews 6:11.

For a discussion of these forms of assurance, see B. M. Palmer's *The Threefold Fellowship and The Threefold Assurance*.

# CHAPTER XXI

# Of the Law of God

## Part One: The Law in General

CONFESSION OF FAITH XXI:1-7
LARGER CATECHISM 91-97, (98) · SHORTER CATECHISM 39-40, (41)

| THE WESTMINSTER CONFESSION OF FAITH | THE WESTMINSTER LARGER CATECHISM | THE WESTMINSTER SHORTER CATECHISM |
|---|---|---|
| | HAVING SEEN WHAT THE SCRIPTURES PRINCIPALLY TEACH US TO BELIEVE CONCERNING GOD, IT FOLLOWS TO CONSIDER WHAT THEY REQUIRE AS THE DUTY OF MAN | |

**Larger Catechism**

Q. 91. *What is the duty which God requireth of man?*

A. The duty which God requireth of man is obedience to his revealed will.[1]

(1) Deut. 29:29; Micah 6:8; I Sam. 15:22.

**Shorter Catechism**

Q. 39. *What is the duty which God requireth of man?*

A. The duty which God requireth of man, is, obedience to his revealed will.[1]

(1) Deut. 29:29; Micah 6:8; I Sam. 15:22.

**Confession of Faith**

GOD gave to Adam a law, as a covenant of works, by which he bound him and all his posterity to personal, entire, exact, and perpetual obedience; promised life upon the fulfilling, and threatened death upon the breach of it; and endued him with power and ability to keep it.[1]

(1) Gal. 3:12; Hos. 6:7; Gen. 2:16, 17. Compare Rom. 5:12-14; I Cor. 15:22; Luke 10:25-28, and the covenants made with Noah and Abraham. Gen. 1:26; Deut. 30:19; John 7:17; Rev. 22:17; James 1:14.

**Larger Catechism**

Q. 92. *What did God at first reveal unto man as the rule of his obedience?*

A. The rule of obedience revealed to Adam in the estate of innocence, and to all mankind in him, besides a special command, not to eat of the fruit of the tree of the knowledge of good and evil, was the moral law.[1]

(1) Rom. 10:5; Rom. 2:14, 15; Gen. 2:17.

Q. 93. *What is the moral law?*

A. The moral law is the declaration of the will of God to mankind, directing and binding everyone to personal, perfect, and perpetual conformity and obedience thereunto, in the frame and disposition of the

**Shorter Catechism**

Q. 40. *What did God at first reveal to man for the rule of his obedience?*

A. The rule which God at first revealed to man for his obedience, was the moral law.[1]

(1) Rom. 2:14, 15; Rom. 10:5.

| THE WESTMINSTER CONFESSION OF FAITH | THE WESTMINSTER LARGER CATECHISM | THE WESTMINSTER SHORTER CATECHISM |
|---|---|---|
| | whole man, soul and body, and in performance of all those duties of holiness and righteousness which he oweth to God and man:[1] promising life upon the fulfilling, and threatening death upon the breach of it.[2]<br><br>(1) James 2:10; Deut. 5:1, 31, 33; Luke 10:26, 27; I Thess. 5:23.<br>(2) Rom. 10:5; Gal. 3:10. | |
| 2. This law, after his fall, continued to be a perfect rule of righteousness; and, as such, was delivered by God upon mount Sinai in ten commandments, and written in two tables;[1] the first four commandments containing our duty toward God, and the other six our duty to man.[2]<br><br>(1) James 1:25; James 2:8, 10; Rom. 3:19; Deut. 5:32; Deut. 10:4; Ex. 34:1; Rom. 13:8, 9.<br>(2) Matt. 22:37-40; Ex. 20:3-18. | (Q. 98. *Wherein is the moral law summarily comprehended?*<br><br>(A. The moral law is summarily comprehended in the ten commandments, which were delivered by the voice of God upon mount Sinai, and written by him on two tables of stone; and are recorded in the twentieth chapter of Exodus; the first four commandments containing our duty to God, and the other six our duty to man.) | (Q. 41. *Wherein is the moral law summarily comprehended?*<br><br>(A. The moral law is summarily comprehended in the ten commandments.) |
| 3. Besides this law, commonly called moral, God was pleased to give to the people of Israel, as a church under age, ceremonial laws, containing several typical ordinances, partly of worship, prefiguring Christ, his graces, actions, sufferings, and benefits;[3] and partly holding forth divers instructions of moral duties.[4] All which ceremonial laws are now abrogated under the New Testament.[5]<br><br>(3) Heb. 10:1; Gal. 4:1-3; Col. 2:17; Heb. 9.<br>(4) See Lev. 5:1-6; 6:1-7 and similar passages.<br>(5) Mark 7:18, 19; Gal. 2:4; Col. 2:17; Eph. 2:15, 16. | | |
| 4. To them also, as a body politic, he gave sundry judicial laws, which expired together with the state of that people, not obliging any other, now, further than the general equity thereof may require.[6]<br><br>(6) Matt. 5:38, 39; I Cor. 9:8-10; Ex. 21, 22. | | |

| THE WESTMINSTER CONFESSION OF FAITH | THE WESTMINSTER LARGER CATECHISM | THE WESTMINSTER SHORTER CATECHISM |
|---|---|---|

## THE WESTMINSTER CONFESSION OF FAITH

5. The moral law doth forever bind all, as well justified persons as others, to the obedience thereof; and that not only in regard of the matter contained in it, but also in respect of the authority of God the Creator who gave it.[7] Neither doth Christ in the gospel any way dissolve, but much strengthen, this obligation.[8]

(7) Rom. 13:8, 9; I John 2:3, 4, 7; Rom. 3:31; Rom. 6:15.
   See citations under Section 2 above.
(8) Matt. 5:18, 19; James 2:8; Rom. 3:31.

## THE WESTMINSTER LARGER CATECHISM

Q. 94. *Is there any use of the moral law to man since the fall?*

A. Although no man since the fall can attain to righteousness and life by the moral law,[1] yet there is great use thereof, as well common to all men, as peculiar either to the unregenerate, or the regenerate.[2]

(1) Rom. 8:3; Gal. 2:16.
(2) I Tim. 1:8; Gal. 3:19, 24.

Q. 95. *Of what use is the moral law to all men?*

A. The moral law is of use to all men, to inform them of the holy nature and will of God,[1] and of their duty binding them to walk accordingly;[2] to convince them of their disability to keep it, and of the sinful pollution of their nature, hearts, and lives,[3] to humble them in the sense of their sin and misery,[4] and thereby help them to a clearer sight of the need they have of Christ,[5] and of the perfection of his obedience.

(1) Rom. 7:12.
(2) Micah 6:8; Luke 10:26, 28, 37.
(3) Psa. 19:11, 12; Rom. 3:20; Rom. 7:7.
(4) Rom. 3:9, 23; Rom. 7:9, 13.
(5) Gal. 3:21, 22.

| THE WESTMINSTER CONFESSION OF FAITH | THE WESTMINSTER LARGER CATECHISM | THE WESTMINSTER SHORTER CATECHISM |
|---|---|---|

**THE WESTMINSTER LARGER CATECHISM**

Q. 96. *What particular use is there of the moral law to unregenerate men?*

A. The moral law is of use to unregenerate men, to awaken their consciences to flee from the wrath to come,[1] and to drive them to Christ;[2] or, upon their continuance in the estate and way of sin, to leave them inexcusable,[3] and under the curse thereof.[4]

(1) Rom. 7:9; I Tim. 1:9, 10.
(2) Gal. 3:24.
(3) Rom. 1:20. Compared with Rom. 2:15.
(4) Gal. 3:10.

Q. 97. *What special use is there of the moral law to the regenerate?*

A. Although they that are regenerate and believe in Christ be delivered from the moral law as a covenant of works, so as thereby they are neither justified nor condemned: yet, besides the general uses thereof common to them with all men, it is of special use to show them how much they are bound to Christ for his fulfilling it, and enduring the curse thereof, in their stead and for their good;[1] and thereby to provoke them to more thankfulness, and to express the same in their greater care to conform themselves thereunto as the rule of their obedience.[2]

(1) Rom. 7:4, 6; Rom. 6:14; Rom. 3:20; Rom. 8:1, 34; Gal. 3:13, 14; Rom. 8:3, 4; II Cor. 5:21.
(2) Col. 1:12, 13, 14; Rom. 7:22; Tit. 2:11-14.

**THE WESTMINSTER CONFESSION OF FAITH**

6. Although true believers be not under the law as a covenant of works, to be thereby justified or condemned;[9] yet is it of great use to them, as well as to others; in that, as a rule of life, informing them of the will of God and their duty, it directs and binds them to walk accordingly;[10] discovering also the sinful pollutions of their nature, hearts, and lives;[11] so as, examining themselves thereby, they may come to further conviction of, humiliation for, and hatred against sin;[12] together with a clearer sight of the need they have of Christ, and the perfection of his obedience.[13] It is likewise of use to the regenerate, to restrain their corruptions, in that it forbids sin,[14] and the threatenings of it serve to show what even their sins deserve, and what afflictions in this life they may expect for them, although freed from the curse thereof threatened in the law.[15] The promises of it, in like manner, show them God's approbation of obedience, and what blessings they may expect upon the performance thereof;[16] although not as due to them by the law as a covenant of works: so as a man's doing good, and refraining from evil, because the law en-

| THE WESTMINSTER CONFESSION OF FAITH | THE WESTMINSTER LARGER CATECHISM | THE WESTMINSTER SHORTER CATECHISM |
|---|---|---|

courageth to the one, and deterreth from the other, is no evidence of his being under the law, and not under grace.[17]

(9) Rom. 6:14; Rom. 8:1; Gal. 4:4, 5; Acts 13:39.
(10) Rom. 7:12; Psa. 119:5; I Cor. 7:19; Gal. 5:14, 18, 23.
(11) Rom. 7:7; Rom. 3:20.
(12) Rom. 7:9, 14, 24.
(13) Gal. 3:24; Rom. 8:3, 4; Rom. 7:24, 25.
(14) James 2:11; Psa. 119:128.
(15) Ezra 9:13, 14; Psa. 89:30-34.
(16) Psa. 37:11; Psa. 19:11; Lev. 26:3-13; Eph. 6:2; Matt. 5:5.
(17) Rom. 6:12, 14; Heb. 12:28, 29; I Pet. 3:8-12; Psa. 34:12-16.

7. Neither are the forementioned uses of the law contrary to the grace of the gospel, but do sweetly comply with it:[18] the Spirit of Christ subduing and enabling the will of man to do that freely and cheerfully, which the will of God, revealed in the law, requireth to be done.[19]

(18) See citations under Section 6 above.
(19) See citations under Chapter X, Section 1.
Gal. 3:13.

## EXPLANATORY NOTES

THE chapters of the Confession have been divided into three groups:

1. Matters of Faith, I-XX, XXXIV-XXXV.
2. Matters of Practice, XXI-XXVI.
3. Matters of Administration and Discipline, XXVII-XXXIII.

With Chapter XX we finish the first major division of the Standards, with exception of chapters XXXIV and XXXV of the Confession and the corresponding parts of the Catechisms. Both Catechisms finish what we are to believe before begin-

ning what we are to do, but as we are following the order of the Confession the parts of the Catechisms relating to the state after death, the resurrection, and the judgment are transferred to the end to harmonize with the final chapters of the Confession.

So having seen what the Scriptures principally teach concerning God, we now proceed to consider what they require as the duty of man. It is interesting and instructive to observe how often and in what connections the Standards treat of the Word of God. All three parts of the Standards deal at the beginning with the Holy Scripture, "the word of God written," which contains the total will of

God. Near the middle they present the law of God as containing the inspired code of morals. Then again farther on, as we discuss "the means of grace" the Word of God comes up for further consideration. The Word of God thus receives a threefold emphasis.

### L.C. 91; S.C. 39

The Law of God now claims our attention. Law is one of the great facts and factors of life. Law has conditioned man's life in its every period.

At the first, man was under the law of nature or the law of creation. Later he came under law as modified by the covenant of works, and later still under law as further modified by the covenant of grace.

### S.C. 40

The Standards recognize law in all three stages. The first stage is referred to in Shorter Catechism question 40. This law, called moral, was at first written on the heart. It was later re-enacted in the Ten Commandments, which were inscribed on tablets of stone, and to which was added in the fourth commandment a positive element.

### CONF. XXI:1-2; L.C. 92-93

Both the first and second stages of law are implicated in the Larger Catechism answers to questions 92 and 93, and in the Confession sections 1 and 2. In the Covenant of Works a positive law was added to the moral law. What is the difference between moral law and positive law? Moral law inheres in the nature of things. It expresses the nature of God and is impressed on the nature of man. Positive law is a creation of God's will. It is made to serve a certain end, and passes away when that end has been accomplished. That is, positive law is provisional and temporary, while moral law is elemental and eternal. It abides unchanged so long as God's nature and man's remain the same. Positive law may be local and national, whereas moral law is universal, being without boundary in time or space.

### CONF. XXI:3

One form of positive law is the subject of the third section of the Confession, *viz.,* ceremonial laws. They were given to Israel as a church. Name the uses of ceremonial laws and tell why and when they were abrogated.

### CONF. XXI:4

Another kind of positive law is specified in the fourth section of the Confession. The judicial laws were given to the people of Israel as a state or nation. These laws were not binding outside of Israel except as they may have embodied principles of general equity. In such cases the positive law contained a moral element.

### CONF. XXI:5; L.C. 93

Moral law is the subject of the Confession in its fifth section and in Larger Catechism question 93. They assert the authority of the moral law over all peoples in all ages, and declare that it binds all to conformity and obedience both in the inner state and disposition and in the outer acts. The sanctions of the moral law are the promise of life in case of obedience and the threat of death in case of disobedience. What is meant by sanctions in this connection?

### CONF. XXI:6-7; L.C. 94-97

Sections 6 and 7 of the Confession and questions 94-97 of the Larger Catechism relate to the uses of the moral law. The law is of no use toward life and salvation (L.C. 94), but is of much use in giving knowledge of *need* of salvation as it makes men aware of sin, inability, and lostness (L.C. 95-96).

Five uses of the law to all men are specified in the infinitive clauses in answer to question 95. Three particular uses of the law to the unregenerate are pointed out by the infinitives in answer to question 96. Of what special use is the law to the regenerate as stated under question 97?

The Catechism is clearer and more specific than the Confession here. The Confession does not include the unregenerate in its statement of the uses of the law, though the long section 6 would lead the reader to think so. Near the middle of the section it says: "It [the law] is *likewise* of use to the regenerate . . ." That language implies that the foregoing statement is about the use of the *law* to the *unregenerate*. But examination of the statement reveals the fact that it is about the use of the law to *"true* believers." But true believers are regenerate. This section would be clarified if the word "further" were substituted for the word "likewise"; or, if the first half of the statement were so framed as to apply to the unregenerate.

What are the uses of the law to the regenerate according to the Confession? May they not be summed up under three heads: informing, restraining, encouraging?

The last section of the Confession on the law declares that the forementioned uses of the law are consistent with the grace of the gospel, as the fifth section declares that the grace of the gospel in no wise weakens, but rather strengthens, the obligation of the law. There is no conflict between law and gospel, but each when rightly used re-enforces the other.

# Of the Law of God

## Part Two: The Law in Particular . . . The Ten Commandments

### (CONFESSION OF FAITH XXIII:7-8)
### LARGER CATECHISM 98-152 · SHORTER CATECHISM 41-84

| THE WESTMINSTER CONFESSION OF FAITH | THE WESTMINSTER LARGER CATECHISM | THE WESTMINSTER SHORTER CATECHISM |
|---|---|---|

**THE WESTMINSTER LARGER CATECHISM**

**Q. 98.** *Wherein is the moral law summarily comprehended?*

**A.** The moral law is summarily comprehended in the ten commandments,[1] which were delivered by the voice of God upon mount Sinai, and written by him on two tables of stone;[2] and are recorded in the twentieth chapter of Exodus; the first four commandments containing our duty to God, and the other six our duty to man.

(1) Matt. 19:17, 18, 19.
(2) Deut. 10:4; Ex. 34:1-4.

**Q. 99.** *What rules are to be observed for the right understanding of the ten commandments?*

**A.** For the right understanding of the ten commandments, these rules are to be observed:

1. That the law is perfect, and bindeth everyone to full conformity in the whole man unto the righteousness thereof, and unto entire obedience forever; so as to require the utmost perfection of every duty, and to forbid the least degree of every sin.[1]

(1) Psa. 19:7; James 2:10; Matt. 5:22, 28, 37, 44.

2. That it is spiritual, and so reacheth the understanding, will, affections, and all other powers of

**THE WESTMINSTER SHORTER CATECHISM**

**Q. 41.** *Wherein is the moral law summarily comprehended?*

**A.** The moral law is summarily comprehended in the ten commandments.[1]

(1) Matt. 19:17, 18, 19.

THE WESTMINSTER
**CONFESSION OF FAITH**

THE WESTMINSTER
**LARGER CATECHISM**

THE WESTMINSTER
**SHORTER CATECHISM**

the soul; as well as words, works, and gestures.[1]

(1) Rom. 7:14; Deut. 6:5; Matt. 22:37-39; Matt. 12:36, 37.
See citations under Rule 1 above.

3. That one and the same thing, in divers respects, is required or forbidden in several commandments.[1]

(1) Col. 3:5; I Tim. 6:10; Ex. 20:3-5; Amos 8:5.

4. That as, where a duty is commanded, the contrary sin is forbidden;[1] and where a sin is forbidden, the contrary duty is commanded:[2] so, where a promise is annexed, the contrary threatening is included;[3] and where a threatening is annexed, the contrary promise is included.[4]

(1) Isa. 58:13; Matt. 15:4, 5, 6; Deut. 6:13. Compare with Matt. 4:9, 10.
(2) Eph. 4:28.
(3) Ex. 20:12.
(4) Jer. 18:7, 8; Ex. 20:7. Compared with Psa. 15:1, 4, 5; Psa. 24:4, 5.

5. That what God forbids, is at no time to be done;[1] what he commands is always our duty;[2] and yet every particular duty is not to be done at all times.[3]

(1) Rom. 3:8; Heb. 11:25.
(2) Deut. 4:9.
(3) Matt. 12:7; Mark 14:7.

6. That, under one sin or duty, all of the same kind are forbidden or commanded; together with all the causes, means, occasions, and appearances thereof, and provocations thereunto.[1]

(1) I Thess. 5:22; Gal. 5:26; Heb. 10:24; Col. 3:21.

7. That what is forbidden or commanded to ourselves, we are bound, according to our places, to endeavor that it may be avoided or performed by others, according to the duty of their places.[1]

(1) Ex. 20:10; Deut. 6:6, 7; Josh. 24:15.

| THE WESTMINSTER CONFESSION OF FAITH | THE WESTMINSTER LARGER CATECHISM | THE WESTMINSTER SHORTER CATECHISM |
|---|---|---|
| | 8. That in what is commanded to others, we are bound, according to our places and callings, to be helpful to them;[1] and to take heed of partaking with others in what is forbidden them.[2]<br>(1) Heb. 10:24.<br>(2) I Tim. 5:22; Eph. 5:11. | |

**LARGER CATECHISM**

Q. 100. *What special things are we to consider in the ten commandments?*

A. We are to consider in the ten commandments: the preface, the substance of the commandments themselves, and the several reasons annexed to some of them the more to enforce them.

Q. 101. *What is the preface to the ten commandments?*

A. The preface to the ten commandments is contained in these words: *I am the Lord thy God, which have brought thee out of the land of Egypt, out of the house of bondage.*[1] Wherein God manifesteth his sovereignty, as being Jehovah, the eternal, immutable, and almighty God; having his being in and of himself, and giving being to all his words and works; and that he is a God in covenant, as with Israel of old, so with all his people: who as he brought them out of their bondage in Egypt, so he delivered us from our spiritual thralldom; and that therefore we are bound to take him for our God alone, and to keep all his commandments.
(1) Ex. 20:2.

Q. 102. *What is the sum of the four commandments which contain our duty to God?*

A. The sum of the four commandments containing our duty to God is, to love the Lord our God with

**SHORTER CATECHISM**

Q. 43. *What is the preface to the ten commandments?*

A. The preface to the ten commandments is in these words, *I am the Lord thy God, which have brought thee out of the land of Egypt, out of the house of bondage.*[1]
(1) Ex. 20:2.

Q. 44. *What doth the preface to the ten commandments teach us?*

A. The preface to the ten commandments teacheth us, that because God is the Lord, and our God, and Redeemer, therefore we are bound to keep all his commandments.

Q. 42. *What is the sum of the ten commandments?*

A. The sum of the ten commandments is, to love the Lord our God, with all our heart, with all our soul, with all our strength, and with all

| THE WESTMINSTER CONFESSION OF FAITH | THE WESTMINSTER LARGER CATECHISM | THE WESTMINSTER SHORTER CATECHISM |
|---|---|---|
| | all our heart, and with all our soul, and with all our strength, and with all our mind.[1]<br>(1) Luke 10:27. | our mind; and our neighbor as ourselves.[1]<br>(1) Matt. 22:37, 38, 39, 40. |
| | **Q. 103.** *Which is the first commandment?*<br>A. The first commandment is, *Thou shalt have no other gods before me.*[1]<br>(1) Ex. 20:3. | **Q. 45.** *Which is the first commandment?*<br>A. The first commandment is, *Thou shalt have no other gods before me.*[1]<br>(1) Ex. 20:3. |
| | **Q. 104.** *What are the duties required in the first commandment?*<br>A. The duties required in the first commandment[1] are: the knowing and acknowledging of God to be the only true God, and our God;[2] and to worship and glorify him accordingly;[3] by thinking,[4] meditating,[5] remembering,[6] highly esteeming,[7] honoring,[8] adoring,[9] choosing,[10] loving,[11] desiring,[12] fearing of him;[13] believing him;[14] trusting,[15] hoping,[16] delighting,[17] rejoicing in him;[18] being zealous for him;[19] calling upon him, giving all praise and thanks,[20] and yielding all obedience and submission to him with the whole man;[21] being careful in all things to please him,[22] and sorrowful when in anything he is offended;[23] and walking humbly with him.[24]<br>(1) The exposition of the Ten Commandments contained in the answers to Questions 104 to 148 are deduced from the commandments themselves, and from the "Rules" set forth in Question 99. Texts under the specifications are given in order to show that the specifications are in accord with the general teaching of the Scriptures,<br>(2) I Chron. 28:9; Deut. 26:17; Isa. 43:10; Jer. 14:22.<br>(3) Psa. 95:6, 7; Matt. 4:10; Psa. 29:2.<br>(4) Mal. 3:16.<br>(5) Psa. 63:6.<br>(6) Eccl. 12:1.<br>(7) Psa. 18:1, 2. | **Q. 46.** *What is required in the first commandment?*<br>A. The first commandment requireth us[1] to know and acknowledge God to be the only true God, and our God,[2] and to worship and glorify him accordingly.[3]<br>(1) The exposition of the Ten Commandments found in answers to Questions 46-81 are deductions from the commandments themselves and the rules set forth in the Larger Catechism, Q. 99. The texts under the specifications are given to show that they are in accord with the general teaching of the Scriptures.<br>(2) I Chron. 28:9; Deut. 26:17.<br>(3) Matt. 4:10; Psa. 95:6, 7; Psa. 29:2. |

| THE WESTMINSTER CONFESSION OF FAITH | THE WESTMINSTER LARGER CATECHISM | THE WESTMINSTER SHORTER CATECHISM |
|---|---|---|

**LARGER CATECHISM**

(8) Mal. 1:6.
(9) Isa. 45:23; Psa. 96.
(10) Josh. 24:22.
(11) Deut. 6:5.
(12) Psa. 73:25.
(13) Isa. 8:13.
(14) Ex. 14:31; Rom. 10:11; Acts 10:43.
(15) Isa. 26:4; Psa. 40:4.
(16) Psa. 130:7.
(17) Psa. 37:4.
(18) Psa. 32:11.
(19) Rom. 12:11; Rev. 3:19; Num. 25:11.
(20) Phil. 4:6.
(21) Jer. 7:23; James 4:7; Rom. 12:1.
(22) I John 3:22.
(23) Neh. 13:8; Psa. 73:21; Psa. 119:136; Jer. 31:18, 19.
(24) Micah 6:8.

Q. 105. *What are the sins forbidden in the first commandment?*

A. The sins forbidden in the first commandment are: atheism, in denying or not having a God;[1] idolatry, in having or worshipping more gods than one, or any with, or instead of the true God;[2] the not having and vouching him for God, and our God;[3] the omission or neglect of anything due to him, required in this commandment;[4] ignorance,[5] forgetfulness,[6] misapprehensions, false opinions,[7] unworthy and wicked thoughts of him;[8] bold and curious searchings into his secrets;[9] all profaneness,[10] hatred of God,[11] self-love,[12] self-seeking,[13] and all other inordinate and immoderate setting of our mind, will, or affections upon other things, and taking them off from him in whole or in part;[14] vain credulity,[15] unbelief,[16] heresy,[17] misbelief,[18] distrust,[19] despair,[20] incorrigibleness, and insensibleness under judgments,[21] hardness of heart,[22] pride,[23] presumption,[24] carnal security,[25] tempting of God;[26] using unlawful means,[27] and trusting in lawful means;[28] carnal delights and joys,[29] corrupt, blind, and indiscreet zeal;[30] lukewarmness,[31] and dead-

**SHORTER CATECHISM**

Q. 47. *What is forbidden in the first commandment?*

A. The first commandment forbiddeth the denying,[1] or not worshipping and glorifying, the true God, as God,[2] and our God;[3] and the giving the worship and glory to any other, which is due to him alone.[4]

(1) Psa. 14:1.
(2) Rom. 1:20, 21.
(3) Psa. 81:11.
(4) Rom. 1:25.

| THE WESTMINSTER CONFESSION OF FAITH | THE WESTMINSTER LARGER CATECHISM | THE WESTMINSTER SHORTER CATECHISM |
|---|---|---|
| | ness in the things of God;[32] estranging ourselves, and apostatizing from God;[33] praying or giving any religious worship to saints, angels, or any other creatures;[34] all compacts and consulting with the devil,[35] and hearkening to his suggestions;[36] making men the lords of our faith and conscience;[37] slighting and despising God, and his commands;[38] resisting and grieving of his Spirit,[39] discontent and impatience at his dispensations, charging him foolishly for the evils he inflicts on us;[40] and ascribing the praise of any good, we either are, have, or can do, to fortune, idols,[41] ourselves,[42] or any other creature.[43] | |

(1) Psa. 14:1.
(2) Jer. 2:27, 28. Compared with I Thess. 1:9.
(3) Psa. 81:11.
(4) Isa. 43:22, 23.
(5) Jer. 4:22; Hos. 4:1, 6.
(6) Jer. 2:32; Psa. 50:22.
(7) Acts 17:23, 29.
(8) Psa. 50:21.
(9) Deut. 29:29.
(10) Tit. 1:16; Heb. 12:16.
(11) Rom. 1:30.
(12) II Tim. 3:2.
(13) Phil. 2:21.
(14) I John 2:15; I Sam. 2:29; Col. 3:2, 5.
(15) I John 4:1.
(16) Heb. 3:12.
(17) Gal. 5:20; Tit. 3:10.
(18) Acts 26:9.
(19) Psa. 78:22.
(20) Ezek. 37:11.
(21) Jer. 5:3.
(22) Rom. 2:5.
(23) Jer. 13:15.
(24) Psa. 19:13.
(25) Zeph. 1:12.
(26) Matt. 4:7.
(27) Rom. 3:8.
(28) Jer. 17:5.
(29) II Tim. 3:4.
(30) Gal. 4:17; Rom. 10:2; John 16:2; Luke 9:54, 55.
(31) Rev. 3:16.
(32) Rev. 3:1.
(33) Ezek. 14:5; Isa. 1:4, 5.
(34) Hos. 4:12; Rev. 19:10; Col. 2:18; Rom. 1:25.

| THE WESTMINSTER CONFESSION OF FAITH | THE WESTMINSTER LARGER CATECHISM | THE WESTMINSTER SHORTER CATECHISM |
|---|---|---|
| | (35) Lev. 20:6; I Sam. 28:7-11. Compared with I Chron. 10:13, 14.<br>(36) Acts 5:3.<br>(37) Matt. 23:9.<br>(38) Deut. 32:15; Prov. 13:13; II Sam. 12:9.<br>(39) Acts 7:51; Eph. 4:30.<br>(40) Psa. 73:2, 3.<br>See verses 13-15, 22.<br>(41) Dan. 5.23.<br>(42) Deut. 8:17; Dan. 4:30.<br>(43) Hab. 1:16. | |

**Q. 106.** *What are we especially taught by these words (before me) in the first commandment?*

A. These words (*before me*, or before my face) in the first commandment, teach us, that God, who seeth all things, taketh special notice of, and is much displeased with, the sin of having any other god: that so it may be an argument to dissuade from it, and to aggravate it as a most impudent provocation;[1] as also to persuade us to do as in his sight, whatever we do in his service.[2]

(1) Psa. 44:20, 21; Ezek. 8:5-18.
(2) I Chron. 28:9.

**Q. 48.** *What are we especially taught by these words, "before me," in the first commandment?*

A. These words, *"before me,"* in the first commandment, teach us that God, who seeth all things, taketh notice of, and is much displeased with, the sin of having any other god.[1]

(1) I Chron. 27:9; Psa. 44:20, 21.

**Q. 107.** *Which is the second commandment?*

A. The second commandment is, *Thou shalt not make unto thee any graven image, or any likeness of any thing that is in heaven above, or that is in the earth beneath, or that is in the water under the earth: thou shalt not bow down thyself to them, nor serve them: for I the Lord thy God am a jealous God, visiting the iniquity of the fathers upon the children unto the third and fourth generation of them that hate me; and showing mercy unto thousands of them that love me, and keep my commandments.*[1]

(1) Ex. 20:4-6.

**Q. 49.** *Which is the second commandment?*

A. The second commandment is, *Thou shalt not make unto thee any graven image, or any likeness of any thing that is in heaven above, or that is in the earth beneath, or that is in the water under the earth: thou shalt not bow down thyself to them, nor serve them: for I the Lord thy God am a jealous God, visiting the iniquity of the fathers upon the children unto the third and fourth generation of them that hate me; and showing mercy unto thousands of them that love me, and keep my commandments.*[1]

(1) Ex. 20:4-6.

| THE WESTMINSTER CONFESSION OF FAITH | THE WESTMINSTER LARGER CATECHISM | THE WESTMINSTER SHORTER CATECHISM |
|---|---|---|
| | Q. 108. *What are the duties required in the second commandment?*<br><br>A. The duties required in the second commandment are: the receiving, observing, and keeping pure and entire, all such religious worship and ordinances as God hath instituted in his word;[1] particularly prayer and thanksgiving in the name of Christ;[2] the reading, preaching, and hearing of the word;[3] the administration and receiving of the sacraments;[4] church government and discipline;[5] the ministry and maintenance thereof;[6] religious fasting;[7] swearing by the name of God;[8] and vowing unto him:[9] as also the disapproving, detesting, opposing all false worship;[10] and, according to each one's place and calling, removing it, and all monuments of idolatry.[11]<br><br>(1) Deut. 32:46; Matt. 28:20; I Tim. 6:13, 14; Acts 2:42.<br>(2) Phil. 4:6; Eph. 5:20.<br>(3) Deut. 17:18, 19; Acts 15:21; II Tim. 4:2; James 1:21, 22; Acts 10:33.<br>(4) Matt. 28:19; I Cor. 11:23-30.<br>(5) Matt. 16:19; Matt. 18:17; I Cor. 5; I Cor. 12:28; John 20:23.<br>(6) Eph. 4:11, 12; I Tim. 5:17, 18; I Cor. 9:1-15.<br>(7) Joel 2:12; I Cor. 7:5.<br>(8) Deut. 6:13.<br>(9) Psa. 76:11; Isa. 19:21; Psa. 116:14, 18.<br>(10) Acts 17:16, 17; Psa. 16:4.<br>(11) Deut. 7:5; Isa. 30:22. | Q. 50. *What is required in the second commandment?*<br><br>A. The second commandment requireth the receiving, observing, and keeping pure and entire, all such religious worship and ordinances as God hath appointed in his word.[1]<br><br>(1) Deut. 12:32; Deut. 32:46; Matt. 28:20. |
| | Q. 109. *What are the sins forbidden in the second commandment?*<br><br>A. The sins forbidden in the second commandment are: all devising,[1] counselling,[2] commanding,[3] using,[4] and any wise approving any religious worship not instituted by God himself;[5] the making any representation of God, of all, or of any of the three Persons, either inwardly | Q. 51. *What is forbidden in the second commandment?*<br><br>A. The second commandment forbiddeth the worshipping of God by images,[1] or any other way not appointed in his word.[2]<br><br>(1) Deut. 4:15, 16.<br>See verses 17-19; Acts 17:29.<br>(2) Deut. 12:30, 31, 32. |

| THE WESTMINSTER CONFESSION OF FAITH | THE WESTMINSTER LARGER CATECHISM | THE WESTMINSTER SHORTER CATECHISM |
|---|---|---|

**THE WESTMINSTER LARGER CATECHISM**

in our mind, or outwardly in any kind of image or likeness of any creature whatsoever;[6] all worshipping of it,[7] or God in it or by it;[8] the making of any representation of feigned deities,[9] and all worship of them, or service belonging to them;[10] all superstitious devices,[11] corrupting the worship of God,[12] adding to it, or taking from it,[13] whether invented and taken up of ourselves,[14] or received by tradition from others,[15] though under the title of antiquity,[16] custom,[17] devotion,[18] good intent, or any other pretense whatsoever;[19] simony,[20] sacrilege;[21] all neglect,[22] contempt,[23] hindering,[24] and opposing the worship and ordinances which God hath appointed.[25]

(1) Num. 15:39.
(2) Deut. 13:6, 8.
(3) Hos. 5:11; Micah 6:16.
(4) I Kings 11:33; I Kings 12:33.
(5) Deut. 12:30, 32.
(6) Deut. 4:15, 16; Acts 17:29; Rom. 1:21-25.
(7) Gal. 4:8; Dan. 3:18.
(8) Ex. 32:5.
(9) Ex. 32:8.
(10) I Kings 18:26, 28; Isa. 65:11.
(11) Acts 19:19.
(12) Mal. 1:7, 8, 14.
(13) Deut. 4:2.
(14) Psa. 106:39.
(15) Matt. 15:9.
(16) I Pet. 1:18.
(17) Jer. 44:17.
(18) Isa. 65:3, 4, 5; Gal. 1:13, 14.
(19) I Sam. 13:12; I Sam. 15:21.
(20) Acts 8:18, 19, 22.
(21) Rom. 2:22; Mal. 3:8.
(22) Ex. 4:24, 25, 26.
(23) Matt. 22:5; Mal. 1:7, 12, 13.
(24) Matt. 23:13.
(25) Acts 13:45; I Thess. 2:15, 16.

Q. 110. *What are the reasons annexed to the second commandment, the more to enforce it?*

A. The reasons annexed to the second commandment, the more to enforce it, contained in these words,

**THE WESTMINSTER SHORTER CATECHISM**

Q. 52. *What are the reasons annexed to the second commandment?*

A. The reasons annexed to the second commandment are: God's sovereignty over us,[1] his propriety in

| THE WESTMINSTER CONFESSION OF FAITH | THE WESTMINSTER LARGER CATECHISM | THE WESTMINSTER SHORTER CATECHISM |
|---|---|---|
| | *For I the Lord thy God am a jealous God, visiting the iniquity of the fathers upon the children unto the third and fourth generation of them that hate me; and showing mercy unto thousands of them that love me, and keep my commandments;*[1] are, besides God's sovereignty over us, and propriety in us, his revengeful indignation against all false worship, as being a spiritual whoredom;[3] accounting the breakers of this commandment such as hate him, and threatening to punish them unto divers generations,[4] and esteeming the observers of it such as love him and keep his commandments, and promising mercy to them unto many generations.[5] | us,[2] and the zeal he hath to his own worship.[3] |
| | | (1) Psa. 95:2, 3. |
| | | (2) Psa. 45:2. |
| | | (3) Ex. 34:14. |
| | (1) Ex. 20:5, 6. | |
| | (2) Ex. 34:13, 14. | |
| | (3) I Cor. 10:20, 21, 22; Deut. 32:16-19; Jer. 7:18-20; Ezek. 16:26, 27. | |
| | (4) Hos. 2:2, 3, 4. | |
| | (5) Deut. 5:29. | |
| | **Q. 111.** *Which is the third commandment?* | **Q. 53.** *Which is the third commandment?* |
| | **A.** The third commandment is, *Thou shalt not take the name of the Lord thy God in vain; for the Lord will not hold him guiltless that taketh his name in vain.*[1] | **A.** The third commandment is, *Thou shalt not take the name of the Lord thy God in vain; for the Lord will not hold him guiltless that taketh his name in vain.*[1] |
| | (1) Ex. 20:7. | (1) Ex. 20:7. |
| | **Q. 112.** *What is required in the third commandment?* | **Q. 54.** *What is required in the third commandment?* |
| | **A.** The third commandment requires, that the name of God, his titles, attributes,[1] ordinances,[2] the word,[3] sacraments,[4] prayer,[5] oaths,[6] vows,[7] lots,[8] his works,[9] and whatsoever else there is whereby he makes himself known, be holily and reverently used in thought,[10] meditation,[11] word,[12] and writing;[13] by an holy profession,[14] and answerable conversation,[15] to the glory of God,[16] | **A.** The third commandment requireth the holy and reverent use of God's names,[1] titles, attributes,[2] ordinances,[3] word,[4] and works.[5] |
| | | (1) Psa. 29:2; Matt. 6:9. |
| | | (2) Rev. 15:3, 4. |
| | | (3) Mal. 1:14. |
| | | (4) Psa. 138:2. |
| | | (5) Psa. 107:21, 22. |

and the good of ourselves[17] and others.[18]

(1) Matt. 6:9; Deut. 28:58; Psa. 68:4; Psa. 29:2; Rev. 15:3, 4.
(2) Mal. 1:14.
(3) Psa. 138:2.
(4) I Cor. 11:28, 29. See context.
(5) I Tim. 2:8.
(6) Jer. 4:2.
(7) Psa. 76:11.
(8) Acts 1:24, 26.
(9) Psa. 107:21, 22.
(10) Mal. 3:16.
(11) Psa. 8.
(12) Psa. 105:2, 5; Col. 3:17.
(13) Psa. 102:18.
(14) I Pet. 3:15; Micah 4:5.
(15) Phil. 1:27.
(16) I Cor. 10:31.
(17) Jer. 32:39.
(18) I Pet. 2:12.

**Q. 113.** *What are the sins forbidden in the third commandment?*

A. The sins forbidden in the third commandment are: the not using of God's name as is required;[1] and the abuse of it in an ignorant,[2] vain,[3] irreverent, profane,[4] superstitious,[5] or wicked mentioning or otherwise using the titles, attributes,[6] ordinances,[7] or works;[8] by blasphemy;[9] perjury;[10] all sinful cursing,[11] oaths,[12] vows,[13] and lots;[14] violating our oaths and vows, if lawful;[15] and fulfilling them, if of things unlawful;[16] murmuring and quarreling at,[17] curious prying into,[18] and misapplying of God's decrees[19] and providence;[20] misinterpreting,[21] misapplying,[22] or any way perverting the word, or any part of it,[23] to profane jests,[24] curious and unprofitable questions, vain janglings, or the maintaining of false doctrines;[25] abusing it, the creatures, or anything contained under the name of God, to charms,[26] or sinful lusts and practices;[27] the maligning,[28] scorning,[29] reviling,[30] or any way opposing of God's truth, grace, and ways;[31] making profession of religion in hypocrisy, or for sinister

**Q. 55.** *What is forbidden in the third commandment?*

A. The third commandment forbiddeth all profaning or abusing of anything whereby God maketh himself known.[1]

(1) Mal. 2:2; Isa. 5:12.

| THE WESTMINSTER CONFESSION OF FAITH | THE WESTMINSTER LARGER CATECHISM | THE WESTMINSTER SHORTER CATECHISM |
|---|---|---|
| | ends;[32] being ashamed of it,[33] or a shame to it, by uncomfortable,[34] unwise,[35] unfruitful,[36] and offensive walking[37] or backsliding from it.[38] | |

(1) Mal. 2:2.
(2) Acts 17:23.
(3) Prov. 30:9.
(4) Mal. 1:6, 7, 12; Mal. 3:14.
(5) Jer. 7:4 (see context); Col. 2:20-22.
(6) Ex. 5:2; Psa. 139:20.
(7) Psa. 50:16, 17.
(8) Isa. 5:12.
(9) II Kings 19:22; Lev. 24:11.
(10) Zech. 5:4.
(11) Rom. 12:14; I Sam. 17:43; II Sam. 16:5.
(12) Jer. 5:7; Jer. 23:10.
(13) Deut. 23:18; Acts 23:12.
(14) Esth. 3:7; Esth. 9:24.
(15) Psa. 24:4; Ezek. 17:19. See context.
(16) Mark 6:26; I Sam. 25:22, 32-34.
(17) Rom. 9:14, 19, 20.
(18) Deut. 29:29.
(19) Rom. 3:5, 7. See context.
(20) Psa. 73:12, 13.
(21) Matt. 5:21-48.
(22) Ezek. 13:22.
(23) II Pet. 3:16; Matt. 22:29. See context, verses 23-32.
(24) Eph. 5:4.
(25) I Tim. 6:4, 5, 20; II Tim. 2:14; Tit. 3:9.
(26) Deut. 18:10, 11. See context. Acts 19:13.
(27) II Tim. 4:3, 4; Jude 4; Rom. 13:13, 14; I Kings 21:9, 10.
(28) Acts 13:45.
(29) II Pet. 3:3; Psa. 1:1.
(30) I Pet. 4:4.
(31) Acts 13:50. See verses 45, 46. Acts 4:18; Acts 19:9; I Thess. 2:16; Heb. 10:29.
(32) II Tim. 3:5; Matt. 23:14; Matt. 6:1, 2, 3, 5, 16.
(33) Mark 8:38.
(34) Psa. 73:14, 15.
(35) Eph. 5:15, 17; I Cor. 6:5, 6.
(36) Isa. 5:4; II Pet. 1:8, 9.
(37) Rom. 2:23, 24.
(38) Gal. 3:1, 3; Heb. 6:6.

Q. 114. *What reasons are annexed to the third commandment?*

A. The reasons annexed to the third commandment, in these words: *"the*

Q. 56. *What is the reason annexed to the third commandment?*

A. The reason annexed to the third commandment is, that however the

| THE WESTMINSTER CONFESSION OF FAITH | THE WESTMINSTER LARGER CATECHISM | THE WESTMINSTER SHORTER CATECHISM |
|---|---|---|

**LARGER CATECHISM:**

*Lord thy God,"* and, *"for the Lord will not hold him guiltless that taketh his name in vain,"*[1] are because he is the Lord and our God, therefore his name is not to be profaned, or any way abused by us;[2] especially because he will be so far from acquitting and sparing the transgressors of this commandment, as that he will not suffer them to escape his righteous judgment,[3] albeit many such escape the censures and punishments of men.[4]

(1) Ex. 20:7.
(2) Lev. 19:12.
(3) Deut. 28:58, 59; Zech. 5:2, 3, 4; Ezek. 36:21, 22, 23.
(4) I Sam. 2:12, 17, 22.

Q. 115. *Which is the fourth commandment?*

A. The fourth commandment is, *Remember the sabbath day, to keep it holy. Six days shalt thou labour, and do all thy work: but the seventh day is the sabbath of the Lord thy God: in it thou shalt not do any work, thou, nor thy son, nor thy daughter, thy manservant, nor thy maidservant, nor thy cattle, nor thy stranger that is within thy gates: for in six days the Lord made heaven and earth, the sea, and all that in them is, and rested the seventh day: wherefore the Lord blessed the sabbath day, and hallowed it.*[1]
(1) Ex. 20:8-11.

Q. 116. *What is required in the fourth commandment?*

A. The fourth commandment requireth of all men the sanctifying or keeping holy to God such set times as he hath appointed in his word, expressly one whole day in seven;[1] which was the seventh from the beginning of the world to the resurrection of Christ,[2] and the first day of the week ever since, and so to continue to the end of the world;

**SHORTER CATECHISM:**

breakers of this commandment may escape punishment from men, yet the Lord our God will not suffer them to escape his righteous judgment.[1]

(1) Deut. 28:58, 59.

Q. 57. *Which is the fourth commandment?*

A. The fourth commandment is, *Remember the sabbath day, to keep it holy. Six days shalt thou labour, and do all thy work: but the seventh day is the sabbath of the Lord thy God: in it thou shalt not do any work, thou, nor thy son, nor thy daughter, thy manservant, nor thy maidservant, nor thy cattle, nor thy stranger that is within thy gates:for in six days the Lord made heaven and earth, the sea, and all that in them is, and rested the seventh day: wherefore the Lord blessed the sabbath day, and hallowed it.*[1]
(1) E. 20:8-11.

Q. 58. *What is required in the fourth commandment?*

A. The fourth commandment requireth the keeping holy to God such set times as he hath appointed in his word; expressly one whole day in seven, to be a holy Sabbath to himself.[1]
(1) Lev. 19:30; Deut. 5:12; Isa. 56:2-7.

Q. 59. *Which day of the seven hath God appointed to be the weekly Sabbath?*

**CONFESSION OF FAITH:**

(7. As it is of the law of nature that, in general, a due proportion of time be set apart for the worship of God; so, in his word, by a positive, moral, and perpetual commandment, binding all men in all ages, he hath particularly appointed one day in seven for a Sabbath, to be kept holy unto him: which, from the beginning of the world to the resurrection of Christ, was the last day of the week; and, from the res-

| THE WESTMINSTER **CONFESSION OF FAITH** | THE WESTMINSTER **LARGER CATECHISM** | THE WESTMINSTER **SHORTER CATECHISM** |
|---|---|---|

urrection of Christ, was changed into the first day of the week, which in Scripture is called the Lord's day, and is to be continued to the end of the world as the Christian Sabbath.

— *Conf. of Faith, XXIII:7.)*

which is the Christian Sabbath,[3] and in the New Testament called *The Lord's day.*
(1)  Isa. 56:2, 4, 6, 7.
(2)  Gen. 2:3; Luke 23:56.
(3)  I Cor. 16:2; Acts 20:7; John 20:19-27.

A. From the beginning of the world to the resurrection of Christ, God appointed the seventh day of the week to be the weekly Sabbath;[1] and the first day of the week, ever since, to continue to the end of the world, which is the Christian Sabbath.[2]
(1)  Gen. 2:3; Luke 23:56.
(2)  Acts 20:7; I Cor. 16:1, 2; John 20:19-26.

(8. This Sabbath is then kept holy unto the Lord when men, after a due preparing of their hearts, and ordering of their common affairs beforehand, do not only observe an holy rest all the day from their own works, words, and thoughts about their worldly employments and recreations; but also are taken up the whole time in the public and private exercises of his worship, and in the duties of necessity and mercy.

— *Conf. of Faith, XXIII:8.)*

Q. 117. *How is the Sabbath or Lord's day to be sanctified?*

A. The Sabbath, or Lord's day, is to be sanctified by an holy resting all that day,[1] not only from such works as are at all times sinful, but even from such worldly employments and recreations as are on other days lawful;[2] and making it our delight to spend the whole time (except so much of it as is to be taken up in works of necessity and mercy)[3] in the public and private exercise of God's worship.[4] And, to that end, we are to prepare our hearts, and with such foresight, diligence, and moderation, to dispose, and seasonably to dispatch our worldly business, that we may be the more free and fit for the duties of the day.[5]
(1)  Ex. 20:8, 10.
(2)  Jer. 17:21, 22; Ex. 16:25-29; Neh. 13:15-22.
(3)  Matt. 12:1-14.
(4)  Lev. 23:3; Isa. 58:13; Luke 4:16; Acts 20:7.
(5)  Ex. 20:8; Luke 23:54, 56; Neh. 13:19.

Q. 118. *Why is the charge of keeping the Sabbath more specially directed to governors of families and other superiors?*

A. The charge of keeping the Sabbath is more specially directed to governors of families and other superiors, because they are bound not only to keep it themselves, but to see that it be observed by all those

Q. 60. *How is the Sabbath to be sanctified?*

A. The Sabbath is to be sanctified by a holy resting all that day, even from such worldly employments and recreations as are lawful on other days;[1] and spending the whole time in the public and private exercises of God's worship,[2] except so much as is to be taken up in the works of necessity and mercy.[3]
(1)  Lev. 23:3; Ex. 16:25-29; Jer. 17:21, 22.
(2)  Psa. 92:1, 2; Luke 4:16; Isa. 58:13; Acts 20:7.
(3)  Matt. 12:11, 12. See context.

| THE WESTMINSTER<br>**CONFESSION OF FAITH** | THE WESTMINSTER<br>**LARGER CATECHISM** | THE WESTMINSTER<br>**SHORTER CATECHISM** |
|---|---|---|
| | that are under their charge; and because they are prone ofttimes to hinder them by employments of their own.[1]<br><br>(1) These statements are necessary inferences from the relations which exist between governors and the governed. | |

**Q. 119.** *What are the sins forbidden in the fourth commandment?*

A. The sins forbidden in the fourth commandment are: all omissions of the duties required,[1] all careless, negligent, and unprofitable performing of them, and being weary of them;[2] all profaning the day by idleness, and doing that which is in itself sinful;[3] and by all needless works, words, and thoughts about our worldly employments and recreations.[4]

(1) Ezek. 22:26.
(2) Ezek. 33:31, 32; Mal. 1:13; Amos 8:5.
(3) Ezek. 23:38.
(4) Jer. 17:27. See context. Isa. 58:13, 14.

**Q. 61.** *What is forbidden in the fourth commandment?*

A. The fourth commandment forbiddeth the omission, or careless performance, of the duties required,[1] and the profaning the day by idleness, or doing that which is in itself sinful,[2] or by unnecessary thoughts, words, or works, about our worldly employments or recreations.[3]

(1) Ezek. 22:26; Mal. 1:13; Amos 8:5.
(2) Ezek. 23:38.
(3) Isa. 58:13; Jer. 17:24, 27.

**Q. 120.** *What are the reasons annexed to the fourth commandment, the more to enforce it?*

A. The reasons annexed to the fourth commandment, the more to enforce it, are taken from the equity of it, God allowing us six days of seven for our own affairs, and reserving but one for himself, in these words, *six days shalt thou labour, and do all thy work:*[1] from God's challenging a special propriety in that day, *the seventh day is the sabbath of the Lord thy God:*[2] from the example of God who *in six days . . . made heaven and earth, the sea, and all that in them is, and rested the seventh day:* and from that blessing which God put upon that day, not only in sanctifying it to be

**Q. 62.** *What are the reasons annexed to the fourth commandment?*

A. The reasons annexed to the fourth commandment are, God's allowing us six days of the week for our own employments,[1] his challenging a special propriety in the seventh,[2] his own example,[3] and his blessing the Sabbath day.[4]

(1) Ex. 31:15, 16.
(2) Lev. 23:3.
(3) Ex. 31:17.
(4) Gen. 2:3.

| THE WESTMINSTER CONFESSION OF FAITH | THE WESTMINSTER LARGER CATECHISM | THE WESTMINSTER SHORTER CATECHISM |
|---|---|---|

**LARGER CATECHISM (continued)**

a holy day for his service, but in ordaining it to be a means of blessing to us in our sanctifying it, *wherefore the Lord blessed the sabbath day, and hallowed it.*[3]

(1) Ex. 20:9.
(2) Ex. 20:10.
(3) Ex. 20:11.

Q. 121. *Why is the word* remember *set in the beginning of the fourth commandment?*

A. The word *remember* is set in the beginning of the fourth commandment,[1] partly because of the great benefit of remembering it, we being thereby helped in our preparation to keep it;[2] and, in keeping it, better to keep all the rest of the commandments,[3] and to continue a thankful remembrance of the two great benefits of creation and redemption, which contain a short abridgment of religion:[4] and partly because few are ready to forget it,[5] for that there is less light of nature for it, and yet it restraineth our natural liberty in things at other times lawful;[6] that it cometh but once in seven days, and many worldly businesses come between, and too often take off our minds from thinking of it, either to prepare for it, or to sanctify it;[7] and that Satan with his instruments much labor to blot out the glory, and even the memory of it, and to bring in all irreligion and impiety.[8]

(1) Ex. 20:8.
(2) Ex. 16:23; Luke 23:54, 56; compared with Mark 14:42; Neh. 13:19.
(3) Ezek. 20:12, 20.
(4) Gen. 2:2, 3; Psa. 118:22, 24; Heb. 4:9.
(5) Num. 15:37, 38, 40. See context.
(6) Ex. 34:21.
(7) See citation under figure 5 above.
(8) Lam. 1:7; Neh. 13:15-23; Jer. 17:21-23.

| THE WESTMINSTER CONFESSION OF FAITH | THE WESTMINSTER LARGER CATECHISM | THE WESTMINSTER SHORTER CATECHISM |
|---|---|---|
| | Q. 122. *What is the sum of the six commandments which contain our duty to man?* | (Q. 42. *What is the sum of the ten commandments?* |
| | A. The sum of the six commandments which contain our duty to man is, to love our neighbor as ourselves,[1] and to do to others what we would have them to do to us.[2]<br>(1) Matt. 22:39.<br>(2) Matt. 7:12. | (A. The sum of the ten commandments is, to love the Lord our God, with all our heart, with all our soul, with all our strength, and with all our mind; and our neighbor as ourselves.) |
| | Q. 123. *Which is the fifth commandment?* | Q. 63. *Which is the fifth commandment?* |
| | A. The fifth commandment is, *Honour thy father and thy mother: that thy days may be long upon the land which the Lord thy God giveth thee.*[1]<br>(1) Ex. 20:12. | A. The fifth commandment is, *Honour thy father and thy mother: that thy days may be long upon the land which the Lord thy God giveth thee.*[1]<br>(1) Ex. 20:12. |
| | Q. 124. *Who are meant by* father *and* mother, *in the fifth commandment?* | |
| | A. By *father* and *mother,* in the fifth commandment, are meant not only natural parents, but all superiors in age[1] and gifts;[2] and especially such as by God's ordinance are over us in place of authority, whether in family,[3] church,[4] or commonwealth.[5]<br>(1) I Tim. 5:1, 2.<br>(2) Gen. 4:20, 21; Gen. 45:8.<br>(3) II Kings 5:13.<br>(4) Gal. 4:19; II Kings 2:12; II Kings 13:14.<br>(5) Isa. 49:23. | |
| | Q. 125. *Why are superiors styled* father *and* mother? | |
| | A. Superiors are styled *father* and *mother,* both to teach them in all duties towards their inferiors, like natural parents, to express love and tenderness to them, according to their several relations,[1] and to work inferiors to a greater willingness and cheerfulness in performing their duties to their superiors, as to their parents.[2]<br>(1) Eph. 6:4; I Thess. 2:7, 8, 11; Num. 11:11, 12, 16.<br>(2) I Cor. 4:14, 15, 16. | |

## THE WESTMINSTER CONFESSION OF FAITH

## THE WESTMINSTER LARGER CATECHISM

Q. 126. *What is the general scope of the fifth commandment?*

A. The general scope of the fifth commandment is, the performance of those duties which we mutually owe in our several relations, as inferiors, superiors, or equals.[1]

(1) Eph. 5:21; I Pet. 2:17; Rom. 12:10.

Q. 127. *What is the honor which inferiors owe to their superiors?*

A. The honor which inferiors owe to their superiors is: all due reverence in heart,[1] word,[2] and behavior;[3] prayer and thanksgiving for them;[4] imitation of their virtues and graces;[5] willing obedience to their lawful commands and counsels,[6] due submission to their corrections;[7] fidelity to,[8] defense and maintenance of their persons and authority, according to their several ranks, and the nature of their places;[9] bearing with their infirmities, and covering them in love,[10] that so they may be an honor to them and to their government.[11]

(1) Mal. 1:6; Lev. 19:3.
(2) Prov. 31:28; I Pet. 3:6.
(3) Lev. 19:32; I Kings 2:19.
(4) I Tim. 2:1, 2.
(5) Heb. 13:7; Phil. 3:17.
(6) Eph. 6:1, 5, 6, 7; I Pet. 2:13, 14; Rom. 13:1-6; Heb. 13:17; Prov. 4:3, 4; Prov. 23:22.
(7) Heb. 12:9; I Pet. 2:18-20.
(8) Tit. 2:9, 10.
(9) Matt. 22:21; Rom. 13:6, 7; I Tim. 5:17, 18; Gal. 6:6; Gen. 45:11; Gen. 47:12.
(10) Gen. 9:23; I Pet. 2:18; Prov. 23:22.
(11) Psa. 127:3, 5; Prov. 31:23.

Q. 128. *What are the sins of inferiors against their superiors?*

A. The sins of inferiors against their superiors are: all neglect of the duties required toward them;[1] envying at,[2] contempt of,[3] and rebellion[4] against their persons[5] and places,[6] in their lawful counsels,[7]

## THE WESTMINSTER SHORTER CATECHISM

Q. 64. *What is required in the fifth commandment?*

A. The fifth commandment requireth the preserving the honor, and performing the duties, belonging to everyone in their several places and relations, as superiors, inferiors, or equals.[1]

(1) Eph. 5:21, 22; Eph. 6:1, 5, 9; Rom. 13:1; Rom. 12:10.

Q. 65. *What is forbidden in the fifth commandment?*

A. The fifth commandment forbiddeth the neglecting of, or doing anything against, the honor and duty which belongeth to everyone in their several places and relations.[1]

(1) Rom. 13:7, 8.

THE WESTMINSTER
**CONFESSION OF FAITH**

THE WESTMINSTER
**LARGER CATECHISM**

THE WESTMINSTER
**SHORTER CATECHISM**

commands, and corrections;[8] cursing, mocking,[9] and all such refractory and scandalous carriage, as proves a shame and dishonor to them and their government.[10]

(1) Matt. 15:5, 6.
(2) Psa. 106:16.
(3) I Sam. 8:7; Isa. 3:5.
(4) II Sam. 15:1-12.
(5) Ex. 21:15.
(6) I Sam. 10:27.
(7) I Sam. 2:25.
(8) Deut. 21:18, 20, 21.
(9) Prov. 30:11, 17.
(10) Prov. 19:26.

Q. 129. *What is required of superiors towards their inferiors?*

A. It is required of superiors, according to that power they receive from God, and that relation wherein they stand, to love,[1] pray for,[2] and bless their inferiors;[3] to instruct,[4] counsel, and admonish them;[5] countenancing,[6] commending, and rewarding such as do well;[7] and discountenancing,[8] reproving, and chastising such as do ill;[9] protecting, and providing for them all things necessary for soul and body;[10] and, by grave, wise, holy, and exemplary carriage, to procure glory to God,[11] honor to themselves,[12] and so to preserve that authority which God hath put upon them.[13]

(1) Col. 3:19; Tit. 2:4.
(2) I Sam. 12:23; Job 1:5.
(3) I Kings 8:55, 56; Gen. 49:28.
(4) Deut. 6:6, 7.
(5) Eph. 6:4.
(6) I Pet. 3:7.
(7) Rom. 13:3; I Pet. 2:14.
(8) Rom. 13:4.
(9) Prov. 29:15; Rom. 13:4.
(10) I Tim. 5:8; Isa. 1:10, 17; Eph. 6:4.
(11) I Tim. 4:12; Tit. 2:2-14.
(12) I Kings 3:28.
(13) Tit. 2:15.

Q. 130. *What are the sins of superiors?*

A. The sins of superiors are, besides the neglect of the duties required of

| THE WESTMINSTER CONFESSION OF FAITH | THE WESTMINSTER LARGER CATECHISM | THE WESTMINSTER SHORTER CATECHISM |
|---|---|---|

them,[1] an inordinate seeking of themselves,[2] their own glory,[3] ease, profit, or pleasure;[4] commanding things unlawful,[5] or not in the power of inferiors to perform;[6] counseling,[7] encouraging,[8] or favoring them in that which is evil;[9] dissuading, discouraging, or discountenancing them in that which is good;[10] correcting them unduly;[11] careless exposing or leaving them to wrong, temptation, and danger;[12] provoking them to wrath;[13] or any way dishonoring themselves, or lessening their authority, by an unjust, indiscreet, rigorous, or remiss behavior.[14]

(1) Ezek. 34:2, 4.
(2) Phil. 2:21.
(3) John 5:44; John 7:18.
(4) Isa. 56:10, 11; Deut. 17:17.
(5) Acts 4:18; Dan. 3:4-6.
(6) Ex. 5:10-19; Matt. 23:2, 4.
(7) Matt. 14:8 compared with Mark 6:24.
(8) Jer. 5:30, 31; II Sam. 13:28.
(9) Jer. 6:13, 14; Ezek. 13:9, 10.
(10) John 7:46, 47, 48, 49; John 9:28.
(11) I Pet. 2:19, 20; Heb. 12:10; Deut. 25:3.
(12) Lev. 19:29; Isa. 58:7; Gen. 38:11, 26.
(13) Eph. 6:4.
(14) Gen. 9:21; I Kings 12:13, 14; I Kings 1:6; I Sam. 3:13.

Q. 131. *What are the duties of equals?*

A. The duties of equals are: to regard the dignity and worth of each other,[1] in giving honor to go one before another;[2] and to rejoice in each other's gifts and advancement as their own.[3]

(1) I Pet. 2:17.
(2) Rom. 12:10; Phil. 2:3.
(3) Rom. 12:15, 16; Phil. 2:4.

Q. 132. *What are the sins of equals?*

A. The sins of equals are, besides the neglect of the duties required,[1] the undervaluing of the worth,[2] envying the gifts,[3] grieving at the ad-

THE WESTMINSTER
**CONFESSION OF FAITH**

THE WESTMINSTER
**LARGER CATECHISM**

THE WESTMINSTER
**SHORTER CATECHISM**

vancement or prosperity one of an-other;[4] and usurping pre-eminence one over another.[5]

(1) Rom. 13:8.
(2) Prov. 14:21; Isa. 65:5; II Tim. 3:3.
(3) Acts 7:9; Gal. 5:26.
(4) I John 3:12; Matt. 20:15; Num. 12:2; Luke 15:28, 29.
(5) Matt. 20:25, 26, 27; III John 9; Luke 22:24, 25, 26.

Q. 133. *What is the reason an-nexed to the fifth command-ment, the more to enforce it?*

A. The reason annexed to the fifth commandment in these words: *"that thy days may be long upon the land which the Lord thy God giveth thee,"*[1] is an express promise of long life and prosperity, as far as it shall serve for God's glory and their own good, to all such as keep this com-mandment.[2]

(1) Ex. 20:12.
(2) Eph. 6:2, 3; Deut. 5:16; I Kings 8:25.

Q. 134. *Which is the sixth com-mandment?*

A. The sixth commandment is, *Thou shalt not kill.*[1]
(1) Ex. 20:13.

Q. 135. *What are the duties re-quired in the sixth command-ment?*

A. The duties required in the sixth commandment are: all careful studies, and lawful endeavors, to preserve the life of ourselves[1] and others,[2] by resisting all thoughts and purposes,[3] subduing all passions,[4] and avoiding all occasions,[5] tempta-tions,[6] and practices, which tend to the unjust taking away the life of any;[7] by just defense thereof against violence;[8] patient bearing of the hand of God;[9] quietness of mind,[10] cheerfulness of spirit,[11] a sober use of meat,[12] drink,[13] physic,[14] sleep,[15]

Q. 66. *What is the reason annexed to the fifth commandment?*

A. The reason annexed to the fifth commandment is, a promise of long life and prosperity (as far as it shall serve for God's glory, and their own good) to all such as keep this com-mandment.[1]

(1) Eph. 6:2, 3.

Q. 67. *Which is the sixth com-mandment?*

A. The sixth commandment is, *Thou shalt not kill.*[1]
(1) Ex. 20:13.

Q. 68. *What is required in the sixth commandment?*

A. The sixth commandment re-quireth all lawful endeavors to pre-serve our own life,[1] and the life of others.[2]

(1) Eph. 5:29; Matt. 10:23.
(2) Psa. 82:3, 4; Job 29:13; I Kings 18:4.

| THE WESTMINSTER CONFESSION OF FAITH | THE WESTMINSTER LARGER CATECHISM | THE WESTMINSTER SHORTER CATECHISM |
|---|---|---|
| | labor,[16] and recreation;[17] by charitable thoughts,[18] love,[19] compassion,[20] meekness, gentleness, kindness;[21] peaceable,[22] mild, and courteous speeches and behavior;[23] forbearance, readiness to be reconciled, patient bearing and forgiving of injuries, and requiting good for evil;[24] comforting and succoring the distressed, and protecting and defending the innocent.[25]<br>(1) Eph. 5:29; Matt. 10:23.<br>(2) Psa. 82:4; Deut. 22:8.<br>(3) Matt. 5:22; Jer. 26:15, 16.<br>(4) Eph. 4:26.<br>(5) Prov. 22:24, 25; I Sam. 25:32, 33; Deut. 22:8.<br>(6) Prov. 1:10, 11, 15; Matt. 4:6, 7.<br>(7) I Kings 21:9, 10, 19; Gen. 37:21, 22; I Sam. 24:12, and 26:9, 10, 11.<br>(8) Prov. 24:11, 12; I Sam. 14:45.<br>(9) Luke 21:19; James 5:8; Heb. 12:5.<br>(10) Psa. 37:8, 11; I Pet. 3:3, 4.<br>(11) Prov. 17:22; I Thess. 5:16.<br>(12) Prov. 23:20; Prov. 25:16.<br>(13) Prov. 23:29, 30; I Tim. 5:23.<br>(14) Matt. 9:12; Isa. 38:21.<br>(15) Psa. 127:2.<br>(16) II Thess. 3:10, 12.<br>(17) Mark 6:31; I Tim. 4:8.<br>(18) I Cor. 13:4, 5; I Sam. 19:4, 5.<br>(19) Rom. 13:10; Prov. 10:12.<br>(20) Zech. 7:9; Luke 10:33, 34.<br>(21) Col. 3:12.<br>(22) Rom. 12:18.<br>(23) I Pet. 3:8, 9; I Cor. 4:12, 13.<br>(24) Col. 3:13; James 3:17; I Pet. 2:20; Rom. 12:20, 21; Matt. 5:24.<br>(25) I Thess. 5:14; Matt. 25:35, 36; Prov. 31:8, 9; Isa. 58:7.<br><br>**Q. 136.** *What are the sins forbidden in the sixth commandment?*<br><br>**A.** The sins forbidden in the sixth commandment are: all taking away the life of ourselves,[1] or of others,[2] except in case of public justice,[3] lawful war,[4] or necessary defense;[5] the neglecting or withdrawing the lawful or necessary means of preservation of life;[6] sinful anger,[7] hatred,[8] envy,[9] desire of revenge;[10] all excessive passions;[11] distracting cares;[12] immoderate use of meat, drink,[13] labor,[14] and recreations;[15] provok- | **Q. 69.** *What is forbidden in the sixth commandment?*<br><br>**A.** The sixth commandment forbiddeth the taking away of our own life,[1] or the life of our neighbor unjustly,[2] or whatsoever tendeth thereunto.[3]<br><br>(1) Acts 16:28.<br>(2) Gen. 9:6.<br>(3) Matt. 5:22; I John 3:15; Gal. 5:15; Prov. 24:11, 12; Ex. 21:18-32. |

THE WESTMINSTER
CONFESSION OF FAITH

THE WESTMINSTER
LARGER CATECHISM

THE WESTMINSTER
SHORTER CATECHISM

ing words;[16] oppression,[17] quarreling,[18] striking, wounding,[19] and whatsoever else tends to the destruction of the life of any.[20]

(1) Acts 16:28; Prov. 1:18.
(2) Gen. 9:6.
(3) Ex. 21:14; Num. 35:31, 33.
(4) Deut. 20 throughout; Heb. 11:32, 33, 34; Jer. 48:10.
(5) Ex. 22:2.
(6) Matt. 25:42, 43; James 2:15, 16.
(7) Matt. 5:22.
(8) I John 3:15; Prov. 10:12; Lev. 19:17.
(9) Prov. 14:30.
(10) Rom. 12:19.
(11) James 4:1; Eph. 4:31.
(12) Matt. 6:34.
(13) Luke 21:34.
(14) Ex. 20:9, 10.
(15) I Pet. 4:3, 4.
(16) Prov. 15:1; Prov. 12:18.
(17) Isa. 3:15; Ex. 1:14.
(18) Gal. 5:15.
(19) Num. 35:16.
(20) Prov. 28:17; Ex. 21:18-36.

Q. 137. *Which is the seventh commandment?*

A. The seventh commandment is, *Thou shalt not commit adultery.*[1]
(1) Ex. 20:14.

Q. 138. *What are the duties required in the seventh commandment?*

A. The duties required in the seventh commandment are: chastity in body, mind, affections,[1] words,[2] and behavior;[3] and the preservation of it in ourselves and others;[4] watchfulness over the eyes and all the senses;[5] temperance,[6] keeping of chaste company,[7] modesty in apparel,[8] marriage by those that have not the gift of continency,[9] conjugal love,[10] and cohabitation;[11] diligent labor in our callings;[12] shunning of all occasions of uncleanness, and resisting temptations thereunto.[13]
(1) I Thess. 4:4, 5.
(2) Eph. 4:29; Col. 4:6.
(3) I Pet. 3:2.
(4) I Cor. 7:2; Tit. 2:4, 5.

Q. 70. *Which is the seventh commandment?*

A. The seventh commandment is, *Thou shalt not commit adultery.*[1]
(1) Ex. 20:14.

Q. 71. *What is required in the seventh commandment?*

A. The seventh commandment requireth the preservation of our own[1] and our neighbor's chastity,[2] in heart,[3] speech,[4] and behavior.[5]
(1) I Thess. 4:4, 5.
(2) I Cor. 7:2; Eph. 5:11, 12.
(3) Matt. 5:28.
(4) Eph. 4:29; Col. 4:6.
(5) I Pet. 3:2.

THE WESTMINSTER
## CONFESSION OF FAITH

THE WESTMINSTER
## LARGER CATECHISM

THE WESTMINSTER
## SHORTER CATECHISM

(5) Matt. 5:28.
(6) Prov. 23:31, 33; Jer. 5:7.
(7) Prov. 2:16, 20; I Cor. 5:9.
(8) I Tim. 2:9.
(9) I Cor. 7:9.
(10) Prov. 5:18, 19.
(11) I Pet. 3:7; I Cor. 7:5.
(12) I Tim. 5:13, 14; Prov. 31:27.
(13) Prov. 5:8.

**Q. 139.** *What are the sins forbidden in the seventh commandment?*

A. The sins forbidden in the seventh commandment, besides the neglect of the duties required,[1] are: adultery, fornication,[2] rape, incest,[3] sodomy, and all unnatural lusts;[4] all unclean imaginations, thoughts, purposes, and affections;[5] all corrupt or filthy communications, or listening thereunto;[6] wanton looks,[7] impudent or light behavior, immodest apparel;[8] prohibiting of lawful,[9] and dispensing with unlawful marriages;[10] allowing, tolerating, keeping of stews, and resorting to them;[11] entangling vows of single life,[12] undue delay of marriage;[13] having more wives or husbands than one at the same time;[14] unjust divorce[15] or desertion;[16] idleness, gluttony, drunkenness,[17] unchaste company;[18] lascivious songs, books, pictures, dancings, stage-plays,[19] and all other provocations to, or acts of, uncleanness either in ourselves or others.[20]

(1) Prov. 5:7; Prov. 4:23, 27.
(2) Heb. 13:4; Eph. 5:5; Gal. 5:19.
(3) II Sam. 13:14; Mark 6:18; I Cor. 5:1, 13.
(4) Rom. 1:26, 27; Lev. 20:15, 16.
(5) Matt. 15:19; Col. 3:5; Matt. 5:28.
(6) Eph. 5:3, 4; Prov. 7:5, 21; Prov. 19:27.
(7) Isa. 3:16; II Pet. 2:14.
(8) Prov. 7:10, 13.
(9) I Tim. 4:3.
(10) Lev. 18:1-21.
(11) II Kings 23:7; Lev. 19:29; Jer. 5:7.
(12) Matt. 19:10, 11, 12.
(13) I Tim. 5:14, 15; Gen. 38:26.
(14) Matt. 19:5; I Cor. 7:2.
(15) Matt. 5:32; Mal. 2:16.

**Q. 72.** *What is forbidden in the seventh commandment?*

A. The seventh commandment forbiddeth all unchaste thoughts,[1] words,[2] and actions.[3]

(1) Matt. 5:28.
(2) Eph. 5:4.
(3) Eph. 5:3.

| THE WESTMINSTER CONFESSION OF FAITH | THE WESTMINSTER LARGER CATECHISM | THE WESTMINSTER SHORTER CATECHISM |
|---|---|---|

**THE WESTMINSTER LARGER CATECHISM**

(16) See citations under Question 138. I Cor. 7:12, 13.
(17) Ezek. 16:49; Jer. 5:7.
(18) Eph. 5:11; Prov. 5:8.
(19) Rom. 13:13; I Pet. 4:3; Mark 6:22.
(20) Rom. 13:14; II Pet. 2:17, 18.

**Q. 140.** *Which is the eighth commandment?*

A. The eighth commandment is, *Thou shalt not steal.*[1]

(1) Ex. 20:15.

**Q. 141.** *What are the duties required in the eighth commandment?*

A. The duties required in the eighth commandment are: truth, faithfulness, and justice in contracts and commerce between man and man;[1] rendering to everyone his due;[2] restitution of goods unlawfully detained from the right owners thereof;[3] giving and lending freely, according to our abilities, and the necessities of others;[4] moderation of our judgments, wills, and affections, concerning worldly goods;[5] a provident care and study to get,[6] keep, use, and dispose of those things which are necessary and convenient for the sustentation of our nature, and suitable to our condition;[7] a lawful calling,[8] and diligence in it;[9] frugality;[10] avoiding unnecessary lawsuits,[11] and suretyship, or other like engagements;[12] and an endeavor by all just and lawful means to procure, preserve, and further the wealth and outward estate of others, as well as our own.[13]

(1) Psa. 15:2, 4; Micah 6:8; Zech. 8:16.
(2) Rom. 13:7.
(3) Lev. 6:4, 5; Luke 19:8.
(4) Deut. 15:7, 8, 10; Gal. 6:10; Luke 6:30, 38.
(5) I Tim. 6:8, 9.
(6) I Tim. 5:8.
(7) Prov. 27:23, 24; I Tim. 6:17, 18.
(8) Eph. 4:28; Rom. 12:5-8.
(9) Prov. 10:4; Rom. 12:11.

**THE WESTMINSTER SHORTER CATECHISM**

**Q. 73.** *Which is the eighth commandment?*

A. The eighth commandment is, *Thou shalt not steal.*[1]

(1) Ex. 20:15.

**Q. 74.** *What is required in the eighth commandment?*

A. The eighth commandment requireth the lawful procuring and furthering the wealth and outward estate of ourselves[1] and others.[2]

(1) II Thess. 3:10, 11, 12; Rom. 12:17; Prov. 27:23.
(2) Lev. 25:35; Phil. 2:4; Prov. 13:4; Prov. 20:4; Prov. 24:30-34.

| THE WESTMINSTER CONFESSION OF FAITH | THE WESTMINSTER LARGER CATECHISM | THE WESTMINSTER SHORTER CATECHISM |
|---|---|---|
| | (10) Prov. 12:27; Prov. 21:20; John 6:12.<br>(11) I Cor. 6:7.<br>(12) Prov. 11:15; Prov. 6:1-5.<br>(13) Lev. 25:35; Phil. 2:4; Deut. 22:1-4; Ex. 23:4, 5. | |

**Q. 142.** *What are the sins forbidden in the eighth commandment?*

A. The sins forbidden in the eighth commandment, besides the neglect of the duties required,[1] are: theft,[2] robbery,[3] man-stealing,[4] and receiving anything that is stolen;[5] fraudulent dealing,[6] false weights and measures,[7] removing landmarks,[8] injustice and unfaithfulness in contracts between man and man,[9] or in matters of trust;[10] oppression,[11] extortion, usury,[12] bribery,[13] vexatious lawsuits,[14] unjust enclosures and depopulations;[15] engrossing commodities to enhance the price,[16] unlawful callings,[17] and all other unjust or sinful ways of taking or withholding from our neighbor what belongs to him, or of enriching ourselves;[18] covetousness,[19] inordinate prizing and affecting worldly goods;[20] distrustful and distracting cares and studies in getting, keeping, and using them;[21] envying at the prosperity of others;[22] as likewise idleness,[23] prodigality, wasteful gaming, and all other ways whereby we do unduly prejudice our own outward estate;[24] and defrauding ourselves of the due use and comfort of that estate which God hath given us.[25]

(1) Prov. 23:21; I John 3:17; James 2:15, 16.
(2) Eph. 4:28.
(3) Psa. 62:10.
(4) I Tim. 1:10; Ex. 21:16.
(5) Prov. 29:24; Psa. 50:18.
(6) I Thess. 4:6.
(7) Prov. 11:1; Prov. 20:10.
(8) Deut. 19:14; Prov. 23:10.
(9) Amos 8:5; Psa. 37:21.
(10) Luke 16:11.
(11) Ezek. 22:29; Lev. 25:17.
(12) Matt. 23:25; Ezek. 22:12.

**Q. 75.** *What is forbidden in the eighth commandment?*

A. The eighth commandment forbiddeth whatsoever doth, or may, unjustly hinder our own[1] or our neighbor's wealth or outward estate.[2]

(1) I Tim. 5:8.
(2) Eph. 4:28; Prov. 21:6; II Thess. 3:7-10.

| THE WESTMINSTER CONFESSION OF FAITH | THE WESTMINSTER LARGER CATECHISM | THE WESTMINSTER SHORTER CATECHISM |
|---|---|---|

**Larger Catechism:**

(13) Isa. 33:15.
(14) Prov. 3:30; I Cor. 6:7.
(15) Isa. 5:8; Micah 2:2.
(16) Prov. 11:26.
(17) Acts 19:19. See context.
(18) James 5:4; Prov. 21:6.
(19) Luke 12:15; Prov. 1:19.
(20) I John 2:15, 16; Prov. 23:5; Psa. 62:10.
(21) Matt. 6:25, 34.
(22) Psa. 73:3; James 5:9.
(23) II Thess. 3:11; Prov. 18:9.
(24) Prov. 21:17; Prov. 23:20, 21; Prov. 28:19.
(25) Deut. 12:7; Deut. 16:14.

Q. 143. *Which is the ninth commandment?*

A. The ninth commandment is, *Thou shalt not bear false witness against thy neighbour.*[1]
(1) Ex. 20:16.

Q. 144. *What are the duties required in the ninth commandment?*

A. The duties required in the ninth commandment are: the preserving and promoting of truth between man and man,[1] and the good name of our neighbor, as well as our own;[2] appearing and standing for the truth;[3] and from the heart, sincerely,[4] freely,[5] clearly,[6] and fully,[7] speaking the truth, and only the truth, in matters of judgment and justice,[8] and in all other things whatsoever;[9] a charitable esteem of our neighbors;[10] loving, desiring, and rejoicing in their good name;[11] sorrowing for,[12] and covering of their infirmities;[13] freely acknowledging of their gifts and graces,[14] defending their innocency;[15] a ready receiving of a good report,[16] and unwillingness to admit of an evil report concerning them;[17] discouraging tale-bearers,[18] flatterers,[19] and slanderers;[20] love and care of our own good name, and defending it when need requireth;[21] keeping of lawful promises;[22] studying and

**Shorter Catechism:**

Q. 76. *Which is the ninth commandment?*

A. The ninth commandment is, *Thou shalt nor bear false witness against thy neighbor.*[1]
(1) Ex. 20:16.

Q. 77. *What is required in the ninth commandment?*

A. The ninth commandment requireth the maintaining and promoting of truth between man and man,[1] and of our own[2] and our neighbor's good name,[3] especially in witness-bearing.[4]
(1) Zech. 8:16.
(2) I Pet. 3:16; Acts 25:10.
(3) III John 12.
(4) Prov. 14:5, 25.

| THE WESTMINSTER CONFESSION OF FAITH | THE WESTMINSTER LARGER CATECHISM | THE WESTMINSTER SHORTER CATECHISM |
|---|---|---|

### THE WESTMINSTER LARGER CATECHISM

practicing of whatsoever things are true, honest, lovely, and of good report.[23]

(1) Eph. 4:25.
(2) III John 12.
(3) Prov. 31:9.
(4) Psa. 15:2.
(5) Jer. 9:3.
(6) Jer. 42:4; Acts 20:20.
(7) Acts 20:27.
(8) Lev. 19:15; Prov. 14:5.
(9) Isa. 63:8; Col. 3:9; II Cor. 1:17.
(10) Heb. 6:9; I Cor. 13:4, 5.
(11) III John 4; Rom. 1:8.
(12) II Cor. 12:21; Psa. 119:158.
(13) Prov. 17:9; I Pet. 4:8.
(14) I Cor. 1:4, 5; II Tim. 1:4, 5.
(15) Psa. 82:3.
(16) I Cor. 13:4, 6, 7.
(17) Psa. 15:3.
(18) Prov. 25:23.
(19) Prov. 26:24, 25.
(20) Psa. 101:5.
(21) II Cor. 11:18, 23; Prov. 22:1; John 8:49.
(22) Psa. 15:4.
(23) Phil. 4:8.

Q. 145. *What are the sins forbidden in the ninth commandment?*

A. The sins forbidden in the ninth commandment are: all prejudicing of the truth, and the good name of our neighbors as well as our own,[1] especially in public judicature;[2] giving false evidence,[3] suborning false witnesses,[4] wittingly appearing and pleading for an evil cause, outfacing and overbearing the truth;[5] passing unjust sentence,[6] calling evil good, and good evil; rewarding the wicked according to the work of the righteous, and the righteous according to the work of the wicked;[7] forgery,[8] concealing the truth, undue silence in a just cause,[9] and holding our peace when iniquity calleth for either a reproof from ourselves,[10] or complaint to others;[11] speaking the truth unseasonably,[12] or maliciously to a wrong end,[13] or perverting it to a wrong meaning,[14] or in doubtful and equivocal expression, to the prejudice of truth or

### THE WESTMINSTER SHORTER CATECHISM

Q. 78. *What is forbidden in the ninth commandment?*

A. The ninth commandment forbiddeth whatsoever is prejudicial to truth,[1] or injurious to our own or our neighbor's good name.[2]

(1) Prov. 19:5; Prov. 6:16-19.
(2) Luke 3:14; Psa. 15:3.

| THE WESTMINSTER CONFESSION OF FAITH | THE WESTMINSTER LARGER CATECHISM | THE WESTMINSTER SHORTER CATECHISM |
|---|---|---|
| | justice;[15] speaking untruth,[16] lying,[17] slandering,[18] backbiting,[19] detracting,[20] tale-bearing,[21] whispering,[22] scoffing,[23] reviling;[24] rash,[25] harsh,[26] and partial censuring;[27] misconstruing intentions, words, and actions;[28] flattering,[29] vainglorious boasting,[30] thinking or speaking too highly or too meanly of ourselves or others; denying the gifts and graces of God;[31] aggravating smaller faults;[32] hiding, excusing, or extenuating of sins, when called to a free confession;[33] unnecessarily discovering of infirmities;[34] raising false rumors;[35] receiving and countenancing evil reports,[36] and stopping our ears against just defense;[37] evil suspicion;[38] envying or grieving at the deserved credit of any;[39] endeavoring or desiring to impair it,[40] rejoicing in their disgrace and infamy;[41] scornful contempt,[42] fond admiration;[43] breach of lawful promises;[44] neglecting such things as are of good report;[45] and practicing or not avoiding ourselves, or not hindering what we can in others, such things as procure an ill name.[46] | |

(1) Luke 3:14.
(2) Lev. 19:15; Hab. 1:4.
(3) Prov. 19:5; Prov. 6:16, 19.
(4) Acts 6:13.
(5) Jer. 9:3; Psa. 12:3, 4; Psa. 52:1-4.
(6) Prov. 17:15.
(7) Isa. 5:23.
(8) I Kings 21:8.
(9) Lev. 5:1; Acts 5:3.
(10) Lev. 19:17; Isa. 58:1.
(11) Isa. 59:4.
(12) Prov. 29:11.
(13) I Sam. 22:9, 10; Psa. 52:1.
(14) Psa. 56:5; Matt. 26:60, 61. Compare John 2:19.
(15) Gen. 3:5; Gen. 26:7, 9.
(16) Isa. 59:13.
(17) Col. 3:9; Lev. 19:11.
(18) Psa. 50:20.
(19) Psa. 15:3; Rom. 1:30.
(20) James 4:11; Tit. 3:2.
(21) Lev. 19:16.
(22) Rom. 1:29; Prov. 16:28.
(23) Isa. 28:22; Gen. 21:9; Gal. 4:29.
(24) I Cor. 6:10.
(25) Matt. 7:1.

| THE WESTMINSTER CONFESSION OF FAITH | THE WESTMINSTER LARGER CATECHISM | THE WESTMINSTER SHORTER CATECHISM |
|---|---|---|
| | (26) James 2:13.<br>(27) John 7:24; Rom. 2:1.<br>(28) Rom. 3:8; Psa. 69:10.<br>(29) Psa. 12:2, 3.<br>(30) II Tim. 3:2.<br>(31) Luke 18:11; Gal. 5:26; Ex. 4:10, 14; Acts 12:22.<br>(32) Isa. 29:20, 21; Matt. 7:3.<br>(33) Gen. 3:12, 13; Prov. 28:13; Gen. 4:9.<br>(34) Prov. 25:9; Gen. 9:22.<br>(35) Ex. 23:1.<br>(36) Jer. 20:10; Prov. 29:12.<br>(37) Acts 7:57.<br>(38) I Cor. 13:4, 5; I Tim. 6:4.<br>(39) Matt. 21:15; Num. 11:29.<br>(40) Dan. 6:3, 4; Ezra 4:12, 13.<br>(41) Jer. 48:27.<br>(42) Matt. 27:28, 29; Psa. 35:15, 16.<br>(43) I Cor. 3:21; Jude 16; Acts 12:22.<br>(44) Rom. 1:31; II Tim. 3:3.<br>(45) II Sam. 12:14; I Sam. 2:24.<br>(46) Phil. 3:18, 19; II Pet. 2:2; II Sam. 12:13, 14. | |
| | Q. 146. *Which is the tenth commandment?*<br><br>A. The tenth commandment is, *Thou shalt not covet thy neighbour's house, thou shalt not covet thy neighbour's wife, nor his manservant, nor his maidservant, nor his ox, nor his ass, nor any thing that is thy neighbour's.*[1]<br>(1) Ex. 20:17. | Q. 79. *Which is the tenth commandment?*<br><br>A. The tenth commandment is, *Thou shalt not covet thy neighbour's house, thou shalt not covet thy neighbour's wife, nor his manservant, nor his maidservant, nor his ox, nor his ass, nor any thing that is thy neighbour's.*[1]<br>(1) Ex. 20:17. |
| | Q. 147. *What are the duties required in the tenth commandment?*<br><br>A. The duties required in the tenth commandment are: such a full contentment with our own condition,[1] and such a charitable frame of the whole soul towards our neighbor, as that all our inward motions and affections touching him, tend unto and further all that good which is his.[2]<br>(1) Heb. 13:5; I Tim. 6:6.<br>(2) Rom. 12:15; Phil. 2:4; I Tim. 1:5. | Q. 80. *What is required in the tenth commandment?*<br><br>A. The tenth commandment requireth full contentment with our own condition,[1] with a right and charitable frame of spirit toward our neighbor, and all that is his.[2]<br>(1) Heb. 13:5.<br>(2) Rom. 12:15; Phil. 2:4; I Cor. 13:4-6. |
| | Q. 148. *What are the sins forbidden in the tenth commandment?*<br><br>A. The sins forbidden in the tenth commandment are: discontentment | Q. 81. *What is forbidden in the tenth commandment?*<br><br>A. The tenth commandment forbiddeth all discontentment with our |

| THE WESTMINSTER CONFESSION OF FAITH | THE WESTMINSTER LARGER CATECHISM | THE WESTMINSTER SHORTER CATECHISM |
|---|---|---|
| | with our own estate;[1] envying,[2] and grieving at the good of our neighbor,[3] together with all inordinate motions and affections to anything that is his.[4]<br>(1) I Cor. 10:10.<br>(2) Gal. 5:26; James 3:14, 16.<br>(3) Psa. 112:9, 10; Neh. 2:10.<br>(4) Rom. 7:7; Deut. 5:21; Col. 3:5; Rom. 13:9.<br><br>Q. 149. *Is any man able perfectly to keep the commandments of God?*<br><br>A. No man is able, either of himself,[1] or by any grace received in this life, perfectly to keep the commandments of God;[2] but doth daily break them in thought,[3] word, and deed.[4]<br>(1) James 3:2; John 15:5.<br>(2) I Kings 8:46; Psa. 17:15; I John 1:8–2:6.<br>(3) Gen. 8:21; James 1:14; Gen. 6:5. See citations under figure 2 above.<br>(4) Psa. 19:12; James 3:2, 8.<br><br>Q. 150. *Are all transgressions of the law of God equally heinous in themselves, and in the sight of God?*<br><br>A. All transgressions of the law of God are not equally heinous; but some sins in themselves, and by reason of several aggravations, are more heinous in the sight of God than others.[1]<br>(1) Heb. 2:2, 3; Ezra 9:14; Psa. 78:17, 32, 56.<br><br>Q. 151. *What are those aggravations that make some sins more heinous than others?*<br><br>A. Sins receive their aggravations,<br>1. From the persons offending:[1] if they be of riper age, greater experience, or grace;[2] eminent for profession,[3] gifts,[4] place, office,[5] guides to others,[6] and whose example is likely to be followed by others.[7]<br>2. From the parties offended:[8] if immediately against God,[9] his attributes,[10] and worship;[11] against | own estate,[1] envying or grieving at the good of our neighbor,[2] and all inordinate motions and affections to anything that is his.[3]<br>(1) I Cor. 10:10.<br>(2) Gal. 5:26.<br>(3) Col. 3:5.<br><br>Q. 82. *Is any man able perfectly to keep the commandments of God?*<br><br>A. No mere man, since the fall, is able, in this life, perfectly to keep the commandments of God;[1] but doth daily break them, in thought,[2] word,[3] and deed.[4]<br>(1) I Kings 8:46; I John 1:8–2:6.<br>(2) Gen. 8:21.<br>(3) James 3:8.<br>(4) James 3:2.<br><br>Q. 83. *Are all transgressions of the law equally heinous?*<br><br>A. Some sins in themselves, and by reason of several aggravations, are more heinous in the sight of God than others.[1]<br>(1) Psa. 19:13; John 19:11. |

| THE WESTMINSTER CONFESSION OF FAITH | THE WESTMINSTER LARGER CATECHISM | THE WESTMINSTER SHORTER CATECHISM |
|---|---|---|

**LARGER CATECHISM**

Christ, and his grace;[12] the Holy Spirit, his witness, and workings;[13] against superiors, men of eminency,[14] and such as we stand especially related and engaged unto;[15] against any of the saints,[16] particularly weak brethren, the souls of them or any other;[17] and the common good of all or many.[18]

3. From the nature and quality of the offense:[19] if it be against the express letter of the law,[20] break many commandments, contain in it many sins:[21] if not only conceived in the heart, but break forth in words and actions,[22] scandalize others,[23] and admit of no reparation:[24] if against means,[25] mercies,[26] judgments,[27] light of nature,[28] conviction of conscience,[29] public or private admonition,[30] censures of the church,[31] civil punishments;[32] and our prayers, purposes, promises, vows, covenants, and engagements to God or men:[33] if done deliberately, willfully,[34] presumptuously, impudently, boastingly,[35] maliciously,[36] frequently,[37] obstinately,[38] with light,[39] continuance,[40] or relapsing after repentance.[41]

4. From circumstances of time,[42] and place:[43] if on the Lord's day,[44] or other times of divine worship;[45] or immediately before,[46] or after these,[47] or other helps to prevent or remedy such miscarriages:[48] if in public, or in the presence of others, who are thereby likely to be provoked or defiled.[49]

(1) Jer. 2:8.
(2) I Kings 11:9.
(3) II Sam. 12:14; I Cor. 5:1.
(4) James 4:17; Luke 12:47.
(5) John 3:10; Jer. 5:4, 5; II Sam. 12:7-9; Ezek. 8:11, 12.
(6) Rom. 2:21, 22, 24.
(7) Gal. 2:14; II Pet. 2:2.
(8) I John 5:10; Matt. 21:38, 39.
(9) I Sam. 2:25; Acts 5:4.
(10) Rom. 2:4.
(11) Mal. 1:14; I Cor. 10:21, 22.
(12) John 3:18, 36; Heb. 12:25.
(13) Heb. 6:4, 5, 6; Heb. 10:29; Matt. 12:31, 32; Eph. 4:30.

| THE WESTMINSTER CONFESSION OF FAITH | THE WESTMINSTER LARGER CATECHISM | THE WESTMINSTER SHORTER CATECHISM |
|---|---|---|
| | | |

**THE WESTMINSTER LARGER CATECHISM**

(14) Num. 12:8; Jude 8.
(15) Prov. 30:17; Psa. 41:9; 55:12-14.
(16) Zech. 2:8.
(17) I Cor. 8:11-12; Rom. 14:13, 15, 21.
(18) I Thess. 2:15, 16; Matt. 23:34-38.
(19) Isa. 3:9.
(20) Ezek. 20:12, 13.
(21) Col. 3:5; I Tim. 6:10.
(22) Micah 2:1, 2.
(23) Rom. 2:23, 24; Matt. 18:7.
(24) Prov. 6:32-35; Matt. 16:26.
(25) Matt. 11:21-24; John 15:22.
(26) Deut. 32:6; Isa. 1:2, 3; Ezra 9:13, 14.
(27) Jer. 5:3; Amos 4:8-11.
(28) Rom. 1:20, 21.
(29) Rom. 1:32; Dan. 5:22.
(30) Prov. 29:1.
(31) Matt. 18:17; Tit. 3:10.
(32) Rom. 13:1-5.
(33) Psa. 78:34, 36, 37; Jer. 42:5, 6, 20-22; Prov. 20:25; Lev. 26:25; Jer. 31:32; Prov. 2:17; Ezek. 17:18.
(34) Psa. 36:4; Jer. 6:16.
(35) Num. 15:30; Jer. 6:15; Psa. 52:1.
(36) Ezek. 35:5, 6; III John 10.
(37) Num. 14:22.
(38) Zech. 7:11, 12.
(39) Prov. 2:14.
(40) Jer. 9:3, 5; Isa. 57:17.
(41) II Pet. 2:20, 21; Heb. 6:4, 6.
(42) Isa. 22:12, 13, 14; II Kings 5:26.
(43) Jer. 7:10, 11.
(44) Ezek. 23:38.
(45) Isa. 58:3, 4.
(46) I Cor. 11:20, 21; Jer. 7:9, 10.
(47) Prov. 7:14, 15.
(48) Neh. 9:13-16; II Chron. 36:15-16.
(49) Isa. 3:9; I Sam. 2:22, 23, 24.

Q. 152. *What doth every sin deserve at the hands of God?*

A. Every sin, even the least,[1] being against the sovereignty,[2] goodness,[3] and holiness of God,[4] and against his righteous law,[5] deserveth his wrath and curse,[6] both in this life,[7] and that which is to come;[8] and cannot be expiated but by the blood of Christ.[9]
(1) James 2:10, 11.
(2) Mal. 1:14.
(3) Deut. 32:6.
(4) Hab. 1:13; I Pet. 1:15-16; Lev. 11:45.
(5) I John 3:4; Rom. 7:12.
(6) Gal. 3:10; Eph. 5:6.
(7) Deut. 28:15-68; Prov. 13:21.
(8) Matt. 25:41; Rom. 6:21, 23.
(9) Heb. 9:22; I John 1:7; I Pet. 1:18-19.

**THE WESTMINSTER SHORTER CATECHISM**

Q. 84. *What doth every sin deserve?*

A. Every sin deserveth God's wrath and curse, both in this life, and that which is to come.[1]
(1) Gal. 3:10; Matt. 25:41.

# EXPLANATORY NOTES

ALL three parts of the Standards treat of the Law of God. The Confession discusses the law in general, describing the giving and uses not only of the moral law, but also of the positive laws. The Catechisms confine attention to the moral law. The Larger Catechism merely mentions parenthetically that a positive law was included with moral law in the Covenant of Works. (L.C. 92.)

This Catechism is peculiar in naming eight rules to be observed in the interpretation of the Ten Commandments. They should be studied with care. (L.C. 99.)

Of these eight rules the third seems least clear. It means that the law is a unity, and, as a consequence, the prohibition of any sin or the requirement of any duty really implies the prohibition of every sin or the requirement of every duty in one aspect or another. For example, the first and second commandments forbid idolatry and the tenth commandment forbids covetousness. But covetousness is idolatry. (Col. 3:5.) So that the first and second commandments in a way forbid covetousness and the tenth in a way forbids idolatry. It is sin in divers respects that is forbidden in all the commandments, and it is duty in divers respects that is required in all the commandments. So it would be a misunderstanding of any commandment to suppose that it is concerned with one sin alone or with one duty alone. All sins are interrelated, as also are all duties or virtues.

## L.C. 100

It is interesting and instructive to observe what things are designated by the Larger Catechism as worthy of special consideration. They are three:

1. *The Preface.*

   Why should the preface receive special attention? Because in it the Giver of the Commandments introduces Himself to the receivers of the Commandments, and names the grounds of His claim on their obedience. He calls Himself their God, and by what right? By a threefold right:

   a. By right of His nature. He is the eternal, self-existent, sovereign one, source of all being. This is implied in His name, Jehovah, the I AM.

   b. By right of His covenant relation to them. In the covenant God promised to be their God and the people promised to be His people. (Exod. 19:5; 24:7-8.)

   c. By right of service to them; right of redemption.

2. *The Substance.*

   Does "substance" here mean the same as "sum" in answer 102? These words are commonly used interchangeably, but a distinction seems to be implied here. "Sum" is used with reference to the tables of the law, whereas "substance" is used with reference to the several commandments. The sum of the first table, which comprises the first four commandments, is love to God. What is the measure of that love? The sum of the second table, which comprises the last six commandments, is love to man. What is the measure of this love? The substance of each commandment is brought out by two questions: one asking what is forbidden and the other what is required therein. From question and answer 91 and question and answer 102 and question and answer 122 we learn that the total requirements of God may be expressed in two words: obedience and love. These words are intimately related, love being cause and obedience the effect.

   So the comprehensive duty may be defined as either love or obedience. Obedience roots in love and love fruits in obedience. Together they make a whole.

   The Jews called the Ten Commandments the Ten Words. These ten words were compressed into two: love to God and love to man. These two were reduced by the Apostle Paul into one: love. The will of God in ten words, in two words, in one word. What condensation! How portable and reportable! Condensed for wayfarers and warfarers.

The whole law requires obedience and each part of the law requires obedience.

Duty, then, in its nature is one, but in its forms it is many. The whole decalogue requires love and obedience — a unity — and each separate commandment requires love and obedience; but love expresses itself in many ways and obedience takes many forms. So the Catechisms in connection with each commandment give a bill of particulars. For example: What is required in the first commandment? The answer is not general, but specific — goes into details, thus making the meaning plain and the application strong.

Similarly specific, plain, and strong is the answer to the question, What is forbidden in any given commandment? For sin, like duty, while one in principle is manifold in its expression. So the Catechism answer spreads it out before the reader in its manifold forms.

3. *The Reasons Annexed* to some of the commandments.

What commandments have reasons annexed to them? Some are reminders, some are warnings or threatenings, and some are promises. They appeal some to memory, others to conscience, others to fear, still others to wise and legitimate self-interest.

These "reasons" are sanctions meant to enforce the commandments. Are these particular commandments more in need of re-enforcement? Or are they re-enforced because they are of more importance than the rest? If you were making a comparative study of the commandments, which, if any, would you select for special emphasis?

It is generally agreed that the Decalogue is divisible into two tables, but there is a difference of opinion as to the limits of the tables. Some assign three commandments to the first table and seven to the second. Some assign four to the first table

and six to the second. Others divide the commandments equally between the tables, giving five to each. The first view is without warrant of Scripture or reason. For the last view three reasons may be given.

1. The fact of symmetry, proportion, balance.
2. The pattern of the Lord's Prayer. It contains six petitions: three in the first half which refer to God, and three in the second half which refer to man.
3. The fifth commandment, though it refers to human parents, may properly be placed in the first table, if human parents may be regarded as representing God, the Divine Parent, to their children.

But the second view as to the division of the commandments is to be preferred. According to it the first table of four laws clearly comprises our duties to God, and the second table of six commandments contains our duties to man. In favor of this view may be quoted Jesus and Paul. When Jesus said to the rich young ruler, "Thou knowest the commandments," He named several from the second table, the fifth among them. (Luke 18:20.)

When Paul said, "Children, obey your parents . . . Honor thy father and mother," he added, "which is the first commandment with promise." (Eph. 6:1-2.) Now as a matter of fact, the fifth commandment is not the first commandment with promise, for the second commandment has a promise annexed to it. So we must understand the apostle as meaning that the fifth commandment is the first commandment of the second table.

These notes on the law, I deem sufficient to awaken interest in the Decalogue and to afford the reader some guidance in the study of it. No Christian can afford to neglect the treatment of the law by the Catechisms. It is the briefest and best treatise in existence on Christian ethics. Ethics is scarcely less important than theology. Each finds its complement in the other. If no layman can afford to neglect the Catechisms on the law, much less can any minister. The minister who leaves this source of information and stimulation untapped impoverishes himself and his ministry.

### L.C. 149; S.C. 82

Having studied the Ten Commandments under the guidance of the Catechisms and learned to appreciate the length and breadth and depth of their prohibitions and requirements, one is prepared for the answers of the Catechisms to this question: Is any man able perfectly to keep the commandments of God? (L.C. 149 and S.C. 82.) The answers seem to some to be extreme. But consider just what the question is. Note the word "perfectly," and let it stand in the fullness and strength of its proper meaning. Now consider the limitations in the answer: "No *mere* man"; that excepts our Lord Jesus Christ, who did keep the law perfectly. "Since the fall"; that allows that man before the fall was able to keep the law.

Finally, look carefully at the words with which the answer closes. Does any man think a whole day through without any least taint or error or fault attaching to his thought? Can any man honestly say that for a whole day his speech has been perfectly free from any offense to truth or kindness or justice? At the close of any day can any man of moral discrimination and spiritual discernment claim that his actions toward himself, man, and God have been free from all defect and full of every excellence?

The Catechetical statements are not too strong for anyone who knows his Bible and his own heart. Sanctification is imperfect in this life, and this life is imperfect in its thoughts, words, and deeds. The Catechisms deny the full *ability* of man, natural or spiritual, but they do not deny his *liberty*, which means his power and opportunity of choice.

### L.C. 150-152; S.C. 83-84

The Larger Catechism's discussion of degrees of guilt will repay careful study. The aim of the framers of these statements was to enable us to see our actions in the full light of all the circumstances of their commission. Not many are competent unaided to determine the degree of their guilt in a given instance. Paragraph one under "aggravations" should enlighten and sensitize the consciences of ministers, elders, deacons, teachers, and parents.

The second paragraph is meant to teach us how to estimate offenses against dignitaries and, also, against frailties.

The last two paragraphs direct attention to the many considerations which must be taken into account if we would know the real nature and quality of our sins. Note the number of Scripture citations in support of these paragraphs.

The last question under the head of the law is the 84th of the Shorter Catechism and 152nd of the Larger Catechism, relating to the demerit or ill-desert of sin. The Shorter Catechism statement is without qualification or explanation. The Larger Catechism enlarges by specification, explanation, and addition. It declares that every sin, even the least, deserves the wrath and curse of God, now and forever. And explains that this is so because sin is measured not against the author of the sin but against the object of it, namely God — His character, His law, His sovereignty. So measured, even the least sin is seen to be immeasurable, *i.e.*, infinite. Our church rejects the Catholic classification of sins as "mortal" and "venial." Every sin is mortal — deadly. Every sin is a capital offense, being a violation of the whole law of God, opposition to the whole character of God, rebellion against the whole will of God. Sin is lawlessness, and lawlessness in little is not different in principle from lawlessness in much.

The Larger Catechism adds that sin, even the least, cannot be expiated or atoned for but by the blood of Christ. Behold the gravity of sin! Only God can save from sin, and He in only one way — by the blood of His Son! He that hath ears to hear, let him hear.

# CHAPTER XXII

# Of Christian Liberty, and Liberty of Conscience

CONFESSION OF FAITH XXII:1-4

| THE WESTMINSTER<br>CONFESSION OF FAITH | THE WESTMINSTER<br>LARGER CATECHISM | THE WESTMINSTER<br>SHORTER CATECHISM |
|---|---|---|

THE liberty which Christ hath purchased for believers under the gospel consists in their freedom from the guilt of sin, the condemning wrath of God, the curse of the moral law;[1] and in their being delivered from this present evil world, bondage to Satan, and dominion of sin,[2] from the evil of afflictions, the sting of death, the victory of the grave, and everlasting damnation;[3] as also in their free access to God,[4] and their yielding obedience unto him, not out of slavish fear, but a childlike love, and a willing mind.[5] All which were common also to believers under the law;[6] but under the New Testament, the liberty of Christians is further enlarged in their freedom from the yoke of the ceremonial law, to which the Jewish church was subjected;[7] and in greater boldness of access to the throne of grace,[8] and in fuller communications of the free Spirit of God, than believers under the law did ordinarily partake of.[9]

(1) Tit. 2:14; I Thess. 1:10.
(2) Gal. 1:4; Acts 26:18; Col. 1:13; Rom. 6:14.
(3) Psa. 119:71; I Cor. 15:56, 57; Rom. 8:1.
(4) Rom. 5:2.
(5) Rom. 8:14, 15; Eph. 2:18; Gal. 4:6; Heb. 10:19; I John 4:18.
(6) Gal. 3:9, 14.
See citations under Chapter VIII, Section 6.
(7) Gal. 5:1; Acts 15:10; Gal. 4:1, 2, 3, 6.
(8) Heb. 4:14, 16; Heb. 10:19, 20.
(9) John 7:38, 39; II Cor. 3:13, 17, 18.

| THE WESTMINSTER CONFESSION OF FAITH | THE WESTMINSTER LARGER CATECHISM | THE WESTMINSTER SHORTER CATECHISM |
|---|---|---|

2. God alone is Lord of the conscience, and hath left it free from the doctrines and commandments of men which are in anything contrary to his word, or beside it in matters of faith or worship.[10] So that to believe such doctrines, or to obey such commandments out of conscience, is to betray true liberty of conscience;[11] and the requiring an implicit faith, and an absolute and blind obedience, is to destroy liberty of conscience, and reason also.[12]

(10) Rom. 14:4; Acts 4:19; Acts 5:29; I Cor. 7:23; Matt. 23:8-10; II Cor. 1:24; Matt. 15:9.
(11) Gal. 2:3, 4; Col. 2:20, 22, 23; Gal. 5:1.
(12) Hosea 5:11; Rev. 13:12, 16, 17.

3. They who, upon pretense of Christian liberty, do practice any sin, or cherish any lust, do thereby destroy the end of Christian liberty; which is, that, being delivered out of the hands of our enemies, we might serve the Lord without fear, in holiness and righteousness before him, all the days of our life.[13]

(13) Gal. 5:13; I Pet. 2:16; Luke 1:74, 75; II Pet. 2:19; John 8:34.

4. And because the powers which God hath ordained, and the liberty which Christ hath purchased, are not intended by God to destroy, but mutually to uphold and preserve one another; they who, upon pretense of Christian liberty, shall oppose any lawful power, or the lawful exercise of it, whether it be civil or ecclesiastical, resist the ordinance of God.[14] And for their publishing of such opinions, or maintaining of such practices, as are contrary to the light of nature, or to the known principles of Christianity, whether concerning faith, worship, or conversation; or to the power of godliness; or such erroneous opinions or practices as, either in their own

| THE WESTMINSTER CONFESSION OF FAITH | THE WESTMINSTER LARGER CATECHISM | THE WESTMINSTER SHORTER CATECHISM |
| --- | --- | --- |

nature, or in the manner of publishing or maintaining them, are destructive to the external peace and order which Christ hath established in the church: they may lawfully be called to account, and proceeded against by the censures of the church.[15]

(14) I Pet. 2:13, 14, 16; Heb. 13:17; Rom. 13:1-8.
(15) I Cor. 5:1, 5, 11, 13; Titus 1:13; Matt. 18:17, 18; II Thess. 3:14; Titus 3:10.

# EXPLANATORY NOTES

THE Confession treats of liberty in immediate connection with law. The relation between law and liberty is close, and it is important that the relation be understood. Law requires obedience, and obedience is not inconsistent with liberty. Indeed, obedience conditions liberty. Only the obedient are truly free. Any creature that obeys all the laws of its being has all the liberty its Maker intended it should have.

Section 1 teaches two things about Christian liberty:

1. Whence it comes — the source of it. It is a purchase of Christ. "For freedom did Christ set us free."

2. What Christian liberty is — wherein it consists. Christ has purchased for believers a fourfold liberation.
   a. From guilt and its consequences. Name the consequences.
   b. From sin and its consequences. Name the consequences: the evil world, bondage to Satan, dominion of sin, evil of afflictions, the sting of death, the victory of the grave, and everlasting damnation.
   c. From limitation of access to the throne of grace.
   d. From servility of obedience and service. These forms of liberty were enjoyed by believers even under the law. But under the gospel, the liberty of Christians has been enlarged in three respects, as stated in the end of the section.

Section 2 sets forth the true doctrine of liberty of conscience. The Christian conscience recognizes one lordship only, that of God. Any doctrine or commandment contrary to or beside His will in matters religious the Christian not only may but must disobey. Liberty of conscience means the liberty of the individual to obey God rather than man, when the will of man and the will of God conflict. Illustrations are better than definitions. Peter before the Sanhedrin (Acts 4:19-20) and Luther before the Diet of Worms exercised liberty of conscience. Conscience, when Christian, requires submission to the will of God and forbids submission to the will of man, when the latter is contrary to the will of God. In the name of conscience one may betray or destroy conscience. This paragraph is pointed at Catholic precept and practice.

Section 3 teaches that liberty is not license to sin. The liberty of Christ is not emancipation from all moral restraints. True liberty is freedom to do right. To practice any sin is to forfeit liberty. Jesus says, "Every one that committeth sin is the bondservant of sin." (John 8:34.) Christ frees from servitude to Satan that He may enlist in service to God in holiness and righteousness.

Section 4 is closely connected with section 3 as the connective "and" indicates. It conveys a further warning against the misuse of liberty. A Christian is a citizen of the state and a member of the church of Christ. Both are ordained of God. So that they who shall oppose any civil authority lawfully exercised are as guilty of resisting the ordinance of God as they who oppose the principles of the gospel. And if any shall hold and advocate opinions and practices which in their working would endanger the peace and order of either church or state, they may be proceeded against by one or the other of said institutions. True freedom is not liberty to do as you please unless you please to do right. Liberty is not absolute, but limited — limited by the will of God and the rights and interests of men. Those who misuse ought to lose their freedom.

# CHAPTER XXIII

# Of Religious Worship and the Sabbath Day

## Part One: Of Religious Worship . . . Of the Sabbath Day

CONFESSION OF FAITH XXIII:1-8
LARGER CATECHISM (116-117), 178-185 · SHORTER CATECHISM (59-60), 98

| THE WESTMINSTER CONFESSION OF FAITH | THE WESTMINSTER LARGER CATECHISM | THE WESTMINSTER SHORTER CATECHISM |
|---|---|---|

THE light of nature showeth that there is a God, who hath lordship and sovereignty over all; is good, and doeth good unto all; and is therefore to be feared, loved, praised, called upon, trusted in, and served with all the heart, and with all the soul, and with all the might.[1] But the acceptable way of worshipping the true God is instituted by himself, and so limited by his own revealed will, that he may not be worshipped according to the imaginations and devices of men, or the suggestions of Satan, under any visible representation or any other way not prescribed in the Holy Scripture.[2]

(1) Rom. 1:19, 20; Jer. 10:7; Psa. 19:1, 2, 3, 4, 5, 6.
(2) Deut. 12:32; Matt. 15:9; Matt. 4:9, 10; Acts 17:24, 25; Ex. 20:4-6; Deut. 4:15-20; Col. 2:20-23.

2. Religious worship is to be given to God, the Father, Son, and Holy Ghost; and to him alone:[3] not to angels, saints, or any other creature:[4] and since the fall, not without a Mediator; nor in the mediation of any other but of Christ alone.[5]

(3) John 5:23; II Cor. 13:14; Matt. 4:10; Rev. 5:11-13.
(4) Col. 2:18; Rev. 19:10; Rom. 1:25.
(5) John 14:6; I Tim. 2:5; Eph. 2:18.

3. Prayer with thanksgiving, being one special part of religious worship,[6] is by God required of all men;[7] and that it may be accepted, it is to be made in the name of the Son,[8] by the help of his Spirit,[9] according to his will,[10] with understanding, reverence, humility, fervency, faith, love, and perseverance;[11] and, if vocal, in a known tongue.[12]

(6) Phil. 4:6.
(7) Luke 18:1; I Tim. 2:8.
(8) John 14:13, 14.
(9) Rom. 8:26.
(10) I John 5:14.
(11) Psa. 47:7; Heb. 12:28; Gen. 18:27; James 5:16; Eph. 6:18; James 1:6, 7; Mark 11:24; Matt. 6:12, 14, 15; Col. 4:2.
(12) I Cor. 14:14.

Q. 185. *How are we to pray?*

A. We are to pray with an awful apprehension of the majesty of God,[1] and deep sense of our own unworthiness,[2] necessities,[3] and sins;[4] with penitent,[5] thankful,[6] and enlarged hearts;[7] with understanding,[8] faith,[9] sincerity,[10] fervency,[11] love,[12] and perseverance,[13] waiting upon him[14] with humble submission to his will.[15]

(1) Psa. 33:8; Psa. 95:6.
(2) Gen. 18:27; Psa. 144:3.
(3) Psa. 86:1; Luke 15:17-19.
(4) Psa. 130:3; Luke 18:13.
(5) Psa. 51:17; Zech. 12:10-14.
(6) Phil. 4:6; I Thess. 5:18.
(7) Psa. 81:10; Eph. 3:20, 21.
(8) I Cor. 14:15.
(9) Heb. 10:22; James 1:6.
(10) Heb. 10:22; Psa. 145:18; Psa. 17:1; John 4:24.
(11) James 5:16.
(12) I Tim. 2:8; Matt. 5:23, 24.
(13) Eph. 6:18.
(14) Micah 7:7.
(15) Matt. 26:39.

Q. 178. *What is prayer?*

A. Prayer is an offering up of our desires unto God,[1] in the name of Christ,[2] by the help of his Spirit,[3] with confession of our sins,[4] and thankful acknowledgment of his mercies.[5]

(1) Psa. 62:8.
(2) John 16:23, 24.
(3) Rom. 8:26.
(4) Dan. 9:4; Psa. 32:5, 6.
(5) Phil. 4:6.

Q. 179. *Are we to pray unto God only?*

A. God only being able to search the heart,[1] hear the requests,[2] pardon the sins,[3] and fulfill the desires of all,[4] and only to be believed in,[5] and worshipped with religious worship;[6] prayer, which is a special part thereof,[7] is to be made by all to him alone, and to none other.[8]

(1) I Kings 8:39; Acts 1:24; Rom. 8:27.
(2) Psa. 65:2.

Q. 98. *What is prayer?*

A. Prayer is an offering up of our desires unto God,[1] for things agreeable to his will,[2] in the name of Christ,[3] with confession of our sins,[4] and thankful acknowledgment of his mercies.[5]

(1) Psa. 62:8; Psa. 10:17.
(2) I John 5:14; Matt. 26:39; John 6:38.
(3) John 16:23.
(4) Dan. 9:4.
(5) Phil. 4:6.

| THE WESTMINSTER CONFESSION OF FAITH | THE WESTMINSTER LARGER CATECHISM | THE WESTMINSTER SHORTER CATECHISM |
|---|---|---|

(3) Micah 7:18.
(4) Psa. 145:16, 19.
(5) II Sam. 22:32; John 14:1.
(6) Matt. 4:10.
(7) I Cor. 1:2.
(8) Luke 9:8; Isa. 42:8; Jer. 3:23.

Q. 180. *What is it to pray in the name of Christ?*

A. To pray in the name of Christ is, in obedience to his command, and in confidence on his promises, to ask mercy for his sake:[1] not by bare mentioning of his name;[2] but by drawing our encouragement to pray, and our boldness, strength, and hope of acceptance in prayer, from Christ and his mediation.[3]
(1) John 14:13, 14; Dan. 9:17.
(2) Luke 6:46; Matt. 7:21.
(3) Heb. 4:14, 15, 16; I John 5:13-15.

Q. 181. *Why are we to pray in the name of Christ?*

A. The sinfulness of man, and his distance from God by reason thereof, being so great, as that we can have no access into his presence without a mediator, and there being none in heaven or earth appointed to, or fit for, that glorious work but Christ alone, we are to pray in no other name but his only.[1]
(1) John 14:6; Eph. 3:12; I Tim. 2:5; John 6:27; Col. 3:17; Heb. 7:25-27; Heb. 13:15.

Q. 182. *How doth the Spirit help us to pray?*

A. We not knowing what to pray for as we ought, the Spirit helpeth our infirmities, by enabling us to understand both for whom, and what, and how prayer is to be made; and by working and quickening in our hearts (although not in all persons, nor at all times in the same measure) those apprehensions, affections, and graces, which are requisite for the right performance of that duty.[1]
(1) Rom. 8:26; Psa. 80:18; Psa. 10:17; Zech. 12:10.

4. Prayer is to be made for things lawful,[13] and for all sorts of men living, or that shall live hereafter;[14] but not for the dead.[15]

(13) I John 5:14.
(14) I Tim. 2:1, 2; John 17:20; II Sam. 7:29.
(15) I John 5:14.

Q. 183. *For whom are we to pray?*

A. We are to pray for the whole church of Christ upon earth,[1] for magistrates,[2] and ministers,[3] for ourselves,[4] our brethren,[5] yea, our enemies,[6] and for all sorts of men living,[7] or that shall live hereafter;[8] but not for the dead.[9]

(1) Eph. 6:18; Psa. 28:9.
(2) I Tim. 2:1, 2.
(3) II Thess. 3:1; Col. 4:3.
(4) Gen. 32:11.
(5) James 5:16; II Thess. 1:11.
(6) Matt. 5:44.
(7) I Tim. 2:1, 2.
(8) John 17:20; II Sam. 7:29.
(9) This statement is based on the absence of any command to pray for the dead, and of any example in the Scriptures of such prayer.

Q. 184. *For what things are we to pray?*

A. We are to pray for all things tending to the glory of God,[1] the welfare of the church,[2] our own[3] or others' good;[4] but not for anything that is unlawful.[5]

(1) Matt. 6:9.
(2) Psa. 51:18; Psa. 122:6.
(3) Matt. 7:11.
(4) Psa. 125:4; I Thess. 5:23; II Thess. 3:16.
(5) I John 5:14; James 4:3.

5. The reading of the Scriptures with godly fear;[17] the sound preaching,[18] and conscionable hearing of the word, in obedience unto God with understanding, faith, and reverence;[19] singing of psalms with grace in the heart;[20] as, also, the due administration and worthy receiving of the sacraments instituted by Christ; are all parts of the ordinary religious worship of God:[21] besides religious oaths,[22] and vows,[23] solemn fastings,[24] and thanksgivings upon special occasions;[25] which are, in their several times and seasons, to be used in an holy and religious manner.[26]

(17) Acts 15:21; Acts 17:11; Rev. 1:3.

| THE WESTMINSTER CONFESSION OF FAITH | THE WESTMINSTER LARGER CATECHISM | THE WESTMINSTER SHORTER CATECHISM |
|---|---|---|

(18) II Tim. 4:2.
(19) James 1:22; Acts 10:33; Heb. 4:2; Matt. 13:19; Isa. 66:2.
(20) Col. 3:16; Eph. 5:19; James 5:13.
(21) Matt. 28:19; Acts 2:42; I Cor. 11:23-29.
(22) Deut. 6:13.
(23) Psa. 116:14; Isa. 19:21; Neh. 10:29.
(24) Joel 2:12; Matt. 9:15; I Cor. 7:5; Esther 4:16.
(25) Psa. 107.
(26) John 4:24; Heb. 10:22.

6. Neither prayer, nor any other part of religious worship, is now, under the gospel, either tied unto, or made more acceptable by, any place in which it is performed, or towards which it is directed:[27] but God is to be worshipped everywhere[28] in spirit and in truth;[29] as in private families[30] daily,[31] and in secret each one by himself,[32] so more solemnly in the public assemblies, which are not carelessly or willfully to be neglected or forsaken, when God, by his word or providence, calleth thereunto.[33]

(27) John 4:21.
(28) Mal. 1:11; I Tim. 2:8.
(29) John 4:23, 24.
(30) Deut. 6:7; Job 1:5; Acts 10:2.
(31) Matt. 6:11.
(32) Matt. 6:6; Eph. 6:18.
(33) Isa. 56:7; Heb. 10:25; Acts 2:42; Luke 4:16; Acts 13:42.

7. As it is of the law of nature that, in general, a due proportion of time be set apart for the worship of God; so, in his word, by a positive, moral, and perpetual commandment, binding all men in all ages, he hath particularly appointed one day in seven for a Sabbath, to be kept holy unto him:[34] which, from the beginning of the world to the resurrection of Christ, was the last day of the week; and, from the resurrection of Christ, was changed into the first day of the week, which in Scripture is called the Lord's day, and is to be continued to the end

(Q. 116. *What is required in the fourth commandment?*

(A. The fourth commandment requireth of all men the sanctifying or keeping holy to God such set times as he hath appointed in his word, expressly one whole day in seven; which was the seventh from the beginning of the world to the resurrection of Christ, and the first day of the week ever since, and so to continue to the end of the world; which is the Christian Sabbath, and in the New Testament called *The Lord's day.*)

(Q. 59. *Which day of the seven hath God appointed to be the weekly Sabbath?*

(A. From the beginning of the world to the resurrection of Christ, God appointed the seventh day of the week to be the weekly Sabbath; and the first day of the week, ever since, to continue to the end of the world, which is the Christian Sabbath.)

| THE WESTMINSTER CONFESSION OF FAITH | THE WESTMINSTER LARGER CATECHISM | THE WESTMINSTER SHORTER CATECHISM |
|---|---|---|

**THE WESTMINSTER CONFESSION OF FAITH**

of the world as the Christian Sabbath.[35]

(34) Ex. 20:8, 9, 10, 11; Isa. 56:2, 4, 6.
(35) I Cor. 16:1, 2; Acts 20:7.
    These texts are cited in connection with the example of the apostles and the early church.

8. This Sabbath is then kept holy unto the Lord when men, after a due preparing of their hearts, and ordering of their common affairs beforehand, do not only observe an holy rest all the day from their own works, words, and thoughts about their worldly employments and recreations;[36] but also are taken up the whole time in the public and private exercises of his worship, and in the duties of necessity and mercy.[37]

(36) Ex. 16:23, 25, 26, 29, 30; Ex. 31:15, 16; Isa. 58:13; Neh. 13:15-22; Luke 23:56.
(37) Isa. 58:13; Matt. 12:1-13.

**THE WESTMINSTER LARGER CATECHISM**

(Q. 117. *How is the Sabbath or Lord's day to be sanctified?*

(A. The Sabbath, or Lord's day, is to be sanctified by an holy resting all that day, not only from such works as are at all times sinful, but even from such worldly employments and recreations as are on other days lawful; and making it our delight to spend the whole time (except so much of it as is to be taken up in works of necessity and mercy) in the public and private exercise of God's worship. And, to that end, we are to prepare our hearts, and with such foresight, diligence, and moderation, to dispose, and seasonably to despatch our worldly business, that we may be the more free and fit for the duties of the day.)

**THE WESTMINSTER SHORTER CATECHISM**

(Q. 60. *How is the Sabbath to be sanctified?*

(A. The Sabbath is to be sanctified by a holy resting all that day, even from such worldly employments and recreations as are lawful on other days; and spending the whole time in the public and private exercises of God's worship, except so much as is to be taken up in the works of necessity and mercy.)

# EXPLANATORY NOTES

THE previous chapter treated of liberty. It teaches that both liberation and enlargement of liberty come through Christ; yet even Christian liberty has its limitations. The limitation of liberty finds further illustration in this chapter.

## CONF. XXIII:1

The first section teaches two things about religious worship:

1. The duty of worship is clearly seen in the light of nature.
2. The directory of worship is derived only from the Word of God. This teaching is directed, first, at deists who assert the sufficiency of

natural theology, and deny the need of a special revelation. The Standards (the Confession) admit the value of the former but deny its sufficiency for sinners. A sinner cannot learn from nature whether he may approach the holy God whom he has offended. Much less can he learn *how* he may approach Him. The religion of nature was for man in a state of innocence. The religion of revelation and redemption is for man in a state of sin.

This teaching is directed, secondly, at Catholics who use in their worship many forms which are not only not prescribed but are proscribed.

To worship God according to one's own will is will worship, prompted by pride and presumption. To worship God according to His own appointment is true piety and humility, which are in His sight of great price.

Let the reader take from this section a double lesson.

1. The duty of worship has a twofold basis, in nature and in revelation.
2. The directory or rule of worship has only one ground or source — the Scriptures of God. It belongs to God to determine the mode of His worship. Not human invention and imagination but divine institution is to be our guide.

## CONF. XXIII:2

The second section is about the object and medium of acceptable worship. It was framed with reference to Unitarians, Roman Catholics, and idolaters. God alone is to be worshipped. He — one in three — three in one — is the proper object of worship. He may be worshipped in either person. Since the fall He may not be worshipped directly but only through a mediator; and the only mediator appointed and approved of God is Jesus Christ. Moses was a typical or representative mediator of reconciliation and peace. Christ is the only real mediator, who accomplishes the object of mediation. To worship otherwise is a species of will worship. None find access to God but those who approach Him through Christ. (John 14:6; Eph. 2:18.)

## CONF. XXIII:3-5; L.C. 178-184; S.C. 98

The next three sections are about the parts of worship. The first is prayer. Let the reader mark this: it is a lesson in the place and importance of prayer. The Catechisms supplement the Confession here. They both define prayer, and the Larger Catechism questions 179, 180, 181, 182, 184, and 185 enlarge upon the Confession, sections 2, 3, and 4.

Are we to pray unto God only? This question has reference to the practice of Rome, which offers prayers to saints.

What is it to pray in the name of Christ? Study and analyze the answer. To pray in Christ's name is to pray in the right of His merit, under the cover and in the confidence of His righteousness. When closing our prayers we often say, "In His name and for His sake." According to the Larger Catechism that is tautology, for "in His name" means "for His sake."

Why are we to pray in the name of Christ? Because of what we are, and because of what He is, in His character and in His office. We are sinners, therefore excluded. He is in Himself sinless and holy and in His office a mediator, the only mediator appointed of God and accepted; therefore He is admitted and with Him all whom He represents. Our access is in and through Him.

How doth the Spirit help us to pray? Study the answer and give the sense in your own words. Consider what help you need. Being ignorant, you need enlightening. Being dull, you need awakening. Being sluggish, you need quickening.

There are two points in section 3.

1. The requirement of prayer.
2. The conditions of acceptable prayer. (*Cf.* L.C. 185.)
   a. Prayer is not merely a permission or a privilege, it is a duty. The duty is individual, therefore universal, binding unbelievers as well as believers. Prayer in the broad sense includes adoration, confession, supplication or petition, intercession (see section 4), and thanksgiving. If prayer involves all these, or even one of these elements, can the unregenerate pray? And since, to be acceptable, prayer must be in the name of Christ and by the aid of the Holy Spirit, can the unbeliever pray?

   If he cannot pray, is it still his duty to pray? Certainly. Inability does not release from moral obligation. The sinner's responsibility is greater than his ability. In the state of innocence, ability was the measure of duty, but it is not so in the state of sin. The sinner cannot, yet he ought, must! The prayer of the unregenerate is sinful, yet his omission of prayer is more sinful. Most unhappy the man in that case! If he prays, he sins; if he prays not, he sins yet more. The *only* acceptable prayer on the lips of the unwashed sinner is the prayer of the publican. (Luke 18:13.)

   b. No one should neglect the conditions of acceptable prayer. To pray without regard to the conditions of prayer is evidence of ignorance or a form of unbelief and disobedience. Israel in the time of Isaiah did that, and the Lord called their worship wickedness. (Isaiah 1:13.) Unhappy the individual or congregation whose very worship is wickedness! Therefore count and consider the conditions of true prayer. The last words are aimed at the Roman Catholic Church, so much of whose public worship is in Latin.

The subject of the fourth section and of the Larger Catechism questions 183 and 184 is lawful and unlawful subjects of prayer. This counsel is meant to save us from the error of the Church of Rome, which prays for souls in purgatory to hasten their deliverance therefrom. There is no such place as purgatory and therefore there are no souls in it to be prayed out. All the dead have gone either to hell or heaven (see under Chapter XXXIV), where their destinies are fixed. All things that are included in the will of God for us or others now living or yet to be born are proper subjects of prayer. For prayers for the dead there is no warrant of Bible command or Bible example. Prayer without warrant of the Word is not an act of faith but of superstition.

The General Assembly has authorized the omission of the last clause of section 4 of the Confession and of answer 183 of the Larger Catechism.

In section 5 the Confession proceeds to enumerate other ordinances of worship, some of which are ordinary and occasional. Observe it is not said that the mere reading of the Scriptures or preaching or hearing or singing or administering or receiving of the sacrament is worship. Mark the qualifying word or words in each case. These words make self-examination imperative.

The other parts of worship named are less important, being less frequent and more or less optional, being left to the judgment of the persons concerned. For instance, fasting is recognized in Scripture, but not required. Fastings and special thanksgivings are voluntary, from religious motives, not appointed. As to oaths and vows, they are dealt with in the next chapter.

## CONF. XXIII:6

Section 6 is about freedom of worship. By freedom of worship is not meant that worship under the gospel is optional. It is the worship that is free, not the worshipper. The latter must worship, but his worship is not tied to any place or posture. God is present everywhere, and may be worshipped anywhere. The words of Jesus to the woman at Jacob's well free worship not only from places and seasons and outward postures, but from prescribed forms. The state of the soul is the principal thing in worship, for God looketh on the heart. Yet places and forms by reason of sacred associations may be helpful to worship.

The first section of this chapter teaches the duty of worshipping God according to His own appointment; the second section describes the true object and medium of worship; sections 3-5 discuss the ordinances of worship; the sixth section affirms and defines freedom of worship; while the last two sections are concerned with the Sabbath as the appointed time of worship.

## CONF. XXIII:7; (L.C. 116); (S.C. 59)

The seventh section tells us that the light of nature teaches the duty of worshipping God and the necessity of setting apart a portion of time for that purpose, but not what proportion. So revelation supplements nature by naming one day in seven as the time apportioned for religious worship. This day is called the Sabbath, which signifies that it is to be a day of rest as well as of worship.

The truth about the Sabbath law contained in this section of the Confession may be stated in several propositions:

   1. Its ground is in human nature; in man's need and duty.

   2. Its origin is in God's Word.

   3. Its nature is dual — it being both positive and moral.

4. Its obligation is perpetual.

5. Its place in the week has been changed from the seventh day to the first day.

6. Its purpose is to serve as a memorial: first, of creation, and second, of redemption.

7. Its name — Lord's day or Christian Sabbath.

An important aspect of the Sabbath law remains to be considered: *viz.,* its observance. The obligation of Sabbath observance is not difficult to explain and maintain. For consider:

1. It is a memorial of the greatest events known to man, namely, creation finished and redemption accomplished.

2. It is a model for man's life. For the Sabbath law tells us how to employ not one day of the week only, but all the days. We are to use the days of our week as God used the days of His week. He worked six days and rested the seventh; we should do likewise. Being made in His image we should model our life after His.

3. The Sabbath law is a mercy — a mercy to man and to beasts of burden, affording them opportunity to rest and renew their strength.

Man needs to pause for repairs once every day for several hours and once every week for a whole day. After the wear and tear of six days he needs time to lay down the tools of his trade, and to straighten up, clean up, dress up, and look up. The Sabbath is one of God's best gifts to this weary world, and its observance is based upon the threefold authority of the primeval sanction, the Decalogue, and Christian propriety. What better basis for the doctrine and duty of Sabbath law than is laid in divine creation, legislation, and redemption.

### CONF. XXIII:8; (L.C. 117); (S.C. 60)

But *how* to observe the day is far more difficult. The Confession and both Catechisms undertake to tell us how to keep the day. The prescriptions seem overstrict. Yet when you try to relax them without in any measure sacrificing the principle and purpose of the day you soon abandon the attempt. If people would only make conscience of observing the day and do as here directed, "preparing . . . their hearts, and ordering . . . their common affairs beforehand," the fulfillment of the Confessional prescription would not seem so impossible. And the day would be not a loss, but a gain; not a burden, but a delight and a refreshment. Let us not forget that in the fundamental law of our religion it is written, "Remember the sabbath day, to keep it holy."

# Of Religious Worship and the Sabbath Day

## Part Two: Of Religious Worship . . . A Pattern of Prayer

### LARGER CATECHISM 186-196 · SHORTER CATECHISM 99-107

| THE WESTMINSTER CONFESSION OF FAITH | THE WESTMINSTER LARGER CATECHISM | THE WESTMINSTER SHORTER CATECHISM |
|---|---|---|

**THE WESTMINSTER LARGER CATECHISM**

Q. 186. *What rule hath God given for our direction in the duty of prayer?*

A. The whole word of God is of use to direct us in the duty of praying;[1] but the special rule of direction is that form of prayer which our Saviour Christ taught his disciples, commonly called, *The Lord's prayer.*[2]

(1) II Tim. 3:16, 17; I John 5:14.
(2) Matt. 6:9-13; Luke 11:2-4.

Q. 187. *How is the Lord's prayer to be used?*

A. The Lord's prayer is not only for direction, as a pattern according to which we are to make other prayers; but may be also used as a prayer so that it be done with understanding, faith, reverence, and other graces necessary to the right performance of the duty of prayer.[1]

(1) Matt. 6:9; Luke 11:2.

Q. 188. *Of how many parts doth the Lord's prayer consist?*

A. The Lord's prayer consists of three parts: a preface, petitions, and a conclusion.

Q. 189. *What doth the preface of the Lord's prayer teach us?*

A. The preface of the Lord's prayer (contained in these words, *Our Father which art in heaven*)[1] teacheth us, when we pray, to draw near to God with confidence of his fatherly goodness, and our interest therein;[2] with reverence, and all other childlike dispositions,[3] heavenly affections,[4] and due apprehen-

**THE WESTMINSTER SHORTER CATECHISM**

Q. 99. *What rule hath God given for our direction in prayer?*

A. The whole word of God is of use to direct us in prayer;[1] but the special rule of direction is that form of prayer, which Christ taught his disciples, commonly called, *The Lord's prayer.*[2]

(1) II Tim. 3:16, 17; I John 5:14.
(2) Matt. 6:9.

Q. 100. *What doth the preface of the Lord's prayer teach us?*

A. The preface of the Lord's prayer, which is, *"Our Father which art in heaven,"* teacheth us to draw near to God, with all holy reverence and confidence, as children to a father, able and ready to help us;[1] and that we should pray with and for others.[2]

(1) Isa. 64:9; Luke 11:13; Rom. 8:15.
(2) Eph. 6:18; Acts 12:5; Zech. 8:21.

| THE WESTMINSTER CONFESSION OF FAITH | THE WESTMINSTER LARGER CATECHISM | THE WESTMINSTER SHORTER CATECHISM |
|---|---|---|

**LARGER CATECHISM**

sions of his sovereign power, majesty, and gracious condescension:[5] as also to pray with and for others.[6]

(1) Matt. 6:9.
(2) Luke 11:13; Rom. 8:15.
(3) Psa. 95:6, 7; Isa. 64:9.
(4) Psa. 123:1; Lam. 3:41.
(5) Psa. 104:1; Isa. 63:15; Psa. 113:4-6.
(6) Acts 12:5; Zech. 8:21.

**Q. 190.** *What do we pray for in the first petition?*

A. In the first petition (which is, *Hallowed be thy name*),[1] acknowledging the utter inability and indisposition that is in ourselves and all men to honor God aright,[2] we pray: that God would by his grace enable and incline us and others to know, to acknowledge, and highly esteem him,[3] his titles,[4] attributes,[5] ordinances, word,[6] works, and whatsoever he is pleased to make himself known by;[7] and to glorify him in thought, word,[8] and deed;[9] that he would prevent and remove atheism,[10] ignorance,[11] idolatry,[12] profaneness,[13] and whatsoever is dishonorable to him;[14] and by his overruling providence, direct and dispose of all things to his own glory.[15]

(1) Matt. 6:9.
(2) II Cor. 3:5; Psa. 51:15.
(3) Psa. 67:2, 3; Psa. 72:19; Eph. 3:20, 21.
(4) Psa. 83:18.
(5) Psa. 145:6, 7, 8; Psa. 86:10, 15.
(6) II Thess. 3:1; Psa. 107:32; II Cor. 2:14.
(7) Psa. 8 and 145 throughout.
(8) Psa. 19:14.
(9) Phil. 1:11.
(10) Psa. 79:10; Psa. 67:1-4.
(11) Eph. 1:17, 18.
(12) Psa. 97:7.
(13) Psa. 74:18, 22.
(14) Jer. 14:21; II Kings 19:16.
(15) Isa. 64:1, 2; II Chron. 20:6, 10-12.

**Q. 191.** *What do we pray for in the second petition?*

A. In the second petition (which is, *Thy kingdom come*),[1] acknowl-

**SHORTER CATECHISM**

**Q. 101.** *What do we pray for in the first petition?*

A. In the first petition, which is, *"Hallowed be thy name,"* we pray, that God would enable us, and others, to glorify him in all that whereby he maketh himself known,[1] and that he would dispose all things to his own glory.[2]

(1) Psa. 67:1, 2, 3; II Thess. 3:1; Psa. 145.
(2) Isa. 64:1, 2; Rom. 11:36.

**Q. 102.** *What do we pray for in the second petition?*

A. In the second petition, which is, *"Thy kingdom come,"* we pray, that

THE WESTMINSTER
CONFESSION OF FAITH

THE WESTMINSTER
LARGER CATECHISM

THE WESTMINSTER
SHORTER CATECHISM

edging ourselves and all mankind to be by nature under the dominion of sin and Satan,[2] we pray: that the kingdom of sin and Satan may be destroyed,[3] the gospel propagated throughout the world,[4] the Jews called,[5] the fullness of the Gentiles brought in;[6] that the church may be furnished with all gospel-officers and ordinances,[7] purged from corruption,[8] countenanced and maintained by the civil magistrate; that the ordinances of Christ may be purely dispensed, and made effectual to the converting of those that are yet in their sins, and the confirming, comforting, and building up of those that are already converted;[9] that Christ would rule in our hearts here,[10] and hasten the time of his second coming, and our reigning with him forever;[11] and that he would be pleased so to exercise the kingdom of his power in all the world, as may best conduce to these ends.[12]

(1) Matt. 6:10.
(2) Eph. 2:2, 3.
(3) Psa. 68:1; Rev. 12:9.
(4) II Thess. 3:1; Psa. 67:2.
(5) Rom. 10:1.
(6) Rom. 11:25; Psa. 67:1-7.
(7) Matt. 9:38.
(8) Eph. 5:26, 27; Mal. 1:11.
(9) II Cor. 4:2; Acts 26:18; II Thess. 2:16, 17.
(10) Eph. 3:14, 17.
(11) Rev. 22:20.
(12) Isa. 64:1, 2; II Chron. 20:6, 10-12.

Satan's kingdom may be destroyed,[1] and that the kingdom of grace may be advanced, ourselves and others brought into it, and kept in it,[2] and that the kingdom of glory may be hastened.[3]

(1) Psa. 68:1.
(2) II Thess. 3:1; Psa. 51:18; Psa. 67:1-3; Rom. 10:1.
(3) Rev. 22:20; II Pet. 3:11-13.

**Q. 192.** *What do we pray for in the third petition?*

A. In the third petition (which is, *Thy will be done on earth as it is in heaven*),[1] acknowledging that by nature we and all men are not only utterly unable and unwilling to know and do the will of God,[2] but prone to rebel against his word,[3] to repine and murmur against his providence,[4] and wholly inclined to do the will of the flesh, and of the

**Q. 103.** *What do we pray for in the third petition?*

A. In the third petition, which is, *"Thy will be done in earth, as it is in heaven,"* we pray, that God, by his grace, would make us able and willing to know, obey, and submit to his will in all things[1] as the angels do in heaven.[2]

(1) Psa. 119:34, 35, 36; Acts 21:14.
(2) Psa. 103:20, 21, 22.

THE WESTMINSTER
CONFESSION OF FAITH

THE WESTMINSTER
LARGER CATECHISM

THE WESTMINSTER
SHORTER CATECHISM

devil:[5] we pray that God would by his Spirit take away from ourselves and others all blindness,[6] weakness,[7] indisposedness,[8] and perverseness of heart,[9] and by his grace make us able and willing to know, do, and submit to his will in all things,[10] with the like humility,[11] cheerfulness,[12] faithfulness,[13] diligence,[14] zeal,[15] sincerity,[16] and constancy,[17] as the angels do in heaven.[18]

(1) Matt. 6:10.
(2) I Cor. 2:14; Rom. 8:5, 8.
(3) Rom. 8:7.
(4) Matt. 20:11, 12; Psa. 73:3.
(5) Tit. 3:3; Eph. 2:2, 3.
      See Question 191 under figure 2.
(6) Eph. 1:17, 18.
(7) Eph. 3:16.
(8) Matt. 26:40, 41; Rom. 7:24, 25.
(9) Ezek. 11:19; Jer. 31:18.
(10) Psa. 119:35; Acts 21:14; I Sam. 3:18.
(11) Psa. 123:2; Psa. 131:2; Micah 6:8.
(12) Psa. 100:2.
(13) Isa. 38:3; Eph. 6:6.
(14) Psa. 119:4.
(15) Rom. 12:11.
(16) II Cor. 1:12.
(17) Psa. 119:112; Rom. 2:7.
(18) Psa. 103:20, 21, 22; Dan. 7:10.

Q. 193. *What do we pray for in the fourth petition?*

A. In the fourth petition (which is, *Give us this day our daily bread*),[1] acknowledging that in Adam, and by our own sin, we have forfeited our right to all the outward blessings of this life, and deserve to be wholly deprived of them by God, and to have them cursed to us in the use of them;[2] and that neither they of themselves are able to sustain us,[3] nor we to merit,[4] or by our own industry to procure them,[5] but prone to desire,[6] get,[7] and use them unlawfully:[8] we pray for ourselves and others, that both they and we, waiting upon the providence of God from day to day in the use of lawful means may, of his free gift, and as to his fatherly wisdom shall seem

Q. 104. *What do we pray for in the fourth petition?*

A. In the fourth petition, which is, *"Give us this day our daily bread,"* we pray, that, of God's free gift, we may receive a competent portion of the good things of this life,[1] and enjoy his blessing with them.[2]
(1) Prov. 30:8.
(2) I Tim. 4:4, 5; Prov. 10:22.

| THE WESTMINSTER CONFESSION OF FAITH | THE WESTMINSTER LARGER CATECHISM | THE WESTMINSTER SHORTER CATECHISM |
|---|---|---|
| | best, enjoy a competent portion of them,[9] and have the same continued and blessed unto us in our holy and comfortable use of them,[10] and contentment in them;[11] and be kept from all things that are contrary to our temporal support and comfort.[12] | |

Larger Catechism footnotes:

(1) Matt. 6:11.
(2) Gen. 3:17; Lam. 3:22; Deut. 28:15-68.
(3) Deut. 8:3.
(4) Gen. 32:10.
(5) Deut. 8:18; Prov. 10:22.
(6) Luke 12:15; Jer. 6:13.
(7) Hos. 12:7.
(8) James 4:3.
(9) Gen. 28:20, 21; James 4:13, 15; Psa. 90:17; Psa. 144:12-15.
(10) I Tim. 4:4, 5; Prov. 10:22.
(11) I Tim. 6:6, 8.
(12) Prov. 30:8, 9.

**Q. 194.** *What do we pray for in the fifth petition?*

**A.** In the fifth petition (which is, *Forgive us our debts, as we forgive our debtors*),[1] acknowledging that we and all others are guilty both of original and actual sin, and thereby become debtors to the justice of God, and that neither we nor any other creature can make the least satisfaction for that debt:[2] we pray for ourselves and others, that God of his free grace would, through the obedience and satisfaction of Christ apprehended and applied by faith, acquit us both from the guilt and punishment of sin,[3] accept us in his Beloved,[4] continue his favor and grace to us,[5] pardon our daily failings,[6] and fill us with peace and joy, in giving us daily more and more assurance of forgiveness;[7] which we are the rather emboldened to ask, and encouraged to expect, when we have this testimony in ourselves, that we from the heart forgive others their offenses.[8]

(1) Matt. 6:12.
(2) Matt. 18:24; Rom. 5:19; Rom. 3:9, 19 (See context); Psa. 130:3; Micah 6:6, 7.

**Q. 105.** *What do we pray for in the fifth petition?*

**A.** In the fifth petition, which is, *"And forgive us our debts, as we forgive our debtors,"* we pray, that God, for Christ's sake, would freely pardon all our sins;[1] which we are the rather encouraged to ask, because by his grace we are enabled from the heart to forgive others.[2]

(1) Psa. 51:1; Rom. 3:24, 25.
(2) Luke 11:4; Matt. 18:35; Matt. 6:14, 15.

|  | THE WESTMINSTER<br>**CONFESSION OF FAITH** | THE WESTMINSTER<br>**LARGER CATECHISM** | THE WESTMINSTER<br>**SHORTER CATECHISM** |

(3) Rom. 5:19; Rom. 3:24, 25; Acts 13:39.
(4) Eph. 1:6.
(5) II Pet. 1:2.
(6) Hos. 14:2; Psa. 143:2; Psa. 130:3.
(7) Rom. 15:13; Rom. 5:1, 2; Psa. 51:7-12.
(8) Luke 11:4; Matt. 18:35; Matt. 6:14, 15.

**Q. 195.** *What do we pray for in the sixth petition?*

**A.** In the sixth petition (which is, *And lead us not into temptation, but deliver us from evil*),[1] acknowledging that the most wise, righteous, and gracious God, for divers holy and just ends, may so order things that we may be assaulted, foiled, and for a time led captive by temptations;[2] that Satan,[3] the world,[4] and the flesh, are ready powerfully to draw us aside and ensnare us;[5] and that we, even after the pardon of our sins, by reason of our corruption,[6] weakness, and want of watchfulness,[7] are not only subject to be tempted, and forward to expose ourselves unto temptations,[8] but also of ourselves unable and unwilling to resist them, to recover out of them, and to improve them;[9] and worthy to be left under the power of them;[10] we pray: that God would so overrule the world and all in it,[11] subdue the flesh,[12] and restrain Satan,[13] order all things,[14] bestow and bless all means of grace,[15] and quicken us to watchfulness in the use of them, that we and all his people may by his providence be kept from being tempted to sin;[16] or, if tempted, that by his Spirit we may be powerfully supported and enabled to stand in the hour of temptation;[17] or, when fallen, raised again and recovered out of it,[18] and have a sanctified use and improvement thereof;[19] that our sanctification and salvation may be perfected,[20] Satan trodden under our feet,[21] and we

**Q. 106.** *What do we pray for in the sixth petition?*

**A.** In the sixth petition, which is, *"And lead us not into temptation, but deliver us from evil,"* we pray, that God would either keep us from being tempted to sin,[1] or support and deliver us when we are tempted.[2]

(1) Matt. 26:41; Psa. 19:13.
(2) I Cor. 10:13; Psa. 51:10, 12.

THE WESTMINSTER
**CONFESSION OF FAITH**

THE WESTMINSTER
**LARGER CATECHISM**

THE WESTMINSTER
**SHORTER CATECHISM**

fully freed from sin, temptation, and all evil forever.[22]

(1) Matt. 6:13.
(2) II Chron. 32:31; Job 2:6.
(3) I Pet. 5:8; Job 2:2.
(4) Luke 21:34; Mark 4:19.
(5) James 1:14.
(6) Gal. 5:17; Rom. 7:18.
(7) Matt. 26:41.
(8) I Tim. 6:9; Prov. 7:22.
(9) Rom. 7:18, 19.
(10) Psa. 81:11, 12.
(11) John 17:15; Rom. 8:28.
(12) Psa. 51:10; Psa. 119:133.
(13) Heb. 2:18; I Cor. 10:13; II Cor. 12:8.
(14) Rom. 8:28.
(15) Heb. 13:20, 21; Eph. 4:11, 12.
(16) Matt. 26:41; Psa. 19:13.
(17) I Cor. 10:13; Eph. 3:14-16.
(18) Psa. 51:12.
(19) I Pet. 5:10; I Pet. 1:6, 7.
(20) I Thess. 3:13.
(21) Rom. 16:20.
(22) I Thess. 5:23.

Q. 196. *What doth the conclusion of the Lord's prayer teach us?*

A. The conclusion of the Lord's prayer (which is, *For thine is the kingdom, and the power, and the glory, for ever. Amen.*),[1] teacheth us to enforce our petitions with arguments,[2] which are to be taken, not from any worthiness in ourselves, or in any other creature, but from God;[3] and with our prayers to join praises,[4] ascribing to God alone eternal sovereignty, omnipotency, and glorious excellency;[5] in regard whereof, as he is able and willing to help us,[6] so we by faith are emboldened to plead with him that he would,[7] and quietly to rely upon him that he will, fulfill our requests.[8] And to testify our desires and assurance, we say, *Amen.*[9]

(1) Matt. 6:13.
(2) Job 23:3, 4; Jer. 14:20, 21.
(3) Dan. 9:4, 7, 8, 9, 16, 19.
(4) Phil. 4:6.
(5) I Chron. 29:10, 11, 12, 13.
(6) Eph. 3:20, 21; Luke 11:13; Psa. 84:11.
(7) Eph. 3:12; Heb. 10:19, 20, 21, 22.
(8) I John 5:14; Rom. 8:32.
(9) I Cor. 14:16; Rev. 22:20, 21.

Q. 107. *What doth the conclusion of the Lord's prayer teach us?*

A. The conclusion of the Lord's prayer, which is, *"For thine is the kingdom, and the power, and the glory, for ever, Amen,"* teacheth us to take our encouragement in prayer from God only,[1] and in our prayers to praise him, ascribing kingdom, power, and glory to him,[2] and in testimony of our desire and assurance to be heard, we say, *Amen.*[3]

(1) Dan. 9:18, 19.
(2) I Chron. 29:11, 12, 13.
(3) Rev. 22:20, 21; I Cor. 14:16.

# EXPLANATORY NOTES

THE Confession mentions prayer in Chapter XXIII as a part of worship, but does not treat of prayer as a means of grace. Indeed, the Confession has no chapter on the means of grace. It gives ample consideration to the Word and the sacraments, but not specifically as means of grace. Both Catechisms, however, raise and answer this question: "What are the outward and ordinary means whereby Christ communicateth to us the benefits of redemption?" and name prayer among the means of grace. (L.C. 154; S.C. 88.)

Now not all theologians agree with the Westminster divines here. Berkhof dissents and so do Lutherans. Prayer does not belong to the same category as the Word and the sacraments. These latter are objective ordinances. While prayer may be instrumental in promoting the spiritual life, it can hardly be called an "outward means." Prayer is subjective rather than objective. So Berkhof is right when he says that strictly speaking only the Word and the sacraments can be regarded as means of grace in the technical sense. (*Systematic Theology,* Second Edition, p. 604.)

That prayer is properly regarded as an outward means of grace some doubt and others deny, but that prayer is a part of worship all heartily agree. For this reason I have placed the catechetical treatises on prayer in connection with Chapter XXIII of the Confession, which treats of religious worship and the Sabbath day.

It seemed wise, however, to present the Lord's Prayer itself as Part Two of Chapter XXIII. That chapter treats of religious worship, and names prayer as a prominent part of worship. The Lord's Prayer is meant to illustrate, by example, how to pray and what to pray for. This model prayer makes a fitting conclusion to the Confessional treatise on religious worship.

With two exceptions the two Catechisms ask precisely the same questions about this pattern prayer. The Larger Catechism introduces its treatment of the prayer with two questions (187 and 188) which have no parallel in the Shorter Catechism: first, "How is the Lord's prayer to be used?" and second, "Of how many parts doth the Lord's prayer consist?"

From this point onward the two Catechisms ask the same questions: one about the preface, one about each of the six petitions, and one about the conclusion. But the answers of the Larger Catechism are as a rule twice as long as those of the Shorter Catechism. The Larger Catechism's answer to each question about the petitions begins with an instructive acknowledgment, confessing our sins, inabilities, needs, and dangers; and then proceeds to enumerate the things to be prayed for.

Do you ask how you should pray and what you should pray for? Here are the answers. How our prayers would be improved in spirit and enlarged and enriched in content, if we would only take lessons from the Catechisms, especially the Larger. Our prayers would be more specific and varied, and move in wider circles and reach to farther ends. A thoughtful reading of the Catechisms on the Lord's Prayer would be an excellent preparation for prayer. Try it.

I would direct attention to four characteristics of this prayer, commonly called the Lord's Prayer, though it is really the disciples' prayer.

i. The spirit of the prayer.

1. It is filial: "Father."

2. It is social, fraternal: "Our Father."

3. It is reverent: "Which art in heaven." Reverence looks up in recognition of God's exaltation and majesty.

4. It is humble: "Thy will be done,"
   "Give us ... daily bread,"
   "Deliver us from evil."

   Humility looks down in recognition of our weakness and unworthiness. Reverence and humility acting together put "mine" under "thine," and "ours" under "His."

5. It is forgiving: "Forgive us ... *as* we forgive."

II. The order of the prayer.

1. The things of God: His Name (Himself), His Kingdom, His Will.

2. The things of man: the fundamental things — bread for the body, forgiveness for the soul, protection for the life.

This pattern prayer is modeled after the Decalogue. The commandments of the first table relate to God, while the commandments of the second table relate to man. Religion is before morality. It is a lesson in divine emphasis. Men so often reverse the order and turn things upside down.

III. The brevity of the prayer. It is brief, yet inclusive. It is

as high as heaven
as wide as the Kingdom of God
as deep as the needs of man
and as long as eternity.

IV. The symmetry, proportion, of the prayer. It opens with a preface of reverent address. It closes with a warm ascription of praise and adoration. In between is a body of short petitions — six in number, three having reference to God, and three having reference to man.

This prayer is a work of art, a thing of beauty, and a joy forever.

# CHAPTER XXIV

# Of Lawful Oaths and Vows

## CONFESSION OF FAITH XXIV:1-7

| THE WESTMINSTER CONFESSION OF FAITH | THE WESTMINSTER LARGER CATECHISM | THE WESTMINSTER SHORTER CATECHISM |
|---|---|---|

A LAWFUL oath is a part of religious worship,[1] wherein upon just occasion, the person swearing solemnly calleth God to witness what he asserteth or promiseth; and to judge him according to the truth or falsehood of what he sweareth.[2]

(1) Deut. 10:20.
(2) II Cor. 1:23; II Chron. 6:22, 23; Ex. 20:7.

2. The name of God only is that by which men ought to swear, and therein it is to be used with all holy fear and reverence;[3] therefore to swear vainly or rashly by that glorious and dreadful name, or to swear at all by any other thing, is sinful, and to be abhorred.[4] Yet, as, in matters of weight and moment, an oath is warranted by the word of God, under the New Testament, as well as under the Old, so a lawful oath, being imposed by lawful authority, in such matters ought to be taken.[5]

(3) Deut. 6:13.
(4) Jer. 5:7; James 5:12; Matt. 5:37; Ex. 20:7.
(5) I Kings 8:31; Ezra 10:5; Matt. 26:63, 64.

3. Whosoever taketh an oath ought duly to consider the weightiness of so solemn an act, and therein to avouch nothing but what he is fully persuaded is the truth. Neither may any man bind himself by oath to anything but what is good and just, and what he believeth so to be, and what he is able and resolved to perform. Yet it is a sin to refuse an

THE WESTMINSTER
CONFESSION OF FAITH

THE WESTMINSTER
LARGER CATECHISM

THE WESTMINSTER
SHORTER CATECHISM

oath touching anything that is good
and just, being imposed by lawful
authority.[6]

(6)  See citations under Section 2, above.

4. An oath is to be taken in the
plain and common sense of the
words, without equivocation or mental reservation.[7] It cannot oblige to
sin; but in anything not sinful, being taken, it binds to performance,
although to a man's own hurt:[8] nor
is it to be violated, although made
to heretics or infidels.[9]

(7)  Psa. 24:4; Jer. 4:2.
(8)  Psa. 15:4.
(9)  Ezek. 17:16, 18; Josh. 9:18, 19;
     II Sam. 21:1.

5. A vow is of the like nature
with a promissory oath, and ought to
be made with the like religious care,
and to be performed with the like
faithfulness.[10]

(10) Psa. 66:13, 14; Psa. 61:8; Deut.
     23:21, 23.

6. It is not to be made to any
creature, but to God alone:[11] and
that it may be accepted, it is to be
made voluntarily, out of faith and
conscience of duty, in way of thankfulness for mercy received, or for
obtaining of what we want; whereby we more strictly bind ourselves
to necessary duties, or to other
things, so far and so long as they
may fitly conduce thereunto.[12]

(11) Psa. 76:11; Jer. 44:25, 26.
(12) Psa. 50:14; Gen. 28:20, 21, 22.
     Compare with the above I Sam.
     1:11; Psa. 132:2-5.

7. No man may vow to do anything forbidden in the word of God,
or what would hinder any duty
therein commanded, or which is not
in his own power, and for the performance whereof he hath no promise or ability from God.[13] In which
respects, monastical vows of perpet-

| THE WESTMINSTER CONFESSION OF FAITH | THE WESTMINSTER LARGER CATECHISM | THE WESTMINSTER SHORTER CATECHISM |
|---|---|---|

ual single life, professed poverty, and regular obedience, are so far from being degrees of higher perfection, that they are superstitious and sinful snares, in which no Christian may entangle himself.

(13) Num. 30:5, 8, 12, 13.

# EXPLANATORY NOTES

## CONF. XXIV:1

The main idea in section 1 is that of the nature of a lawful oath. It is an act of religious worship. Can an irreligious person perform a really religious act?

There are two subordinate ideas here.

1. Kinds of oaths: assertory and promissory.

2. God's relation to oaths lawfully made. It is double — that of witness and judge.

## CONF. XXIV:2

The first truth in section 2 follows from the first truth in section 1; for if an oath is an act of religious worship, then the only name by which men ought to swear is the name of God. To swear by any other name would be an act of idolatry, for only God is to be worshipped.

There are two subordinate points here also.

1. The Word of God under both Testaments warrants the custom of oath-taking in matters of weight and moment.

2. When required in such matters by lawful authority, the oath ought to be taken.

The two points may be more briefly stated as the propriety and the duty of oath-taking.

## CONF. XXIV:3

Lawful swearing has its limitations. It must be kept within the bounds of truth and right, and of the swearer's ability and intention to perform.

Within these limits it is wrong to refuse an oath when imposed by lawful authority, civil or ecclesiastical.

Comparison of the last part of section 2 with the last part of section 3 reveals that the latter statement is a corollary of the former. If one ought to take an oath touching any matter, it is of course a sin to refuse the oath.

## CONF. XXIV:4

This section relates to the interpretation and obligation of an oath lawfully made. An unlawful oath is better in the breach than in the observance. But a lawful oath, being taken, is to be honestly interpreted and faithfully kept — to whomever made and howsoever it hurts. The man who swears to his own hurt and changeth not is acceptable with God.

Why this elaborate justification of the oath? Because not only the duty but the propriety of the oath under any circumstances has been and still is denied by some groups. But Bible precept and example give the oath a place among the high solemnities of religion.

How are Christ and James to be understood when they say, "Swear not at all"? (Matt. 5:34;

James 5:12.) I think Dummelow has the correct interpretation: "The prohibition 'Swear not at all' is to be taken in its widest sense, and not simply as forbidding the common oaths of conversation. Christ looks forward to a time when truthfulness will be so binding a duty that oaths will no longer be necessary even in courts of justice. This is one of those ideal commands which cannot be fully carried out in the present state of society. Our Lord Himself at His trial allowed Himself to be put on oath (26:63). But one day there will come a time when a man's word will be as good as his oath." (*The One Volume Bible Commentary* on Matthew 5:33-37.)

The necessity for the oath is of the evil one, and when this world is delivered from its corruptor that necessity will cease. It is our duty so to live now that our word will be regarded as good as our oath.

### CONF. XXIV:5-7

Sections 5-7 relate to the vow. The oath and the vow have much in common. They are of like nature, both being acts of worship. The vow, being an act of worship, is to be made only to God according to His will. That it may be acceptable with Him it must be made in sincerity and truth. A vow has an obligation, distinct from that of the law. If you do not wish to add to your obligation do not vow. Read Ecclesiastes 5:4-5.

While the oath and the vow have much in common, they may be distinguished. In the oath, the parties are both men, and God is invoked as a witness and judge. In the vow, God is the party to whom the promise is made.

These sections on the oath and the vow are meant to give sound instruction in regard to their use and to safeguard us from the error of the Church of Rome.

# CHAPTER XXV

# Of the Civil Magistrate

CONFESSION OF FAITH XXV:1-4

| THE WESTMINSTER CONFESSION OF FAITH | THE WESTMINSTER LARGER CATECHISM | THE WESTMINSTER SHORTER CATECHISM |
|---|---|---|

GOD, the Supreme Lord and King of all the world, hath ordained civil magistrates to be under him over the people, for his own glory and the public good; and to this end, hath armed them with the power of the sword, for the defense and encouragement of them that are good, and for the punishment of evildoers.[1]

(1) Rom. 13:1, 3, 4; I Pet. 2:13, 14.

2. It is lawful for Christians to accept and execute the office of a magistrate, when called thereunto;[2] in the managing whereof, as they ought especially to maintain piety, justice, and peace, according to the wholesome laws of each commonwealth,[3] so, for that end, they may lawfully, now under the New Testament, wage war upon just and necessary occasions.[4]

(2) Prov. 8:15, 16.
    See citations under Section 1 above.
(3) Psa. 82:3, 4; I Pet. 2:13.
    See citations under Section 1 above.
(4) Rom. 13:1, 2, 3, 4; Luke 3:14; Matt. 8:9; Acts 10:1, 2.

3. Civil magistrates may not assume to themselves the administration of the word and sacraments; or the power of the keys of the kingdom of heaven; or, in the least, interfere in matters of faith.[5] Yet, as nursing fathers, it is the duty of civil magistrates to protect the church of our common Lord, without giving the preference to any denomination of Christians above the rest, in such a manner that all ecclesiastical persons whatever shall enjoy the full,

THE WESTMINSTER
## CONFESSION OF FAITH

THE WESTMINSTER
## LARGER CATECHISM

THE WESTMINSTER
## SHORTER CATECHISM

free, and unquestioned liberty of discharging every part of their sacred functions, without violence or danger. And, as Jesus Christ hath appointed a regular government and discipline in his church, no law of any commonwealth should interfere with, let, or hinder, the due exercise thereof, among the voluntary members of any denomination of Christians, according to their own profession and belief. It is the duty of civil magistrates to protect the person and good name of all their people, in such an effectual manner as that no person be suffered, either upon pretense of religion or infidelity, to offer any indignity, violence, abuse, or injury to any other person whatsoever: and to take order, that all religious and ecclesiastical assemblies be held without molestation or disturbance.[6]

(5) Matt. 16:19; I Cor. 4:1; John 18:36; Eph. 4:11, 12; II Chron. 26:18.

(6) See General Note, Confession of Faith, Chapter 1.

4. It is the duty of the people to pray for magistrates,[7] to honor their persons,[8] to pay them tribute and other dues,[9] to obey their lawful commands, and to be subject to their authority, for conscience' sake.[10] Infidelity, or difference in religion, doth not make void the magistrate's just and legal authority, nor free the people from their due obedience to him:[11] from which ecclesiastical persons are not exempted;[12] much less hath the Pope any power or jurisdiction over them in their dominions, or over any of their people; and least of all to deprive them of their dominions or lives, if he shall judge them to be heretics, or upon any other pretense whatsoever.[13]

(7) I Tim. 2:1, 2.

(8) I Pet. 2:17.

(9) Rom. 13:6, 7.

| THE WESTMINSTER CONFESSION OF FAITH | THE WESTMINSTER LARGER CATECHISM | THE WESTMINSTER SHORTER CATECHISM |
|---|---|---|

(10) Rom. 13:5; Tit. 3:1.
(11) This is an inference from the duties just stated.
(12) Rom. 13:1; Acts 25:10, 11.
(13) This is an inference from the doctrine of the civil magistrate, and from duties incumbent on believers with respect to him.

# EXPLANATORY NOTES

THIS chapter deals with a subject of great importance and difficulty: namely, the co-existence and interrelation of state and church. The Confession does not use the word "state," but speaks of commonwealth and of magistrate, the head and representative of the commonwealth.

## CONF. XXV:1

The first section contains the answer to three questions in regard to the state.

1. The question of origin. The state is an ordinance of God. It is not meant that God directly ordained the state by saying to man, Thou shalt set up a government or organize a commonwealth. Government of some kind is a necessity of man's nature and life. But God created man's nature and the conditions of its development. Hence it may be truly said that the state is an ordinance of God.

2. The question of design or end. The ultimate end is the glory of God. The state is a means of manifesting God, or revealing His wisdom, power, justice, and goodness. The proximate end is the good of man. What are the benefits of government?

3. The question of means. Of what is the sword a symbol? The uses of the sword are defined.

## CONF. XXV:2

The subject of the second section is the rights and duties of Christians in relation to civil government.

1. They have the right to participate in civic affairs. They may hold office. If eligible to hold office, they are eligible to vote. It is reported that a certain bishop when asked on election day if he had voted, replied, "No, I am a Christian." Does being a Christian absolve a man from the responsibilities of citizenship?

2. When called to the office of magistrate it is the duty of the Christian to use his office "to . . . establish justice, insure domestic tranquillity, provide for the common defense, promote the general welfare, and secure the blessings of liberty." (Preamble to the Constitution of the United States.)

3. To secure these ends it is the Christian's right and may become his duty to employ force, even engage in war. It may not always be easy to decide when a war is just and necessary. But it is generally conceded that the right of self-defense belongs to the individual; if to the individual, then also to the state.

## CONF. XXV:3

This long section is occupied with the duty of the state toward the church. It denies that the state has any right to interfere in matters of faith or discipline or administration. It then affirms that the state has a threefold duty toward the church and religious people:

1. To protect the church as an institution, treating the various denominations impartially, and making it possible for all ecclesiastical persons to worship and serve God in freedom and in peace.

2. To protect the person and good name of all citizens, that they suffer not on account of religion or the lack of it.

3. To take care that all religious and ecclesiastical bodies enjoy freedom of assembly.

### CONF. XXV:4

The last section is concerned with the duties of citizens to the state. I take it that by "the duty of the people" is meant the duty of Christian people. The duty is several-fold, as analysis of the statement shows. Define the meaning of the phrase, "for conscience' sake."

The right of the representatives of the state to receive respect and obedience is not grounded in their character, but in their office; and all persons, including ecclesiastics, even popes, are under their jurisdiction.

Before leaving this subject, consider this question: Why was an article on the civil magistrate included in a religious creed? It was to inculcate the true view and to combat false views of the relation of church and state. There is the extreme doctrine of Erastianism, that the church is subordinate and subservient to the state. There is the opposite extreme doctrine of the Catholics, that the state should be subordinate and subservient to the church. The true view is that these institutions have each its own separate sphere and end, and means to that end; and each is supreme in its own realm. The words which express their relation to each other are: independent and interdependent. They are both ordained of God, and they best serve the purpose of God when they attend each one to its own proper business.

# CHAPTER XXVI

# Of Marriage and Divorce

## CONFESSION OF FAITH XXVI:1-7

| THE WESTMINSTER CONFESSION OF FAITH | THE WESTMINSTER LARGER CATECHISM | THE WESTMINSTER SHORTER CATECHISM |
|---|---|---|

MARRIAGE is a union between one man and one woman, designed of God to last so long as they both shall live.[1]

(1) Gen. 2:23, 24; I Cor. 7:2, 39; Matt. 19:4-6; Eph. 5:28, 31, 33; I Cor. 13:8, 13; Matt. 5:31, 32; Mark 10:5-9; Rom. 7:2, 3.

2. Marriage is designed for the mutual help of husband and wife;[2] for the safeguarding, undergirding, and development of their moral and spiritual character;[3] for the propagation of children and the rearing of them in the discipline and instruction of the Lord.[4]

(2) Gen. 2:18, 24.

(3) Gen. 1:27, 28; Eph. 5:22, 23; Col. 1:18, 19; Gen. 2:18-25; I Cor. 7: 3-5, 9, 36.

(4) Gen. 1:27, 28; Gen. 9:1; Mal. 2:15; Matt. 18:5, 6, 10, 14; Matt. 19:14; Eph. 6:1-4; Col. 3:20, 21; Mark 10:13-16; Luke 18:15-17.

3. All persons who are able with judgment to give their consent may marry,[5] except within the limits of blood relationship forbidden by Scripture,[6] and such marriages are valid before God in the eyes of the church.[7] But no marriage can be fully and securely Christian in spirit or in purpose unless both partners are committed to a common Christian faith and to a deeply shared intention of building a Christian home. Evangelical Christians should seek as partners in marriage only persons who hold in common a sound basis of evangelical faith.[8]

(5) Gen. 1:27, 28.

| THE WESTMINSTER CONFESSION OF FAITH | THE WESTMINSTER LARGER CATECHISM | THE WESTMINSTER SHORTER CATECHISM |
|---|---|---|

(6) Mark 6:18; I Cor. 5:1; Lev. 18:6-18.

(7) Mark 1:30; John 2:1-2; I Tim. 5:14; Heb. 13:4; I Cor. 7:7, 36; I Cor. 9:5; I Tim. 4:3.

(8) I Cor. 7, especially v. 39; II Cor. 6:14, 15.

4. Marriage for the Christian has religious as well as civil significance.[9] The distinctive contribution of the church in performing the marriage ceremony is to affirm the divine institution of marriage;[10] to invoke God's blessing upon those who enter into the marital relationship in accordance with his word;[11] to hear the vows of those who desire to be married; and to assure the married partners of God's grace within their new relationship.[12]

(9) Prov. 18:22; Matt. 19:6; Eph. 5:29, 30, 32; Mark 10:9, 11, 12.

(10) Gen. 1:27, 28.

(11) Mark 10:9.

(12) Eph. 5:22, 23.

5. It is the divine intention that persons entering the marriage covenant become inseparably united, thus allowing for no dissolution save that caused by the death of either husband or wife.[13] However, the weaknesses of one or both partners may lead to gross and persistent denial of the marriage vows so that marriage dies at the heart and the union becomes intolerable; yet only in cases of extreme, unrepented-of, and irremediable unfaithfulness (physical or spiritual) should separation or divorce be considered. Such separation or divorce is accepted as permissible only because of the failure of one or both of the partners, and does not lessen in any way the divine intention for indissoluble union.[14]

(13) Gen. 2:23, 24; Matt. 5:31, 32; Mark 10:5-9; Rom. 7:2, 3; I Cor. 7:2, 10, 11, 39; Eph. 5:28, 31, 33; Matt. 19:4-9; I Cor. 13:4-13.

| THE WESTMINSTER CONFESSION OF FAITH | THE WESTMINSTER LARGER CATECHISM | THE WESTMINSTER SHORTER CATECHISM |
|---|---|---|

(14) Mark 10:4-9; I Cor. 7:12, 13, 15; Matt. 19:7-9.

6. The remarriage of divorced persons may be sanctioned by the church, in keeping with the redemptive gospel of Christ, when sufficient penitence for sin and failure is evident, and a firm purpose of and endeavor after Christian marriage is manifested.[15]

(15) II Sam. 12:13; Neh. 9:17; Ps. 32:5; Ps. 130:4; Matt. 12:31a; Matt. 21:31, 32; John 8:3a, 11b; Rom. 3:23; Gal. 6:1; I Tim. 2:4; Heb. 7:25; I John 1:9; I John 2:1, 2; Luke 7:36-50; Luke 15:11-32; John 3:16, 17; Rom. 10:9, 10.

7. Divorced persons should give prayerful thought to discover if God's vocation for them is to remain unmarried, since one failure in this realm raises serious question as to the rightness and wisdom of undertaking another union.[16]

(16) Matt. 5:31, 32; I Cor. 7:10, 11, 20, 32-35; Mark 10:11; Luke 16:18.

## EXPLANATORY NOTES

MARRIAGE and divorce belong to the history of the family. Marriage lays the foundation of a family, divorce disrupts that foundation. Like the state and the church, the family is an ordinance of God. These three are the fundamental institutions of human society. All other legitimate organizations and associations of men are secondary and ancillary. The family is more fundamental than either of the other two; for it was prior to them, and they derive their members from it. Anything therefore which safeguards or threatens the purity and permanence of the home is of vital concern to both church and state. Hence the importance of this chapter. It contains instruction which, if heeded, would make home life sound and sweet and strong, and prevent many wrongs and much misery.

### CONF. XXVI:1

From the first section we learn the nature of marriage as divinely intended. It is the union of one man and one woman as husband and wife. This is called monogamy as opposed to bigamy or polygamy.

When God created man, He made him, male and female, one whole. They are complete, each in the other; there is no need of a third. When answering a question of the Pharisees about divorce, Jesus took His questioners beyond Moses back to the beginning. What God appointed at the first is decisive. The original is the normal, the ideal. Man marred the divine pattern and changed the home into a harem — a hell.

## CONF. XXVI:2

The second section defines the purpose of marriage. The purpose is fourfold. State and consider the parts of the purpose that you may know how important marriage is. Any one of these ends should exalt it in our thinking. The impact on our minds of the four ends combined should fill us with reverence for the institution and with fear of defiling it.

## CONF. XXVI:3

The third section tells us what sorts of people may marry and what sorts of people Christians ought or ought not to marry.

Man and woman were made for each other, and the normal state for adults is the state of matrimony. Since God has appointed marriage for male and female, no man or institution has the right to forbid it. There is no sanction in these Standards, for there is none in the Scriptures, for the Catholic practice of denying the privilege of marriage to the clergy. Celibacy is dishonoring to woman and dangerous to man. For it is based on an unworthy conception of woman and matrimony, and history bears witness that it is the occasion of corruption in the church.

In relation to marriage there are two causes of evil: omitting to marry and marrying inadvisedly — marrying the wrong person. Christians should marry Christians. And it is best when Christians marry within their own communion. All unhappiness in wedlock, and out of it, is the consequence of disregarding the counsel of God. "Be ye not unequally yoked together with unbelievers." (II Cor. 6:14.) See the whole counsel of the apostle, I Corinthians, seventh chapter.

## CONF. XXVI:4

The subject of the fourth section is the religious significance of marriage for the Christian. Marriage is ordained by God, and its unity and harmony are preserved by His grace.

## CONF. XXVI:5-7

The last three sections deal with the second half of the subject of this chapter — divorce. Divorce in every case is a confession of defeat, an acknowledgment of failure.

The Bible *allows* divorce, not approves it. Moses' law was a regulation, not a justification of divorce. He *suffered* the putting away, but *commanded* the bill of divorcement. He did not approve what he permitted. He was trying to control an evil.

The sections before us state the grounds of divorce. One is "extreme, unrepented-of, and irremediable unfaithfulness (physical or spiritual)." This sin severs the *moral* tie but not the *legal*. The contract on its legal side can be dissolved only by due process of law. The courts of the land ought to grant the innocent party release from the legal tie after the moral tie has been broken irremediably.

The subject of marriage is not receiving the attention to which its importance entitles it. People need guidance here. They need the restraint and the constraint which right instruction and exhortation would supply.

In this chapter are materials for a series of sermons on its double topic. First sermon: subject — Marriage, Its Nature and Purpose. Outline and materials may be drawn from sections 1 and 2, and the Scriptural texts subjoined.

Second sermon: subject — Marriage: Its Personnel.

1. Who may marry, and of course who may not marry. The privilege of marriage.

2. Who ought to marry. The duty of marriage.

3. Whom those contemplating the marriage relation should not marry. Whom they should marry. A condition of successful marriage.

Third sermon: subject — Marriage: Its Wreck and Ruin. Every divorce sought and secured is a confession that a marriage has failed, that a home has been wrecked. The breakdown of an institution so high in its origin and so honorable in its history as marriage is a mournful thing.

How often it happens.
Why it happens.
Why it should not happen.
How keep it from happening.

# CHAPTER XXVII

# Of the Church

CONFESSION OF FAITH XXVII:1-6
LARGER CATECHISM 61-64, (65)

| THE WESTMINSTER CONFESSION OF FAITH | THE WESTMINSTER LARGER CATECHISM | THE WESTMINSTER SHORTER CATECHISM |
|---|---|---|

THE catholic or universal church, which is invisible, consists of the whole number of the elect, that have been, are, or shall be gathered into one, under Christ the head thereof; and is the spouse, the body, the fullness of him that filleth all in all.[1]

(1) Eph. 1:22, 23; Col. 1:18; Eph. 5:23, 27, 32.

Q. 64. *What is the invisible church?*

A. The invisible church is the whole number of the elect, that have been, are, or shall be gathered into one under Christ the head.[1]

(1) John 11:52; John 10:16; Eph. 1:10, 22, 23.

(Q. 65. *What special benefits do the members of the invisible church enjoy by Christ?*

(A. The members of the invisible church, by Christ, enjoy union and communion with him in grace and glory.)

2. The visible church, which is also catholic or universal under the gospel (not confined to one nation as before under the law), consists of all those throughout the world that profess the true religion,[2] together with their children;[3] and is the kingdom of the Lord Jesus Christ;[4] the house and family of God,[5] through which men are ordinarily saved and union with which is essential to their best growth and service.[6]

(2) I Cor. 1:2; I Cor. 12:12, 13; Rom. 15:9-12.
(3) Gen. 17:7. See context. Compare Gal. 3:7, 9, 14; Rom. 4. Acts 2:39; I Cor. 7:14; Mark 10:13, 14, 15, 16.
(4) Matt. 13:47; Col. 1:13; Isa. 9:7.
(5) Eph. 2:19.
(6) Matt. 28:19; Acts 2:38; I Cor. 12:13; Matt. 26:26, 27, 28.

Q. 62. *What is the visible church?*

A. The visible church is a society made up of all such as in all ages and places of the world do profess the true religion,[1] and of their children.[2]

(1) I Cor. 1:2; I Cor. 12:12, 13; Rom. 15:1-12.
(2) Gen. 17:7. Compare Gal. 3:7, 9, 14; Rom. 4. Acts 2:39; I Cor. 7:14; Mark 10:13, 14, 15, 16.

| THE WESTMINSTER CONFESSION OF FAITH | THE WESTMINSTER LARGER CATECHISM | THE WESTMINSTER SHORTER CATECHISM |
|---|---|---|

### THE WESTMINSTER CONFESSION OF FAITH

3. Unto this catholic visible church, Christ hath given the ministry, oracles, and ordinances of God, for the gathering and perfecting of the saints, in this life, to the end of the world: and doth by his own presence and Spirit, according to his promise, make them effectual thereunto.[7]

(7) Eph. 4:11, 12, 13; Isa. 59:21; Matt. 28:19, 20.

4. This catholic church hath been sometimes more, sometimes less, visible.[8] And particular churches, which are members thereof, are more or less pure, according as the doctrine of the gospel is taught and embraced, ordinances administered, and public worship performed more or less purely in them.[9]

(8) Rom. 11:3, 4; Acts 9:31.
(9) I Cor. 5:6, 7; Rev. 2, 3.

5. The purest churches under heaven are subject both to mixture and error:[10] and some have so degenerated as to become apparently no churches of Christ.[11] Nevertheless, there shall be always a church on earth, to worship God according to his will.[12]

(10) Matt. 13:24, 25, 26, 27, 28, 29, 30, 47, 48.
(11) Rom. 11:18, 19, 20, 21, 22; Rev. 18:2.
(12) Matt. 16:18; Psa. 102:28; Matt. 28:19, 20.

### THE WESTMINSTER LARGER CATECHISM

Q. 63. *What are the special privileges of the visible church?*

A. The visible church hath the privilege of being under God's special care and government;[1] of being protected and preserved in all ages, notwithstanding the opposition of all enemies;[2] and of enjoying the communion of saints, the ordinary means of salvation,[3] and offers of grace by Christ, to all members of it, in the ministry of the gospel, testifying that whosoever believes in him shall be saved,[4] and excluding none that will come unto him.[5]

(1) I Cor. 12:28; Eph. 4:11, 12; Acts 13:1, 2; Isa. 49:14-16.
(2) Matt. 16:18; Isa. 31:4, 5; Psa. 115:9-18.
(3) Acts 2:42; Rom. 3:1, 2.
(4) Psa. 147:19, 20; Rom. 9:4; Acts 16:31; Rev. 22:17.
(5) John 6:37.

Q. 61. *Are all they saved who hear the gospel, and live in the church?*

A. All that hear the gospel, and live in the visible church, are not saved; but only they who are true members of the church invisible.[1]

(1) Rom. 9:6; Matt. 7:21; Matt. 13:41, 42.

| THE WESTMINSTER CONFESSION OF FAITH | THE WESTMINSTER LARGER CATECHISM | THE WESTMINSTER SHORTER CATECHISM |
|---|---|---|

6. The Lord Jesus Christ is the only head of the church,[13] and the claim of any man to be the vicar of Christ and the head of the church, is without warrant in fact or in Scripture, even anti-Christian, a usurpation dishonoring to the Lord Jesus Christ.

(13) Col. 1:18.

# EXPLANATORY NOTES

IN the last several chapters we have been almost altogether in the Confession. The subject of this chapter is treated not only by the Confession but also by the Larger Catechism. The Shorter Catechism has no question about the church. In answer to the 95th question, it *names* the "visible church," that, and nothing more. It seems unfortunate that that part of our Standards which is most used, and the only one of the three which is taught to children, should contain nothing about the church. The committee on the revision of the Standards which was appointed in 1935 recommended certain additions to the Shorter Catechism, but they were rejected by the Assembly (by a small majority).

## CONF. XXVII:1-2; L.C. 62, 64

Both Standards that treat of the church divide it into visible and invisible. These distinctions, though not directly Scriptural, are convenient and useful. Two other adjectives are used in extra-Confessional discussions of the church to characterize these divisions: militant and triumphant. Let us be on our guard against taking the impression from these pairs of words that there are two churches. These epithets describe different phases or aspects of the one church.

Four other adjectives are applied to the church, namely, "holy" and "catholic" in the Apostles' Creed, and "one" and "apostolic" in the Nicene

Creed. Of these four, two are found in our creed, viz., "catholic" and "one." Locate them. Do these four adjectives apply to the church visible as well as to the church invisible? "Catholic" does. (See Confession.) "Holy" does in a sense — in what sense? "One" does in a sense. The church in all its evangelical branches acknowledges Jesus Christ as Head of the church and Lord of the kingdom. All churches confess one great Name. "Apostolic" would be accepted by all denominations as truly descriptive of their ultimate origin. For all communions profess to continue steadfastly in the apostles' doctrine and fellowship, and in the breaking of bread* and the prayers.

A Scottish Roman Catholic catechism quoted in Rankin's *The Creed in Scotland,* page 264, says: "There are three conditions of men in the Catholic church: those glorified in heaven, or the church triumphant; those detained in purgatory, or the church suffering; and the faithful on earth, or the church militant. The church on earth is a visible body, because she is a society of men which is distinguished from all other societies, and which has a visible government and visible means of grace, and is the kingdom of Christ on earth." Wherein does that statement differ from our Confession's definition of the church? Wherein does it agree?

---

*The Society of Friends (the Quakers), while recognized as a Protestant group, do not observe "the breaking of bread."

According to Catholic opinion, out of the church there is no possibility of salvation. According to the Westminster Confession of Faith, out of the church there is no *ordinary* possibility of salvation. The Assembly of 1939 changed the last part of Confession XXVII:2 to read: "Through which men are ordinarily saved and union with which is essential to their best growth and service."

### CONF. XXVII:3; L.C. 63

The third section of the Confession sets forth the task of the church and indicates its qualifications for its task. Its task is twofold. State it. Its qualifications are three. Name them. All are gifts of Christ.

The Giver by His presence and Spirit makes His gifts effectual unto the end in view. Here, as elsewhere, gifts without the giver are bare. Let the church, its ministry especially, remember that the dynamic of Christianity, whether in the individual or in the whole body of believers collectively, is Christ working by His Spirit. All the offices and ordinances of the church converge upon the grand object of winning men to obedience and service, but they fail of their objective except as they are attended by the vivifying and energizing Spirit of Christ. (Eph. 4:11-13; 2:18-22.)

Larger Catechism answer 63 corresponds in a way to Confession XXVII:3. The point of view is different. The Confession speaks of the duties of the church, while the Catechism speaks of the privileges of the church. The two views are complementary. Enumerate and estimate the privileges of the visible church.

### CONF. XXVII:4-5; L.C. 61

The fourth and fifth sections of this chapter relate to the purity of the church. What are the tests of purity? They are three as given in section 4. The marks of a true church are sometimes differently stated thus: the sound preaching of the Word, the right administration of the sacraments and of discipline. The supreme judge by which such matters are to be examined and determined can be no other than the Holy Spirit speaking in the Scripture. (Conf. 1:9.)

The best churches are of mixed character, and the worst are so degenerated as to be apparently no churches of Christ. Nevertheless, according to His expressed will, there shall always be a church on earth to worship God. The prophet, speaking of Christ, declared that He would not fail nor be discouraged till He had set justice in the earth. (Isaiah 42:4.)

### CONF. XXVII:6

The last section is about the headship of the church. This section as revised by the Assembly of 1939 reads as follows: "The Lord Jesus Christ is the only head of the church, and the claim of any man to be the vicar of Christ and the head of the church, is without warrant in fact or in Scripture, even anti-Christian, a usurpation dishonoring to the Lord Jesus Christ." This statement affirms what Rome denies, and denies what Rome affirms. Pope means "father," and Jesus forbade His disciples to call any man father on earth; "for," said He, "one is your Father, even he who is in heaven." (Matt. 23:9.)

# CHAPTER XXVIII

# Of the Communion of Saints

CONFESSION OF FAITH XXVIII:1-3
LARGER CATECHISM 65-66, 69, 82-83, 86, (90) • (See also SHORTER CATECHISM 36-38)

---

THE WESTMINSTER
## CONFESSION OF FAITH

---

THE WESTMINSTER
## LARGER CATECHISM

---

THE WESTMINSTER
## SHORTER CATECHISM

---

ALL saints being united to Jesus Christ their head, by his Spirit and by faith, have fellowship with him in his graces, sufferings, death, resurrection, and glory:[1] and, being united to one another in love, they have communion in each other's gifts and graces,[2] and are obliged to the performance of such duties, public and private, as do conduce to their mutual good, both in the inward and outward man.[3]

(1) I John 1:3; Eph. 3:16, 17, 18, 19; John 1:16; Phil. 3:10; Rom. 6:5, 6; Rom. 8:17.
(2) Eph. 4:15, 16; I John 1:3, 7.
(3) I Thess. 5:11, 14; Gal. 6:10; I John 3:16-18.

2. Saints by their profession are bound to maintain an holy fellowship and communion in the worship of God, and in performing such other spiritual services as tend to their mutual edification;[4] as also in relieving each other in outward things, according to their several abilities and necessities. Which communion, as God offereth opportunity, is to be extended unto all those who, in every place, call upon the name of the Lord Jesus.[5]

(4) Heb. 10:24, 25; Acts 2:42, 46; I Cor. 11:20.
(5) I John 3:17; Acts 11:29, 30; II Cor. 8, 9.

3. This communion which the saints have with Christ, doth not make them in any wise partakers of

Q. 65. *What special benefits do the members of the invisible church enjoy by Christ?*

A. The members of the invisible church, by Christ, enjoy union and communion with him in grace and glory.[1]

(1) John 17:21; Eph. 2:5, 6; I John 1:3; John 17:24.

Q. 66. *What is that union which the elect have with Christ?*

A. The union which the elect have with Christ is the work of God's grace,[1] whereby they are spiritually and mystically, yet really and inseparably, joined to Christ as their head and husband;[2] which is done in their effectual calling.[3]

(1) Eph. 2:8.
(2) I Cor. 6:17; John 10:28; Eph. 5:23, 30; John 15:1-5.
(3) I Cor. 1:9; I Pet. 5:10.

| THE WESTMINSTER CONFESSION OF FAITH | THE WESTMINSTER LARGER CATECHISM | THE WESTMINSTER SHORTER CATECHISM |
|---|---|---|

the substance of his Godhead, or to be equal with Christ in any respect: either of which to affirm, is impious and blasphemous.[6] Nor doth their communion one with another as saints, take away or infringe the title or property which each man hath in his goods and possessions.[7]

(6)   Col. 1:18; I Cor. 8:6; Psa. 15:7.
(7)   Acts 5:4.

Q. 69. *What is the communion in grace, which the members of the invisible church have with Christ?*

A. The communion in grace, which the members of the invisible church have with Christ, is their partaking of the virtue of his mediation, in their justification,[1] adoption,[2] sanctification, and whatever else in this life manifests their union with him.[3]

(1)   Rom. 8:30.
(2)   Eph. 1:5.
(3)   I Cor. 1:30.

Q. 82. *What is the communion in glory which the members of the invisible church have with Christ?*

A. The communion in glory which the members of the invisible church have with Christ, is in this life,[1] immediately after death,[2] and at last perfected at the resurrection and day of judgment.[3]

(1)   II Cor. 3:18.
(2)   Luke 23:43.
(3)   I John 3:2; I Thess. 4:17; Rev. 22:3-5.

Q. 83. *What is the communion in glory with Christ, which the members of the invisible church enjoy in this life?*

A. The members of the invisible church have communicated to them, in this life, the first-fruits of glory

(Q. 36. *What are the benefits which in this life do accompany or flow from justification, adoption, and sanctification?*

(A. The benefits which in this life do accompany or flow from justification, adoption, and sanctification,

THE WESTMINSTER
**CONFESSION OF FAITH**

THE WESTMINSTER
**LARGER CATECHISM**

THE WESTMINSTER
**SHORTER CATECHISM**

with Christ, as they are members of him their head, and so in him are interested in that glory which he is fully possessed of;[1] and as an earnest thereof, enjoy the sense of God's love,[2] peace of conscience, joy in the Holy Ghost, and hope of glory.[3] As, on the contrary, the sense of God's revenging wrath, horror of conscience, and a fearful expectation of judgment, are to the wicked the beginning of the torment which they shall endure after death.[4]

(1) Eph. 2:4, 5, 6.
(2) Rom. 5:5; II Cor. 1:22.
(3) Rom. 5:1, 2; Rom. 14:17.
(4) Gen. 4:13; Matt. 27:3, 4, 5; Heb. 10:27; Mark 9:44; Rom. 2:9.

Q. 86. *What is the communion in glory with Christ, which the members of the invisible church enjoy immediately after death?*

A. The communion in glory with Christ, which the members of the invisible church enjoy immediately after death, is in that their souls are then made perfect in holiness, and received into the highest heavens, where they behold the face of God in light and glory;[1] waiting for the full redemption of their bodies,[2] which even in death continue united to Christ,[3] and rest in their graves as in their beds, till at the last day they be again united to their souls.[4] Whereas the souls of the wicked are at their death cast into hell, where they remain in torments and utter darkness; and their bodies kept in their graves, as in their prisons, until the resurrection and judgment of the great day.[5]

(1) Luke 16:23; Luke 23:43; Phil. 1:23; II Cor. 5:6-8.
(2) Rom. 8:23; Psa. 16:9.
(3) I Thess. 4:14.
(4) Rom. 8:23.
(5) Luke 16:23, 24; Acts 1:25; Jude 6.

are: assurance of God's love, peace of conscience, joy in the Holy Ghost, increase of grace, and perseverance therein to the end.)

(Q. 37. *What benefits do believers receive from Christ at death?*

(A. The souls of believers are at their death made perfect in holiness, and do immediately pass into glory; and their bodies, being still united to Christ, do rest in their graves till the resurrection.)

| THE WESTMINSTER **CONFESSION OF FAITH** | THE WESTMINSTER **LARGER CATECHISM** | THE WESTMINSTER **SHORTER CATECHISM** |
|---|---|---|
|  | (Q. 90. *What shall be done to the righteous at the day of judgment?* | (Q. 38. *What benefits do believers receive from Christ at the resurrection?* |
|  | (A. At the day of judgment, the righteous, being caught up to Christ in the clouds, shall be set on his right hand, and, there openly acknowledged and acquitted, shall join with him in the judging of reprobate angels and men; and shall be received into heaven, where they shall be fully and forever freed from all sin and misery; filled with inconceivable joy; made perfectly holy and happy both in body and soul, in the company of innumerable saints and angels, but especially in the immediate vision and fruition of God the Father, of our Lord Jesus Christ, and of the Holy Spirit, to all eternity. And this is the perfect and full communion, which the members of the invisible church shall enjoy with Christ in glory, at the resurrection and day of judgment.) | (A. At the resurrection, believers, being raised up in glory, shall be openly acknowledged, and acquitted in the day of judgment, and made perfectly blessed in the full enjoying of God to all eternity.) |

# EXPLANATORY NOTES

I BELIEVE in the communion of saints." This clause is a late addition to the Apostles' Creed. The aim of this added clause was to remind living believers, who repeat the Creed, of their connection with a far larger company of fellow Christians who have finished their course, and are now in heaven, inheriting the promises. "Communion of saints" embodies a grand spiritual fact, *viz.*, that all godly, believing people from remote ages and distant lands to the here and the now constitute one brotherhood and share substantially the same privileges and hopes. The practice of the communion of saints involves the cultivation of the sense of unity and community with all true believers living and dead. The idea may be too mystical for most, yet the realization of it would greatly enlarge the boundaries of life.

It is interesting and instructive to compare what the Confession and the Larger Catechism have to say on this subject.

### CONF. XXVIII:1-2

In the first section of the Confession are three points of teaching:

1. The basis of communion (whether of Christians with Christ or of Christians one with another) is union. (*Cf.* L.C. 65-66.)

2. The benefits of communion with Christ, with saints. Read and analyze the Confession first.

### L.C. 65, 69, 82-83, 86, (90); (S.C. 36-38)

The Catechisms limit their statements to the benefits of communion with Christ: first, in grace (L.C. 69, S.C. 36); then, in glory (L.C. 82), subdividing the benefits of communion in glory into those received in this life (L.C. 83); those received immediately after death (L.C. 86, S.C. 37); and those received at the judgment (L.C. 90, S.C. 38). Mark the benefits in each case.

3. The duties arising out of union.

The first section of this chapter is about real saints — saints in fact. The second section is about saints by profession. Is it about them only? If so, how do you account for some things said about them? Can those who are saints only in name "maintain an holy fellowship and communion in the worship of God," and perform "such other spiritual services as tend to their mutual edification'? Formal saints can perform only formal service and worship, they are not capable of mutual spiritual edification.

The second section may be analyzed as follows: Saints *by their profession* are bound to the following duties:

1. The duty of fellowship in the worship of God. This involves church attendance, praise, prayer, and giving.

2. The performance of such other spiritual services as tend to edification. For particulars see proof texts.

3. Fellowship in giving and receiving according to their several abilities and necessities.

4. The extension of such communion to all who in every place call upon the name of the Lord. How is this to be done? See proof texts.

### CONF. XXVIII:3

The third section is meant to safeguard the doctrine of communion of saints from two erroneous opinions: one relating to the saints' communion with Christ; the other relating to their communion with one another. A few extremists have held the notions here condemned.

This section has little value for this present time. Its interest is mainly historical.

# CHAPTER XXIX

# Of the Word and the Sacraments[*]

## Part One: The Word

LARGER CATECHISM (153), 154-160 · SHORTER CATECHISM (85), 88-90

| THE WESTMINSTER CONFESSION OF FAITH | THE WESTMINSTER LARGER CATECHISM | THE WESTMINSTER SHORTER CATECHISM |
|---|---|---|
| | (Q. 153. *What doth God require of us, that we may escape his wrath and curse due to us by reason of the transgression of the law?* | (Q. 85. *What doth God require of us, that we may escape his wrath and curse, due to us for sin?* |
| | (A. That we may escape the wrath and curse of God due to us by reason of the transgression of the law, he requireth of us repentance towards God, and faith towards our Lord Jesus Christ, and the diligent use of the outward means whereby Christ communicates to us the benefits of his mediation.) | (A. To escape the wrath and curse of God, due to us for sin, God requireth of us faith in Jesus Christ, repentance unto life, with the diligent use of all the outward means whereby Christ communicateth to us the benefits of redemption.) |
| | Q. 154. *What are the outward means whereby Christ communicates to us the benefits of his mediation?* | Q. 88. *What are the outward and ordinary means whereby Christ communicateth to us the benefits of redemption?* |
| | A. The outward and ordinary means, whereby Christ communicates to his church the benefits of his mediation, are all his ordinances; especially the word, sacraments, and prayer; all which are made effectual to the elect for their salvation.[1] | A. The outward and ordinary means whereby Christ communicateth to us the benefits of redemption are, his ordinances, especially the word, sacraments, and prayer;[1] all of which are made effectual to the elect for salvation. |
| | (1) Matt. 28:19, 20; Acts 2:42, 46; I Tim. 4:16; I Cor. 1:21; Eph. 5:19, 20; Eph. 6:17, 18. | (1) Matt. 28:19, 20; Acts 2:41, 42. |
| | Q. 155. *How is the word made effectual to salvation?* | Q. 89. *How is the word made effectual to salvation?* |
| | A. The Spirit of God maketh the reading, but especially the preaching of the word, an effectual means of enlightening, convincing, and humbling sinners,[1] of driving them out of themselves, and drawing | A. The Spirit of God maketh the reading, but especially the preaching, of the word, an effectual means of convincing and converting sinners,[1] and of building them up in |

[*]At this point we begin a study of the Means of Grace, covering Chapters XXIX-XXXI.

| THE WESTMINSTER CONFESSION OF FAITH | THE WESTMINSTER LARGER CATECHISM | THE WESTMINSTER SHORTER CATECHISM |
|---|---|---|
| | them unto Christ:[2] of conforming them to his image,[3] and subduing them to his will;[4] of strengthening them against temptations and corruptions;[5] of building them up in grace,[6] and establishing their hearts in holiness and comfort through faith unto salvation.[7] | holiness and comfort through faith unto salvation.[2] |

The Larger Catechism column continues:

(1) Jer. 23:28, 29; Heb. 4:12; Acts 17:11, 12; Acts 26:18.
(2) Acts 2:37, 41; Acts 8:27-38.
(3) II Cor. 3:18; Col. 1:27.
(4) II Cor. 10:4, 5; Rom. 6:17.
(5) Psa. 19:11; Col. 1:28; Eph. 6:16, 17; Matt. 4:7, 10.
(6) Eph. 4:11, 12; Acts 20:32; II Tim. 3:15, 16; I Cor. 3:9-11.
(7) Rom. 16:25; I Thess. 3:2, 13; Rom. 10:14-17.

Q. 156. *Is the word of God to be read by all?*

A. Although all are not permitted to read the word publicly to the congregation, yet all sorts of people are bound to read it apart by themselves,[1] and with their families;[2] to which end, the holy Scriptures are to be translated out of the original into the language of every people unto whom they come.[3]

(1) Deut. 17:18, 19; Isa. 34:16; John 5:39; Rev. 1:3.
(2) Deut. 6:6, 7; Psa. 78:5, 6.
(3) I Cor. 14:18, 19.
　　See context.

Q. 157. *How is the word of God to be read?*

A. The holy Scriptures are to be read with an high and reverent esteem of them;[1] with a firm persuasion that they are the very word of God,[2] and that he only can enable us to understand them;[3] with desire to know, believe, and obey, the will of God revealed in them;[4] with diligence,[5] and attention to the matter and scope of them;[6] with meditation,[7] application,[8] self-denial,[9] and prayer.[10]

(1) Psa. 119:97; Neh. 8:5; Isa. 66:2.
(2) I Thess. 2:13; II Pet. 1:16-21.
(3) Psa. 119:18; Luke 24:44-48.

The Shorter Catechism column continues:

(1) Psa. 19:7; Psa. 119:130; Heb. 4:12.
(2) I Thess. 1:6; Rom. 1:16; Rom. 16:25; Acts 20:32.

Q. 90. *How is the word to be read and heard, that it may become effectual to salvation?*

A. That the word may become effectual to salvation, we must attend thereunto with diligence,[1] preparation,[2] and prayer;[3] receive it with faith[4] and love,[5] lay it up in our hearts,[6] and practice it in our lives.[7]

(1) Prov. 8:34.
(2) Luke 8:18; I Pet. 2:1, 2.
(3) Psa. 119:18.
(4) Heb. 4:2.
(5) II Thess. 2:10.
(6) Psa. 119:11.
(7) Luke 8:15; James 1:25.

| THE WESTMINSTER CONFESSION OF FAITH | THE WESTMINSTER LARGER CATECHISM | THE WESTMINSTER SHORTER CATECHISM |
|---|---|---|
| | (4) James 1:21, 22; I Pet. 2:2; Mark 4:20.<br>(5) Acts 17:11; Deut. 11:13.<br>(6) Acts 8:30, 34; Matt. 13:23.<br>(7) Psa. 1:2; Psa. 119:97.<br>(8) Acts 2:38, 39; II Sam. 12:7; II Chron. 34:21.<br>(9) Gal. 1:15, 16; Prov. 3:5.<br>(10) Psa. 119:18; Luke 24:45. | |

**Q. 158.** *By whom is the word of God to be preached?*

A. The word of God is to be preached only by such as are sufficiently gifted,[1] and also duly approved and called to that office.[2]

(1) I Tim. 3:2, 6; II Tim. 2:2; Mal. 2:7.
(2) Rom. 10:15; I Tim. 4:14.

**Q. 159.** *How is the word of God to be preached by those that are called thereunto?*

A. They that are called to labour in the ministry of the word are to preach sound doctrine,[1] diligently, in season, and out of season;[2] plainly,[3] not in the enticing word of man's wisdom, but in demonstration of the Spirit, and of power;[4] faithfully,[5] making known the whole counsel of God;[6] wisely,[7] applying themselves to the necessities and capacities of the hearers;[8] zealously,[9] with fervent love to God,[10] and the souls of his people;[11] sincerely,[12] aiming at his glory,[13] and their conversion,[14] edification,[15] and salvation.[16]

(1) Tit. 2:1, 8.
(2) Acts 18:25; II Tim. 4:2.
(3) I Cor. 14:9.
(4) I Cor. 2:4.
(5) Jer. 23:28; I Cor. 4:1, 2; Matt. 24:45-47.
(6) Acts 20:27.
(7) Col. 1:28; II Tim. 2:15.
(8) I Cor. 3:2; Heb. 5:12-14; I Thess. 2:7; Luke 12:42.
(9) Acts 18:25; II Tim. 4:5.
(10) II Cor. 5:13, 14; Phil. 1:15-17.
(11) II Cor. 12:15; I Thess. 3:12.
(12) II Cor. 4:2; II Cor. 2:17.
(13) John 7:18; I Thess. 2:4-6.
(14) I Cor. 9:19, 20, 21, 22.

| THE WESTMINSTER CONFESSION OF FAITH | THE WESTMINSTER LARGER CATECHISM | THE WESTMINSTER SHORTER CATECHISM |
|---|---|---|

(15) II Cor. 12:19; Eph. 4:12.
(16) I Tim. 4:16; II Tim. 2:10; Acts 26:16-18.

Q. 160. *What is required of those that hear the word preached?*

A. It is required of those that hear the word preached, that they attend upon it with diligence,[1] preparation,[2] and prayer;[3] examine what they hear by the Scriptures;[4] receive the truth with faith,[5] love,[6] meekness,[7] and readiness of mind,[8] as the word of God;[9] meditate,[10] and confer of it;[11] hide it in their hearts,[12] and bring forth the fruit of it in their lives.[13]

(1) Psa. 84:1, 2, 4; Psa. 27:4; Prov. 8:34.
(2) Luke 8:18; I Pet. 2:1, 2; James 1:21.
(3) Psa. 119:18; Eph. 6:18, 19.
(4) Acts 17:11.
(5) Heb. 4:2.
(6) II Thess. 2:10.
(7) James 1:21; Psa. 25:9.
(8) Acts 17:11; Acts 2:41.
(9) I Thess. 2:13.
(10) Heb. 2:1.
(11) Deut. 6:6, 7.
(12) Psa. 119:11; Prov. 2:1-5.
(13) Luke 8:15; James 1:25.

# EXPLANATORY NOTES

THE subject of this chapter is closely connected with the subjects of the immediately preceding chapters. It is in and through the church that the communion of saints is realized, and the word, sacraments, and prayer are appointed as means of sustaining and quickening the communion of saints.

The Confession treats of the word, sacraments, and prayer, but not formally and directly as means of grace. But the Catechisms treat of these aids to piety as means of grace; and with this subject the Catechisms bring their discussions to an end.

## L.C. 154; S.C. 88

The Catechisms introduce their discussion of the sacraments with the same preliminary question. How do the statements of the question differ? How do the answers differ?

Through this chapter, wherever the two Catechisms are parallel, begin with the Shorter Catechism, and then note how the Larger enlarges upon the Shorter.

## L.C. 155; S.C. 89

"How is the word made effectual to salvation?" Note the honor put upon preaching in the answers, and how the supreme place is given to the Spirit.

What effects are ascribed to the Word as preached and attended by the Spirit? Can they be summed up in fewer and better words? Mark the phrases, "driving them out of themselves, and drawing them unto Christ." Two motives, a propulsive and an attractive. Unless a man can be brought out of himself he cannot be saved. If the people had been unwilling to go out of Egypt they could never have been brought into the land of promise. "He brought us out," said Moses, "that he might bring us in." (Deut. 6:23.)

## L.C. 156

Question 156 in the Larger Catechism is peculiar to it. The question and answer are aimed at the Church of Rome which forbids or discourages the private reading of the Word, and therefore does not favor the translation of the Scriptures into the language of the people.

## L.C. 157; S.C. 90

The way the Word is read determines the value of the reading. The reader's attitude toward the Bible is of fundamental importance. The heart of the matter is at the center of this statement. The Holy Scriptures are to be read . . . with desire to know, believe, and obey the will of God revealed therein. If one reads with such a motive and object one will read with attention and diligence, with prayer and meditation, and in a spirit of self-application and self-denial.

A man received a copy of the Bible from a friend. Opening it at the flyleaf he found four words written which told him what to do with it. These words were:

Admit
Commit
Submit (to)
Transmit

Whosoever reads the Bible with the view of doing those four things will find the reading a blessed experience.

## L.C. 158

It is not enough that the Word should be *read by* all, it must be *preached to* all. That it may be preached, there must be preachers. By whom is the Word of God to be preached?

The answer is threefold: only by such as are sufficiently gifted, duly approved, and called thereto.

Would the absence of any one of these disqualify a man for the gospel ministry? Try the process of elimination. Shall we eliminate the gift? the approval? the call? No! No one of the three can be omitted.

There must be not only a call, but two calls — one from God and one from men. Twofold also must be the approval. And the gifts must be of two kinds — natural and spiritual. Of gifts for the ministry some are physical; some are mental and cultural; others are moral and spiritual.

The office of minister of the gospel should be more jealously guarded against unfitness and incompetence by those responsible for passing on the qualifications of candidates.

## L.C. 159

How is the word to be preached? The answer first tells us what is to be preached, namely, "sound doctrine." A healthy life cannot be maintained on an unhealthy diet. If corrupting the food of the body is a crime deserving to be severely punished, how shall we estimate the ill-desert of the sin of adulterating the food of the soul?

The manner of preaching sound doctrine is laid down in six heads. Mark the adverbs, and consider the explanatory clauses which follow. This statement is a good lesson in homiletics. The preacher should return again and again to this paragraph. The "how" is next in importance to the "what."

## L.C. 160

What is required of those who hear the Word is not essentially different from what is required of those who read the Word. (Compare answer to 160 with answer to 157.)

## S.C. 90

You will observe that the Shorter Catechism combines the two questions into one. The progress of the soul in the appropriation of the truth may be stated in several stages. Attention is in order to knowledge; knowledge is in order to faith; faith is in order to obedience; and obedience is in order to holiness, and the image of God.

# Of the Word and the Sacraments

## Part Two: The Sacraments*

CONFESSION OF FAITH XXIX:1-5
LARGER CATECHISM 161-164 · SHORTER CATECHISM 91-93

SACRAMENTS are holy signs and seals of the covenant of grace, immediately instituted by God,[1] to represent Christ and his benefits, and to confirm our interest in him:[2] as also to put a visible difference between those that belong unto the church, and the rest of the world;[3] and solemnly to engage them to the service of God in Christ, according to his word.[4]

(1) Gen. 17:9, 10, 11; Ex. 13:9, 10; Rom. 4:11; Ex. 12:3-20.
(2) I Cor. 10:16; I Cor. 11:25, 26; Gal. 3:27.
(3) Ex. 12:48; Heb. 13:10; I Cor. 11:27, 28, 29.
(4) Rom. 6:3, 4; I Cor. 10:14, 15, 16. See context.

Q. 162. *What is a sacrament?*

A. A sacrament is an holy ordinance instituted by Christ in his church,[1] to signify, seal, and exhibit[2] unto those that are within the covenant of grace,[3] the benefits of his mediation;[4] to strengthen and increase their faith and all other graces;[5] to oblige them to obedience;[6] to testify and cherish their love and communion one with another,[7] and to distinguish them from those that are without.[8]

(1) Matt. 28:19; Matt. 26:26, 27.
(2) Rom. 4:11; I Cor. 11:24, 25.
(3) Rom. 9:8; Gal. 3:27, 29; Gal. 5:6; Gal. 6:15.
(4) Acts 2:38; I Cor. 10:16; Acts 22:16.
(5) I Cor. 11:24-26.
(6) Rom. 6:4; I Cor. 10:21.
(7) I Cor. 12:13; I Cor. 10:17; Eph. 4:3-5.
(8) I Cor. 10:21.

Q. 92. *What is a sacrament?*

A. A sacrament is a holy ordinance instituted by Christ, wherein, by sensible signs, Christ and the benefits of the new covenant are represented,[1] sealed, and applied to believers.[2]

(1) Matt. 28:19; Matt. 26:26, 27, 28.
(2) Rom. 4:11.

2. There is in every sacrament a spiritual relation, or sacramental union, between the sign and the thing signified; whence it comes to pass that the names and effects of the one are attributed to the other.[5]
(5) Gen. 17:10; Matt. 26:27, 28; Tit. 3:5.

*The parts of the Standards listed here relate to the sacraments in general. For the treatises on the sacraments in particular, see Chapters XXX and XXXI.

Q. 163. *What are the parts of a sacrament?*

A. The parts of a sacrament are two: the one, an outward and sensible sign used according to Christ's own appointment; the other, an inward and spiritual grace thereby signified.[1]

(1) See Confession of Faith, Chapter XXIX, Section 2, and passages there cited.

| THE WESTMINSTER CONFESSION OF FAITH | THE WESTMINSTER LARGER CATECHISM | THE WESTMINSTER SHORTER CATECHISM |
|---|---|---|
| 3. The grace which is exhibited in or by the sacraments, rightly used, is not conferred by any power in them; neither doth the efficacy of a sacrament depend upon the piety or intention of him that doth administer it, but upon the work of the Spirit,[6] and the word of institution, which contains, together with a precept authorizing the use thereof, a promise of benefit to worthy receivers.[7]<br><br>(6) Rom. 2:28, 29; I Cor. 3:7; I Cor. 6:11; John 3:5; Acts 8:13-23.<br>(7) John 6:63. | Q. 161. *How do the sacraments become effectual means of salvation?*<br><br>A. The sacraments become effectual means of salvation, not by any power in themselves or any virtue derived from the piety or intention of him by whom they are administered; but only by the working of the Holy Ghost, and the blessing of Christ by whom they are instituted.[1]<br><br>(1) I Pet. 3:21; Acts 8:13, 23; I Cor. 3:7; I Cor. 6:11. | Q. 91. *How do the sacraments become effectual means of salvation?*<br><br>A. The sacraments become effectual means of salvation, not from any virtue in them, or in him that doth administer them; but only by the blessing of Christ, and the working of his Spirit in them that by faith receive them.[1]<br><br>(1) I Pet. 3:21; Acts 8:13, 23. See intervening context. I Cor. 3:7; I Cor. 6:11; I Cor. 12:13. |
| 4. There be only two sacraments ordained by Christ our Lord in the gospel, that is to say, baptism and the supper of the Lord:[8] neither of which may be dispensed by any but by a minister of the word, lawfully ordained.[9]<br><br>(8) Matt. 28:19; I Cor. 11:20, 23.<br>(9) See General Note, Chapter I. | Q. 164. *How many sacraments hath Christ instituted under the New Testament?*<br><br>A. Under the New Testament Christ hath instituted in his church only two sacraments, baptism, and the Lord's supper.[1]<br><br>(1) Matt. 28:19; Matt. 26:26, 27; I Cor. 11:23-26. | Q. 93. *Which are the sacraments of the New Testament?*<br><br>A. The sacraments of the New Testament are, baptism,[1] and the Lord's supper.[2]<br><br>(1) Matt. 28:19.<br>(2) I Cor. 11:23.<br>See the context. |
| 5. The sacraments of the Old Testament, in regard of the spiritual things thereby signified and exhibited, were, for substance, the same with those of the New.[10]<br><br>(10) Col. 2:11, 12; I Cor. 5:7, 8. | | |

# EXPLANATORY NOTES

THE Standards give ample space to the sacraments, thus emphasizing the importance of the subject.

All three parts of the Standards first treat of the sacraments in general, and then of each sacrament in particular.

### CONF. XXIX:1; L.C. 162; S.C. 92

A comparative statement here may prove helpful. The Word is the universal means of grace. The Word is preached to all, believers and unbelievers;

the sacraments are applied to believers only: "Unto those that are within the covenant of grace."

The Word is the instrument of regeneration, the means of begetting faith and repentance, of converting the soul, of further sanctifying the regenerate. The sacraments are meant to edify those who are already in grace. The Word is used to originate the communion of saints, whereas the function of the sacraments is to quicken and sustain that communion.

The Word is effective without the sacraments, but the sacraments would be meaningless and worthless without the Word. The Word is the gospel addressed to the ear; the sacraments are the gospel addressed to the eye. The Word declares the whole counsel of God; the sacraments represent pictorially redemption only — redemption purchased and applied.

Following the Confession, we begin with definition. What is a sacrament? Study the answers beginning with the briefest statement — that of the Shorter Catechism — and then look for amplifications and additions in the other statements.

Analysis of the combined statements yields three teaching points.

1. The origin of the sacraments — instituted by God (Conf.); Instituted by Christ (the Catechisms).

2. The nature of the sacraments — they are holy ordinances.

3. The design of the sacraments — it is several-fold:
   a. To instruct; "to signify"; "to seal."
   b. To edify; "to strengthen and increase" faith and other graces.
   c. "To oblige," "to engage" — whom? to what?
   d. "To testify" and cherish love and communion of saints.
   e. To distinguish saints, "to put a visible difference" between them and others, to serve as a badge of church membership.

If all this is true of a sacrament, how rich its significance! These pregnant statements lie ready to hand for the preacher's use.

## CONF. XXIX:2; L.C. 163

Question 163 of the Larger Catechism relates to the parts of a sacrament, and the second section of the Confession is concerned with the relation between the parts. Give the number and the names of the parts in the two sacraments.

More difficult is the relation between the inward and the outward in the sacraments. There is a natural relationship between them. That is, there is in water a natural fitness to symbolize cleansing — water being the universal cleansing element in nature. And there is a natural fitness in bread and

wine to represent nourishment. This is the relation of the congruity. Upon this natural relationship is erected the spiritual relationship. This sacramental relation or union is established by divine appointment. This is the relation of divine constitution. "From this union arises what has been called sacramental phraseology, or certain expressions in which the names of the sign and the thing signified are exchanged. Thus, the name of the sign is given to the thing signified, when Christ is called 'our passover'; and the name of the thing signified is given to the sign, when the bread is called the body of Christ. The foundation of this interchange is the sacramental union, which so couples them together that the one may be predicated of the other." (Dick, in *Shaw On the Confession*, p. 306.)

## CONF. XXIX:3; L.C. 161; S.C. 91

The Confession and both Catechisms treat of the efficacy of the sacraments. They answer the question: To what is the efficacy of the sacraments due? They all deny what the Church of Rome affirms, namely,

1. That the grace is so tied to the sacrament that when it is rightly administered, the recipient of the rite receives the grace.

2. That the intention of the administrator is essential to a sacrament.

Give reasons why we cannot accept such doctrines.

Then the Standards affirm what we believe to be the truth about this matter. The efficacy of the sacraments, *i.e.*, their power to produce blessed effects, is due to three things according to the Confession, to two, according to the Catechisms. Are the two things named by the Catechisms equivalent to the three things mentioned by the Confession? What is the difference, if any, between the blessing of Christ and the working of the Holy Spirit?

## CONF. XXIX:4; L.C. 164; S.C. 93

Why are the Standards at pains to affirm, each one affirming, thus making a threefold affirmation, that Christ hath instituted only two sacraments? Because Rome teaches that there are seven sacraments. How is the question of the number to be decided? By applying the test of the things essential to a sacrament. The things essential to a sacrament are divine institution, an outward visible sign, and an inward invisible grace. And these are not arbitrarily determined, but are arrived at by a study of the two universally accepted sacraments, baptism and the Lord's Supper. To these two sacraments instituted by Christ the Church of Rome has added five others: marriage, confirmation, penance, orders, extreme unction. These cannot stand the threefold test just given.

This fourth section of the Confession teaches that the sacraments may not be dispensed by any but a minister of the Word, lawfully ordained. This is said in opposition to the Roman Catholic Church, which permits laymen and women to administer the sacrament of baptism in extreme cases.

## CONF. XXIX:5

Why did the framers of the Confession think it necessary to affirm that the sacraments of the Old Testament were, for substance, the same as those of the New? Because the Church of Rome denies this, teaching that the old sacraments are no more than figures and shadows of the new. We hold that the sacraments of the Old Testament were signs and seals of the same covenant as the sacraments of the New Testament, and that they signified the same blessings. There is no Scripture warrant for denying that they actually conveyed the grace which they pointed to.

# CHAPTER XXX

# Of Baptism

CONFESSION OF FAITH XXX:1-7
LARGER CATECHISM 165-167 · SHORTER CATECHISM 94-95

BAPTISM is a sacrament of the New Testament, ordained by Jesus Christ,[1] not only for the solemn admission of the party baptized into the visible church,[2] but also to be unto him a sign and seal of the covenant of grace,[3] of his ingrafting into Christ,[4] of regeneration,[5] of remission of sins,[6] and of his giving up unto God, through Jesus Christ, to walk in newness of life:[7] which sacrament is, by Christ's own appointment, to be continued in his church until the end of the world.[8]

(1) Matt. 28:19.
(2) Acts 2:41; Acts 10:47.
(3) Rom. 4:11. Compare with Gal. 3:29; Col. 2:11, 12.
(4) Gal. 3:27; Rom. 6:3, 4.
(5) Tit. 3:5.
(6) Acts 2:38; Mark 1:4; Acts 22:16.
(7) Rom. 6:3, 4.
(8) Matt. 28:19, 20.

2. The outward element to be used in this sacrament is water, wherewith the party is to be baptized in the name of the Father, and of the Son, and of the Holy Ghost,[9] by a minister of the gospel, lawfully called thereunto.[10]

(9) Acts 10:47; Acts 8:36, 38; Matt. 28:19; Eph. 4:11-13.
(10) See General Note, Chapter I.

3. Dipping of the person into the water is not necessary; but baptism is rightly administered by pouring,

Q. 165. *What is baptism?*

A. Baptism is a sacrament of the New Testament, wherein Christ hath ordained the washing with water in the name of the Father, and of the Son, and of the Holy Ghost,[1] to be a sign and seal of ingrafting into himself,[2] of remission of sins by his blood,[3] and regeneration by his Spirit;[4] of adoption,[5] and resurrection unto everlasting life:[6] and whereby the parties baptized are solemnly admitted into the visible church,[7] and enter into an open and professed engagement to be wholly and only the Lord's.[8]

(1) Matt. 28:19.
(2) Gal. 3:27; Rom. 6:3.
(3) Acts 22:16; Mark 1:4; Rev. 1:5.
(4) John 3:5; Tit. 3:5.
(5) Gal. 3:26, 27.
(6) I Cor. 15:29.
(7) Acts 2:41.
(8) Rom. 6:4.

Q. 94. *What is baptism?*

A. Baptism is a sacrament, wherein the washing with water, in the name of the Father, and of the Son, and of the Holy Ghost,[1] doth signify and seal our ingrafting into Christ, and partaking of the benefits of the covenant of grace,[2] and our engagement to be the Lord's.[3]

(1) See Matt. 28:19 cited under Question 93 above.
(2) Gal. 3:27; Rom. 6:3.
(3) Rom. 6:4.

| THE WESTMINSTER CONFESSION OF FAITH | THE WESTMINSTER LARGER CATECHISM | THE WESTMINSTER SHORTER CATECHISM |
|---|---|---|

**CONFESSION OF FAITH**

or sprinkling water upon the person.[11]

(11) Mark 7:4; Acts 1:5; Acts 2:3, 4, 17; Acts 11:15, 16; Heb. 9:10, 19-21.

4. Not only those that do actually profess faith in and obedience unto Christ,[12] but also the infants of one or both believing parents are to be baptized.[13]

(12) See citations under Section 1 above.
(13) Gen. 17:7, 9, 10; Gal. 3:9, 14; Rom. 4:11, 12; Acts 2:38, 39; Acts 16:14, 15, 33; Col. 2:11, 12; I Cor. 7:14; Mark 10:13-16; Luke 18:15, 16.

5. Although it be a great sin to contemn or neglect this ordinance,[14] yet grace and salvation are not so inseparably annexed unto it as that no person can be regenerated or saved without it,[15] or that all that are baptized are undoubtedly regenerated.[16]

(14) Luke 7:30; Gen. 17:14.
(15) Rom. 4:11; Luke 23:40, 41, 42, 43; Acts 10:45-47.
(16) Acts 8:13, 23.

6. The efficacy of baptism is not tied to that moment of time wherein it is administered;[17] yet, notwithstanding, by the right use of this ordinance the grace promised is not only offered, but really exhibited and conferred by the Holy Ghost, to such (whether of age or infants) as that grace belongeth unto, according to the counsel of God's own will, in his appointed time.[18]

(17) John 3:5, 8; Rom. 4:11.
(18) Gal. 3:27; Eph. 1:4, 5; Eph. 5:25, 26; Acts 2:38-41; Acts 16:31, 33.

7. The sacrament of baptism is but once to be administered to any person.[19]

(19) There is no command, and no adequate example for the repetition of baptism.

**LARGER CATECHISM**

Q. 166. *Unto whom is baptism to be administered?*

A. Baptism is not to be administered to any that are out of the visible church, and so strangers from the covenant of promise, till they profess their faith in Christ, and obedience to him;[1] but infants descending from parents, either both or but one of them, professing faith in Christ, and obedience to him, are, in that respect, within the covenant, and are to be baptized.[2]

(1) Acts 2:41.
(2) Acts 2:38, 39; I Cor. 7:14; Luke 18:16; Rom. 11:16; Gen. 17:7-9, compared with Col. 2:11, 12; Gal. 3:17, 18, 29.

**SHORTER CATECHISM**

Q. 95. *To whom is baptism to be administered?*

A. Baptism is not to be administered to any that are out of the visible church, till they profess their faith in Christ, and obedience to him;[1] but the infants of such as are members of the visible church, are to be baptized.[2]

(1) Acts 2:41.
(2) Gen. 17:7, 10; Gal. 3:17, 18, 29; Acts 2:38, 39.

| THE WESTMINSTER CONFESSION OF FAITH | THE WESTMINSTER LARGER CATECHISM | THE WESTMINSTER SHORTER CATECHISM |
|---|---|---|

**Q. 167.** *How is our baptism to be improved by us?*

A. The needful but much neglected duty of improving our baptism, is to be performed by us all our life long, especially in the time of temptation,[1] and when we are present at the administration of it to others, by serious and thankful consideration of the nature of it, and of the ends for which Christ instituted it, the privileges and benefits conferred and sealed thereby, and our solemn vow made therein;[2] by being humbled for our sinful defilement, our falling short of, and walking contrary to, the grace of baptism and our engagements;[3] by growing up to assurance of pardon of sin, and of all other blessings sealed to us in that sacrament;[4] by drawing strength from the death and resurrection of Christ, into whom we are baptized, for the mortifying of sin, and quickening of grace;[5] and by endeavoring to live by faith,[6] to have our conversation in holiness and righteousness,[7] as those that have therein given up their names to Christ, and to walk in brotherly love, as being baptized by the same Spirit into one body.[8]

(1) Psa. 22:10, 11.
(2) Rom. 6:3-5.
(3) Rom. 6:2, 3; I Cor. 1:11-13.
(4) I Pet. 3:21; Rom. 4:11, 12.
(5) Rom. 6:2, 3, 4.
(6) Gal. 3:26, 27.
(7) Rom. 6:22.
(8) I Cor. 12:13, 25, 26.
See context.

# EXPLANATORY NOTES

## CONF. XXX:1; L.C. 165; S.C. 94

What is baptism?

All three parts of the Standards answer this question.

By combining the answers we get the following points of teaching:

1. The nature of baptism — a sacrament, a washing with water.
2. The origin of baptism — ordained by Christ.
3. The design of baptism:
   a. A rite of initiation into the visible church.
   b. A sign and seal of the covenant of grace.
   c. A sign and seal of ingrafting into Christ, which involves regeneration and remission of sins.
   d. Engagement to be the Lord's and to walk in newness of life.
4. Perpetuity of the sacrament.

## CONF. XXX:2

The second section embraces three points which any reader can name. It may be passed without comment, except the last part: "by a minister of the gospel, lawfully called thereunto." The church recognizes lay preaching of the Word, why not recognize lay administration of the sacraments? A sacrament is only a visible word — the Word pictured to the eye. Are the sacraments more sacred than the Word?

Dr. James Rankin in *The Creed in Scotland*, page 265, says that Dr. Hatch in his book, *Organization of the Early Churches*, proves to demonstration that common members of the early churches (in the absence of ordained men) were in the habit of celebrating the Lord's Supper.

## CONF. XXX:3

The third section relates to the mode of baptism. It says that dipping of the person into the water is not necessary. Not necessary for what? For real and valid baptism. It further says that baptism is rightly administered by pouring or sprinkling water upon the person. If it is rightly administered by this mode, then is it wrongly administered by any other mode?

It is sometimes said that the Westminster Assembly came within one vote of affirming that immersion is the Scriptural way of baptizing. The truth is that the Westminster Assembly refused by one vote to approve immersion as a Scriptural mode.

The Presbyterian church receives into its membership without re-baptism persons who have been immersed, and yet it refuses to practice immersion. Is it inconsistent? No; because it does not regard the method of using the water as essential to valid baptism, and therefore considers it not a necessary condition of church membership. The acceptance of a person who has been baptized by immersion does not imply the approval of the mode of his baptism any more than the acceptance of a Seventh Day Adventist implies the approval of his peculiar views.

Neither of the Catechisms makes a deliverance on the mode of baptism. They describe baptism as a washing with water, and indicate nothing as to the method of the washing.

## CONF. XXX:4; L.C. 166; S.C. 95

The Confession and both Catechisms make declarations concerning the subjects of baptism. They all affirm that adults who profess faith in and obedience to Christ are to be baptized. This is admitted by all evangelical churches. Our Standards declare further that the infants of one or both believing parents are to be baptized. On this question Christendom is divided.

The scope of these notes does not permit a full defense of infant baptism. I will say that the practice is defensible. Infant baptism ought to be preached and it ought to be practiced. The paedobaptists say so little about the matter that anti-paedobaptists take this silence as an admission that there is little to be said. There is so much to be said that I cannot here attempt to say it. But here is a condensed reply to one who may ask why we baptize the infants of a believer:

1. As a sign of the infant's right. As he was born within the covenant, he has the right to receive the seal of the covenant. In his case baptism is a rite, not of initiation, but of recognition.

2. As a sign of his need. The infant has need of the cleansing which baptism signifies. Baptism of infants is a witness to native depravity.

3. As a sign of God's covenant promise. The promise of the covenant is to the children of believing parents.

4. As a seal of God's covenant blessing. Baptism confers grace, and not merely signifies it.

## CONF. XXX:5-6

Sections 5 and 6 are about the efficacy of baptism. The fifth teaches that baptism is neither saving in itself nor essential to salvation. For a person may be saved without it, and a person may be lost with it. This is said in opposition to the Church of Rome which teaches baptismal regeneration, and therefore the necessity of baptism for salvation.

Yet this section teaches that baptism is necessary and its neglect sinful. Why are these things so? Because baptism has been required, appointed. Its omission, therefore, is disobedience, and disobedience is sin.

Both Protestants and Catholics teach the necessity of baptism: the former, the necessity of precept; the latter, the necessity of means; that is, that the blessings which it signifies cannot be otherwise obtained. The distinction is important. (Hodge, III:516-517.)

The sixth section embraces two points:

1. Baptism may not produce its intended effects at the time of its administration; but,

2. If the ordinance is rightly used, the grace promised will be received in the appointed time by those to whom in the purpose of God it belongs.

## CONF. XXX:7

The truth of the last section is seen in the light of the immediately preceding. If the ordinance of baptism rightly used sooner or later accomplishes its object, there can be no need for repeating it. Yes, yes; but suppose a man is not satisfied with his baptism, and requests that he be baptized again by the same or another mode, would any principle be sacrificed if his request were granted?

## L.C. 167

The Larger Catechism has a question in regard to baptism which is peculiar to itself. It is an inquiry concerning the improvement of our baptism, *our* baptism. We can speak thus of baptism, but not so of the Lord's Supper. There is a baptism which is our own, but there is no Lord's Supper which is our own. Baptism is individual, but the supper is social. Baptism is received once for all, but the supper is repeated again and again through the years, so that we have frequent opportunity to improve the sacrament of the supper by repeated participation in it with others. With baptism it is different. If we are to improve our baptism, the best way is to witness the baptism of others, and apply every part and the whole of the ceremony to ourselves. This can be done by recollection, meditation, imagination, and prayer. Read and study the answer to this Larger Catechism question. It affords the worshippers guidance. There is guidance for the preacher also in his counsel and his prayers.

# CHAPTER XXXI

# Of the Lord's Supper

CONFESSION OF FAITH XXXI:1-8
LARGER CATECHISM 168-177 · SHORTER CATECHISM 96-97

## THE WESTMINSTER CONFESSION OF FAITH

OUR Lord Jesus, in the night wherein he was betrayed, instituted the sacrament of his body and blood, called the Lord's Supper, to be observed in his church unto the end of the world; for the perpetual remembrance of the sacrifice of himself in his death, the sealing all benefits thereof unto true believers, their spiritual nourishment and growth in him, their further engagement in and to all duties which they owe unto him; and to be a bond and pledge of their communion with him, and with each other, as members of his mystical body.[1]

(1) I Cor. 11:23, 24, 25, 26; Matt. 26:26, 27; Luke 22:19, 20; I Cor. 10:16, 17, 21; I Cor. 12:13.

2. In this sacrament Christ is not offered up to his Father, nor any real sacrifice made at all for remission of sins of the quick or dead, but a commemoration of that one offering up of himself, by himself, upon the cross, once for all, and a spiritual oblation of all possible praise unto God for the same; so that the so-called sacrifice of the mass is most contradictory to Christ's one sacrifice, the only propitiation for all the sins of the elect.[2]

(2) Heb. 9:22, 25, 26, 28; Matt. 26:26, 27; Luke 22:19, 20; Heb. 10:11, 12, 14, 18.

## THE WESTMINSTER LARGER CATECHISM

Q. 168. *What is the Lord's supper?*
A. The Lord's supper is a sacrament of the New Testament, wherein by giving and receiving bread and wine according to the appointment of Jesus Christ, his death is showed forth;[1] and they that worthily communicate, feed upon his body and blood to their spiritual nourishment and growth in grace;[2] have their union and communion with him confirmed; testify and renew their thankfulness and engagement to God,[3] and their mutual love and fellowship each with other, as members of the same mystical body.[4]

(1) I Cor. 11:26.
(2) Matt. 25:26, 27; I Cor. 11:23-27.
(3) I Cor. 10:16-21.
(4) I Cor. 10:17.

## THE WESTMINSTER SHORTER CATECHISM

Q. 96. *What is the Lord's supper?*
A. The Lord's supper is a sacrament, wherein, by giving and receiving bread and wine, according to Christ's appointment, his death is showed forth;[1] and the worthy receivers are, not after a corporal and carnal manner, but by faith, made partakers of his body and blood, with all his benefits, to their spiritual nourishment and growth in grace.[2]

(1) Matt. 26:26, 27; I Cor. 11:26.
(2) I Cor. 10:16; Eph. 3:17.

{ 210 }

| THE WESTMINSTER CONFESSION OF FAITH | THE WESTMINSTER LARGER CATECHISM | THE WESTMINSTER SHORTER CATECHISM |
|---|---|---|

**CONFESSION OF FAITH**

3. The Lord Jesus hath, in this ordinance, appointed his ministers to declare his word of institution to the people, to pray, and bless the elements of bread and wine, and thereby to set them apart from a common to an holy use; and to take and break the bread, to take the cup, and (they communicating also themselves) to give both to the communicants.[3]

(3) See citations under Sections 1, 2.

4. Private masses, or receiving this sacrament by a priest, or any other, alone; as likewise the denial of the cup to the people; worshipping the elements, the lifting them up, or carrying them about for adoration, and the reserving them for any pretended religious use, are all contrary to the nature of this sacrament, and to the institution of Christ.[4]

(4) Matt. 15:9.
   NOTE.—There is not the least appearance of a warrant for any of these things, either in precept or example, in any part of the word of God. See all the places in which the ordinance is mentioned.

5. The outward elements in this sacrament, duly set apart to the uses ordained by Christ, have such relation to him crucified, as that truly, yet sacramentally only, they are sometimes called by the name of the things they represent, to wit, the body and blood of Christ;[5] albeit, in substance and nature, they still remain truly, and only, bread and wine, as they were before.[6]

(5) Matt. 26:26, 27, 28.
(6) I Cor. 11:26, 27.

**LARGER CATECHISM**

Q. 169. *How hath Christ appointed bread and wine to be given and received in the sacrament of the Lord's supper?*

A. Christ hath appointed the ministers of his word, in the administration of this sacrament of the Lord's supper, to set apart the bread and wine from common use by the word of institution, thanksgiving, and prayer; to take and break the bread, and to give both the bread and the wine to the communicants; who are by the same appointment to take and eat the bread, and to drink the wine; in thankful remembrance that the body of Christ was broken and given, and his blood shed for them.[1]

(1) See General Note, Larger Catechism, Question 1.

| THE WESTMINSTER CONFESSION OF FAITH | THE WESTMINSTER LARGER CATECHISM | THE WESTMINSTER SHORTER CATECHISM |
|---|---|---|

**THE WESTMINSTER CONFESSION OF FAITH**

6. That doctrine which maintains a change of the substance of bread and wine, into the substance of Christ's body and blood (commonly called transubstantiation) by consecration of a priest, or by any other way, is repugnant, not to Scripture alone, but even to common sense and reason; overthroweth the nature of the sacrament; and hath been, and is, the cause of manifold superstitions, yea, of gross idolatries.[7]

(7) These statements are inferences from the doctrine of the sacraments, and do not require specific Scripture proofs.

7. Worthy receivers, outwardly partaking of the visible elements in this sacrament, do then also inwardly by faith, really and indeed, yet not carnally and corporally, but spiritually, receive and feed upon Christ crucified, and all benefits of his death: the body and blood of Christ being then not corporally and carnally in, with, or under the bread and wine; yet as really, but spiritually, present to the faith of believers in that ordinance, as the elements themselves are to their outward senses.[8]

(8) I Cor. 10:16; John 6:53-58. See Note under Section 6 above.

**THE WESTMINSTER LARGER CATECHISM**

Q. 170. *How do they that worthily communicate in the Lord's supper feed upon the body and blood of Christ therein?*

A. As the body and blood of Christ are not corporally or carnally present in, with, or under the bread and wine in the Lord's supper;[1] and yet are spiritually present to the faith of the receiver, no less truly and really than the elements themselves are to their outward senses;[2] so they that worthily communicate in the sacrament of the Lord's supper, do therein feed upon the body and blood of Christ, not after a corporal or carnal, but in a spiritual manner; yet truly and really,[3] while by faith they receive and apply unto themselves Christ crucified, and all the benefits of his death.[4]

(1) The specifications enumerated in answers to Questions 170 to 175 are deduced from the nature of the Lord's Supper as set forth in the New Testament. The texts are given to show that these specifications are in accord with the general tenor of the Scriptures.
Acts 3:21.

(2) Gal. 3:1; Heb. 11:1.

(3) John 6:51, 53.
See context.

(4) I Cor. 10:16.

| | | |
|---|---|---|
| THE WESTMINSTER **CONFESSION OF FAITH** | THE WESTMINSTER **LARGER CATECHISM** | THE WESTMINSTER **SHORTER CATECHISM** |

8. Although ignorant and wicked men receive the outward elements in this sacrament, yet they receive not the thing signified thereby; but by their unworthy coming thereunto are guilty of the body and blood of the Lord, and bring judgment on themselves.[9]

(9) I Cor. 11:27, 29; I Cor. 10:21; I Cor. 5:6, 7, 13; II Thess. 3:6, 14, 15.

Q. 171. *How are they that receive the sacrament of the Lord's supper to prepare themselves before they come unto it?*

A. They that receive the sacrament of the Lord's supper are, before they come, to prepare themselves thereunto: by examining themselves,[1] of their being in Christ,[2] of their sins and wants;[3] of the truth and measure of their knowledge,[4] faith,[5] repentance,[6] love to God and the brethren,[7] charity to all men,[8] forgiving those that have done them wrong;[9] of their desires after Christ,[10] and of their new obedience;[11] and by renewing the exercise of these graces,[12] by serious meditation,[13] and fervent prayer.[14]

(1) I Cor. 11:28.
(2) II Cor. 13:5.
(3) I Cor. 5:7; Ex. 12:15.
(4) I Cor. 11:29.
(5) II Cor. 13:5.
(6) I Cor. 11:31.
(7) I Cor. 10:17.
(8) I Cor. 5:8; I Cor. 11:18, 20.
(9) Matt. 5:23, 24.
(10) John 7:37; Luke 1:53; Isa. 55:1.
(11) I Cor. 5:8.
(12) Heb. 10:21, 22, 24; Psa. 26:6.
(13) I Cor. 11:24.
(14) Matt. 26:26; II Chron. 30:18, 19.

Q. 172. *May one who doubteth of his being in Christ, or of his due preparation, come to the Lord's supper?*

A. One who doubteth of his being in Christ, or of his due preparation

Q. 97. *What is required to the worthy receiving of the Lord's supper?*

A. It is required of them that would worthily partake of the Lord's supper, that they examine themselves, of their knowledge to discern the Lord's body,[1] of their faith to feed upon him,[2] of their repentance,[3] love,[4] and new obedience;[5] lest coming unworthily, they eat and drink judgment to themselves.[6]

(1) I Cor. 11:28, 29.
(2) John 6:53, 54, 55, 56.
(3) Zech. 12:10.
(4) I John 4:19; Gal. 5:6.
(5) Rom. 6:4; Rom. 6:17-22.
(6) I Cor. 11:27.

| THE WESTMINSTER CONFESSION OF FAITH | THE WESTMINSTER LARGER CATECHISM | THE WESTMINSTER SHORTER CATECHISM |
|---|---|---|
|  | to the sacrament of the Lord's supper, may have true interest in Christ, though he be not yet assured thereof;[1] and in God's account hath it, if he be duly affected with the apprehension of the want of it,[2] and unfeignedly desirous to be found in Christ,[3] and to depart from iniquity;[4] in which case (because promises are made, and this sacrament is appointed, for the relief even of weak and doubting Christians)[5] he is to bewail his unbelief,[6] and labor to have his doubts resolved;[7] and so doing, he may and ought to come to the Lord's supper, that he may be further strengthened.[8]<br><br>(1) Isa. 50:10.<br>(2) Isa. 54:7, 8, 10; Matt. 5:3, 4; Psa. 31:22.<br>(3) Psa. 42:11.<br>(4) II Tim. 2:19; Rom. 7:24, 25.<br>(5) Matt. 26:28; Matt. 11:28; Isa. 40:11, 29, 31.<br>(6) Mark 9:24.<br>(7) Acts 16:30; Acts 9:6.<br>(8) I Cor. 11:28; Matt. 11:28.<br><br>Q. 173. *May any who profess the faith, and desire to come to the Lord's supper, be kept from it?*<br><br>A. Such as are found to be ignorant or scandalous, notwithstanding their profession of the faith, and desire to come to the Lord's supper, may and ought to be kept from that sacrament by the power which Christ hath left in his church,[1] until they receive instruction, and manifest their reformation.[2]<br><br>(1) I Cor. 11:29; I Cor. 5:11; Matt. 7:6.<br>(2) I Cor. 5:4, 5; II Cor. 2:5-8.<br><br>Q. 174. *What is required of them that receive the sacrament of the Lord's supper, in the time of the administration of it?*<br><br>A. It is required of them that receive the sacrament of the Lord's supper that during the time of the |  |

administration of it, with all holy reverence and attention, they wait upon God in that ordinance; diligently observe the sacramental elements and actions;[1] heedfully discern the Lord's body,[2] and affectionately meditate on his death and sufferings,[3] and thereby stir up themselves to a vigorous exercise of their graces; in judging themselves,[4] and sorrowing for sin;[5] in earnest hungering and thirsting after Christ,[6] feeding on him by faith,[7] receiving of his fullness;[8] trusting in his merits.[9] rejoicing in his love,[10] giving thanks for his grace;[11] in renewing of their covenant with God,[12] and love to all the saints.[13]

(1) Gal. 3:1.
(2) I Cor. 11:29.
(3) Luke 22:19.
(4) I Cor. 11:31.
(5) Zech. 12:10.
(6) Psa. 63:1, 2.
(7) Gal. 2:20; John 6:35.
(8) John 1:16; Col. 1:19.
(9) Phil. 3:9.
(10) I Pet. 1:8; II Chron. 30:21.
(11) Psa. 22:26.
(12) Jer. 50:5; Psa. 50:5.
(13) I Cor. 10:17; Acts 2:42.

Q. 175. *What is the duty of Christians after they have received the sacrament of the Lord's supper?*

A. The duty of Christians after they have received the sacrament of the Lord's supper, is seriously to consider how they have behaved themselves therein, and with what success:[1] if they find quickening and comfort, to bless God for it,[2] beg the continuance of it, watch against relapse,[3] fulfill their vows,[4] and encourage themselves to a frequent attendance on that ordinance:[5] but if they find no present benefit, more exactly to review their preparation to, and carriage at, the sacrament;[6] in both which if they can approve themselves to God and their own consciences, they are to wait for the fruit of it in due time;[7] but if they see that they have failed in either, they are to be humbled,[8] and to attend upon it afterward with more care and diligence.[9]

(1) I Cor. 11:17, 30, 31.
(2) II Cor. 2:14; Acts 2:42, 46, 47.
(3) I Cor. 10:12; Rom. 11:20.
(4) Psa. 50:14.
(5) I Cor. 11:25, 26; Psa. 27:4; Acts 2:42.
(6) Psa. 77:6; Psa. 139:23, 24.
(7) Psa. 123:1, 2; Isa. 8:17.
(8) Hos. 14:2; Hos. 6:1, 2.
(9) II Cor. 7:11; I Chron. 15:12-14.

Q. 176. *Wherein do the sacraments of baptism and the Lord's supper agree?*

A. The sacraments of baptism and the Lord's supper agree, in that the author of both is God;[1] the spiritual part of both is Christ and his benefits;[2] both are seals of the same covenant,[3] are to be dispensed by ministers of the gospel and by none other,[4] and to be continued in the church of Christ until his second coming.[5]

(1) Matt. 28:19; I Cor. 11:23.
(2) Rom. 6:3, 4; I Cor. 10:16.
(3) Col. 2:11, 12. Compared with Rom. 4:11. Matt. 26:27, 28.
(4) See General Note, Larger Catechism, Question 1.
(5) Matt. 28:20; I Cor. 11:26.

Q. 177. *Wherein do the sacraments of baptism and the Lord's supper differ?*

A. The sacraments of baptism and the Lord's supper differ, in that baptism is to be administered but once, with water, to be a sign and seal of our regeneration and ingrafting into Christ,[1] and that even to infants;[2] whereas the Lord's supper is to be administered often, in the elements of bread and wine, to represent and exhibit Christ as spiritual nourishment to the soul,[3] and to confirm our continuance and growth in

| THE WESTMINSTER CONFESSION OF FAITH | THE WESTMINSTER LARGER CATECHISM | THE WESTMINSTER SHORTER CATECHISM |
| --- | --- | --- |

him,[4] and that only to such as are of years and ability to examine themselves.[5]

(1) Matt. 3:11; Gal. 3:27; Titus 3:5.
(2) Acts 2:38, 39; I Cor. 7:14. See citations under Question 166, figure 2.
(3) I Cor. 11:26; Col. 2:19.
(4) I Cor. 10:16; John 6:51-53.
(5) I Cor. 11:28.

# EXPLANATORY NOTES

A COMPARISON of the Standards on the Lord's Supper impresses the student with the fact that the Larger Catechism dwells upon this sacrament more than does either of the others, devotes as much space to it as both the others. And yet the Larger Catechism is the most neglected of the three Standards.

The sacrament of the supper is the central symbol of the Christian religion. The cross is in it, and just beyond, distinctly visible, is the empty tomb. At the table of the Lord, at the cross of the Son of God, we are at the center of all things in Providence and History and Redemption. Let us put the shoes from off our feet, and walk softly here.

## CONF. XXXI:1; L.C. 168; S.C. 96

These statements combined declare four things:

1. The author of the sacrament.
2. The time of its institution.
3. Its permanence.
4. The ends which it serves.

The student can easily find these elements of instruction. He should dwell upon the fourth, namely, the uses of this sacrament, five or six of them. There is in the two Catechisms cited an element of teaching not found in the first section of the Confession. I refer to the manner of receiving Christ in the supper. This phase of the subject is further dealt with in the seventh section of the Confession and in the Larger Catechism 170.

## CONF. XXXI:2

The sections between the first and the seventh are engaged in refuting the errors of the Church of Rome. The second section denies that the sacrament of the supper is a sacrifice in any sense, especially is it not a re-enactment of the sacrifice of Jesus Christ for the sins of the world; it is a commemoration of that offering up of Himself, by Himself, once for all. In the transaction at Calvary, Christ was both offerer and offering, priest and victim; and what He did needs not to be repeated, cannot be repeated. Christ's offering up of Himself is the supreme act of worship to which nothing can be added; "so that the so-called sacrifice of the mass is most contradictory to Christ's one sacrifice, the only propitiation for all the sins of the elect."

## CONF. XXXI:3

The third section declares the right manner of dispensing the sacrament, and indirectly condemns the wrong manner.

1. It specifies the administrator. He is to be a minister of the Word.
2. It describes the sacramental actions which are essential to this ordinance, and therefore should never be omitted:

   a. The consecration, which includes the reading of the words of institution, and prayer.
   b. The breaking of the bread. This is symbolic of the rending of the body of Christ, and

should be so done as to call attention to the act. It is mentioned in every account of the institution given by the evangelists.

In Acts 2:42 the whole ordinance is designated from this significant action.

c. The giving and the receiving of the elements, not one alone but both. The communicants are to be active. Jesus said, "Take, eat"; "drink all ye of it." The errors repudiated are two. First, that of withholding the cup from the people, called the laity. This error has its roots in a worse error, that of transubstantiation.

Second, the error of using individual wafers which the priest places in the mouths of the communicants. There is no breaking of the bread in a Catholic Communion service and no partaking of the cup. The priest drinks all the wine.

The last statement of section 3 is not to be understood as forbidding our custom of taking this sacrament to private homes for the benefit of shut-ins. For there the sacrament is administered in the presence of a sufficient number of people "to preserve the true character of the ordinance as a communion." (A. A. Hodge, *Commentary on the Confession of Faith,* p. 491.)

## CONF. XXXI:4

In section 4 various Romish abuses of the sacrament are condemned.

## CONF. XXXI:5

Section 5 gives the true explanation of the words of Jesus when He, in instituting the supper, said of the bread, "This is my body," and of the cup, "This is my blood of the covenant." (Matt. 26:26-27.) The Catholics explain the language of Jesus by transubstantiation, the doctrine that by the words of institution the bread and wine are actually changed into the veritable body and blood of Christ. So that when Jesus says, "This is my body," He is to be taken literally. For our explanation of His language, read again this section and also Chapter XXIX, section 2.

## CONF. XXXI:6

The doctrine of transubstantiation is particularly dealt with in section 6. The tenet is here defined,

and then declared to be repugnant, that is, offensive, not only to Scripture, but to common sense and reason. For common sense and reason teach that no substance can be transmuted into another substance and still retain its original attributes or qualities. But the bread and wine, after the alleged transubstantiation takes place, remain truly and only bread and wine, as they were before. They look like bread and wine, smell and taste like bread and wine; every test that can be applied proves that they *are* bread and wine.

This doctrine "overthroweth the nature of the sacrament." How, do you ask? This way: According to Scripture this sacrament in its proper nature is the sign and symbol of something. But according to the doctrine of Rome it is not the sign and symbol of something; it is the thing itself. The bread and wine are not the signs of the body and blood, they *are* the body and blood of Christ. The doctrine of Rome materializes and destroys the sacrament.

## CONF. XXXI:7

The seventh section teaches the manner of the presence of Christ and the manner of partaking of Him. Observe, the Confession does not deny the presence of Christ in the sacrament. The three parties in the purview of this chapter, Reformed, Catholic, and Lutheran, agree in affirming the presence. They differ as to the manner of the presence, and as to the way of receiving and feeding upon the present Christ. Both Catholics and Lutherans hold that Christ is carnally and corporally present, yet not precisely in the same way. According to Lutherans, Christ's body and blood are present in, with, or under the bread and wine; so that he who eats the bread and drinks the wine eats the literal body and drinks the literal blood of Christ. But the Catholics teach that the body and blood of Christ are not present in, with, or under the bread and the wine, but the bread and wine have ceased to be bread and wine, except in appearance, and have become the very body and blood of Christ.

As contradistinguished from Lutherans and Catholics, the Reformed believe that the body and blood of Christ are as really present to the faith of believers, as the elements themselves are to their outward senses. The worthy receivers, while outwardly partaking of the visible elements in this sacrament, do also inwardly, that is, spiritually, by faith, receive and feed upon Christ crucified and all benefits of His death. According to Catholics and Lutherans, unworthy receivers as well as worthy receivers partake of the body and blood of Christ.

It seems an immeasurable misfortune that the sacrament which memorializes the atoning, reconciling death of the Prince of Peace should be the occasion of so much division and bitter controversy.

In connection with this seventh section read and study Larger Catechism 170.

## CONF. XXXI:8

Section 8 contains a denial and a warning. It denies that ignorant and wicked men who receive the outward elements in this sacrament receive also the thing signified — the body and blood of Christ. It warns that by their unworthy coming to this sacrament they become guilty of the body and blood of the Lord. But, in general, to eat the bread and drink the cup of the Lord unworthily is "to come to the Lord's table in a careless, irreverent spirit, without the intention or desire to commemorate the death of Christ as the sacrifice for our sins, and without the purpose of complying with the engagements which we thereby assume. . . . the warning is directly against the careless and profane, and not against the timid and the doubting." (Charles Hodge, *Commentary on First Corinthians*, p. 231.)

Now study Larger Catechism 171-175. They have great value, for they set forth in full and impressive statements the duties of Christians with respect to this ordinance *before*, *at*, and *after* the partaking thereof. Try reading these paragraphs one after another, omitting the questions. From these paragraphs, you may learn the conditions of profitable communion, and how to meet them.

Under questions 176-177 we have a comparison of baptism and the Lord's Supper which brings out their agreements and their differences.

You have probably observed that the Confession in its treatment of the sacraments is polemic and combative, while in the Catechisms the controversial is reduced to a minimum. The object of the framers of the Confession was to confute error as well as to state and establish truth. All the great creeds of Christendom are outgrowths of controversies, and are meant to safeguard truth by exposing and confuting error.

A member of the Committee on Revision of the Standards, a few years ago, thought the Committee should recommend the removal of all controversial matter from the Confession. If all such matter *were* taken out of the Confession, the great document would be torn to shreds. The Westminster divines were much nearer than we are to the Reformation, which was an era of controversy, when feeling was hot and often bitter. That fact accounts for the language of the Confession in certain places.

Let it be noted that in baptism one gives oneself away. Among the Romans, *sacramentum* meant the soldier's oath of allegiance to his commander or government. The sacrament of baptism is our oath of allegiance to God, Father, Son, and Holy Spirit. To violate that oath is to perjure ourselves. Unfaithfulness to baptismal vows is a serious matter. (Ecclesiastes 5:4-5.) How many in the church are virtually perjurers, and know it not? Who is to tell them, who but their ministers?

The sacraments evermore need to be interpreted anew. Let the minister explain *sacramentum*, as the oath of the newly enlisted soldier swearing allegiance to the Captain of his salvation. Let him point out that the two sacraments represent salvation in its doctrine and experience, in its objective and subjective sides. The bread and wine of the supper are emblems of the broken body and shed blood of Christ — symbols of redemption purchased. The water of baptism is the symbol of redemption applied.

Baptism has a divine side. It represents God as doing something for man. It has a human side; it represents man as receiving, and yet as responding with pledges of obedience and service. The supper likewise has its divine side; it represents God or Christ as giving — what? It has a human side; it represents man as receiver, and yet as reacting with vows of gratitude and devotion. Every time the Christian partakes of the Lord's Supper he renews the oath, taken in baptism, to be the Lord's.

The two sacraments thus re-present the message of salvation. They are a pictorial gospel.

# CHAPTER XXXII

# Of Church Censures

## CONFESSION OF FAITH XXXII:1-4

| THE WESTMINSTER **CONFESSION OF FAITH** | THE WESTMINSTER **LARGER CATECHISM** | THE WESTMINSTER **SHORTER CATECHISM** |
|---|---|---|

THE Lord Jesus, as king and head of his church, hath therein appointed a government in the hand of church officers, distinct from the civil magistrate.[1]

(1) John 18:36; Isa. 9:6, 7; I Cor. 12:28; I Tim. 5:17.

2. To these officers the keys of the kingdom of heaven are committed, by virtue whereof they have power respectively to retain and remit sins, to shut that kingdom against the impenitent, both by the word and censures; and to open it unto pentitent sinners, by the ministry of the gospel, and by absolution from censures, as occasion shall require.[2]

(2) Matt. 16:19; Matt. 18:17, 18; John 20:21, 22, 23; II Cor. 2:6, 7, 8.

3. Church censures are necessary for the reclaiming and gaining of offending brethren; for deterring of others from like offenses; for purging out of that leaven which might infect the whole lump; for vindicating the honor of Christ, and the holy profession of the gospel; and for preventing the wrath of God, which might justly fall upon the church, if they should suffer his covenant, and the seals thereof, to be profaned by notorious and obstinate offenders.[3]

(3) I Tim. 5:20; I Tim. 1:20; Jude 23; I Cor. 5; I Cor. 11:27-34; II Sam. 12:14.

| THE WESTMINSTER CONFESSION OF FAITH | THE WESTMINSTER LARGER CATECHISM | THE WESTMINSTER SHORTER CATECHISM |
|---|---|---|

4. For the better attaining of these ends, the officers of the church are to proceed by admonition, suspension from the sacrament of the Lord's supper for a season, and by excommunication from the church, according to the nature of the crime, and demerit of the person.[4]

(4) I Thess. 5:12; II Thess. 3:6, 14; I Cor. 5:4, 5, 13; Matt. 18:17; Titus 3:10.

## EXPLANATORY NOTES

THIS whole chapter is about church censures. The imposition of censures is an act of government.

### CONF. XXXII:1

So this first section relates to the government which is authorized to impose censures. Two things are affirmed here:

1. That Christ appointed a government for His church. This in effect denies that Christ left His church without a government or that He left the government to be determined by the wisdom of men and to be varied according to circumstances. To hold that Christ so left His church would be equivalent to an impeachment of His wisdom, so important is government to the well-being of any society.

2. That the government of the church was placed by Christ in the hands of officers distinct from the civil magistrate. This is affirmed against the Erastians who hold that the government of the church belongs to the civil magistrate. The Erastians were strongly represented in the Westminster Assembly. John Selden, a learned layman, made a powerful premeditated argument for the Erastian view. During the delivery of the speech young George Gillespie's colleagues urged him to reply to Selden and defend the crown rights of Jesus Christ. Meanwhile Gillespie was busy with his pencil writing in his notebook. But he was not taking notes of Selden's speech nor was he outlining an argument in reply; instead he was inscribing brief prayers: Lord, send light; Lord, give assistance; Lord, defend Thine own cause. When Selden had finished, Gillespie arose and made a speech about which Scottish history has cast a halo of glory. By seven distinct lines of evidence he overthrew the argument of his opponent. So complete and convincing was Gillespie's reasoning, so unanswerable in both its learning and logic, that it astonished and confounded Selden. He made no attempt to reply.

This section calls Christ "king and head of his church." It is said by some that the Bible never calls Christ king of the church. It does not do so formally, but it does so virtually. For in Matthew 16:18-19, Jesus said to Peter, "Thou art Peter, and upon this rock I will build my church," and, "I will give unto thee the keys of the kingdom of heaven."

He calls the society He has come to build by two names: my church and the kingdom of heaven. Does not Jesus here identify the church with the kingdom? As Christ is king, He is likewise king of the church. The church is the only visible embodiment the kingdom has in the earth. Hence the Confession says, "The visible church . . . is the kingdom of the Lord Jesus Christ." (XXVII:2.)

## CONF. XXXII:2

This section relates to the authority of church officers. They have the keys of the kingdom of heaven. "The keys" are a symbol of authority. In authority are two ideas: those of right and power. The possessors of the keys have the right and the power to open and close doors. This is a figurative way of saying that they have the right and power to govern and discipline, agreeably, of course, to the will of the Lord. It belongs to them to say what is lawful and what is unlawful in conduct, and what is right and what is wrong in belief. It is their right and duty to impose censures and to absolve from the same, as occasion may require.

Is a church officer puffed up with a sense of his power and importance? Let him rather be bowed and burdened with the sense of his responsibility!

## CONF. XXXII:3

The third section affirms and explains the necessity of church censures, specifying five ends which censures are essential to secure. It is not claimed that discipline is essential to the being of the church, but to its well-being. Church officers have been remiss in not applying the power of the keys to keep the church pure in its faith and in its morals. As a result the church has suffered much loss of prestige and power. All loss of influence for righteousness should be deplored. Is it enough to deplore the loss of such influence? Should not efforts be made at once to recover the loss and repair the damage? But how few have the wisdom and courage for so difficult and delicate a task!

## CONF. XXXII:4

The subject of the fourth section is Forms of Church Censure. It recommends the employment of mild measures first, resorting to severer measures only after the milder have failed. Prompt action is important. Delay may make discipline more difficult and less successful. The longer disciplinary measures are delayed the less successful they are likely to be. A disease is more easily cured in its early stages than in its later.

# CHAPTER XXXIII

# Of Synods and Councils

CONFESSION OF FAITH XXXIII:1-4

| THE WESTMINSTER CONFESSION OF FAITH | THE WESTMINSTER LARGER CATECHISM | THE WESTMINSTER SHORTER CATECHISM |
|---|---|---|

FOR the better government and further edification of the church, there ought to be such assemblies as are commonly called synods or councils: and it belongeth to the overseers and other rulers of the particular churches, by virtue of their office, and the power which Christ hath given them for edification, and not for destruction, to appoint such assemblies; and to convene together in them, as often as they shall judge it expedient for the good of the church.[1]

(1) Acts 15.

2. It belongeth to synods and councils, ministerially, to determine controversies of faith, and cases of conscience; to set down rules and directions for the better ordering of the public worship of God, and government of his church; to receive complaints in cases of mal-administration, and authoritatively to determine the same: which decrees and determinations, if consonant to the word of God, are to be received with reverence and submission, not only for their agreement with the word, but also for the power whereby they are made, as being an ordinance of God, appointed thereunto in his word.[2]

(2) Acts 16:4; Acts 15:15, 19, 24, 27-31; Matt. 18:17-20.

3. All synods or councils since the apostles' times, whether general or particular, may err, and many have erred; therefore they are not

| THE WESTMINSTER CONFESSION OF FAITH | THE WESTMINSTER LARGER CATECHISM | THE WESTMINSTER SHORTER CATECHISM |
|---|---|---|

**CONFESSION OF FAITH**

to be made the rule of faith or prac-tice, but to be used as a help in both.[3]

(3) See General Note, Confession of Faith, Section I, Chapter 1.

4. Synods and councils are to handle or conclude nothing but that which is ecclesiastical: and are not to intermeddle with civil affairs which concern the commonwealth unless by way of humble petition in cases extraordinary; or by way of advice for satisfaction of conscience, if they be thereunto required by the civil magistrate.[4]

(4) Luke 12:13, 14; John 18:36; Matt. 22:21.

# EXPLANATORY NOTES

BY synods and councils here you may under-stand occasional gatherings or regular parts of church organizations and activity. The Presby-terian Church has a series of courts which meet statedly. But besides these there have been many gatherings in church history convened to serve special ends, doctrinal or administrative or mis-sionary. The first example was the synod which met in Jerusalem to settle the question about cir-cumcision. Another was the Westminster Assembly which framed these Standards. It was called, how-ever, by the authority of the state, and not by the authority of any church.

What is said about synods and councils is true of all ecclesiastical assemblies whether regular or occasional, including the Westminster Assembly itself.

## CONF. XXXIII:1

The teaching of this section may be comprehended in two propositions:

1. Synods or councils are needed for the health and growth of the church.

2. The power to convene such assemblies is vested in the overseers and other rulers of the church.

Is this Presbyterianism or Independency? It is according to Presbyterian policy and contrary to independent principles and practice. This section recognizes Government not by congregations but by representative officers.

## CONF. XXXIII:2

This section defines the functions of synods and councils, *i.e.,* states the nature of the matters that may come before them for determination; and declares that their decisions, if agreeable to the Word of God, are to be received as binding.

This is another point of difference between us and the independent churches. The latter admit that congregations may with advantage consult synods of ministers and laymen, but deny that such synods have any authority over the congregations. We hold that the conclusions and decrees of church officers in council assembled, insofar as they are in accord with the mind of Christ, are authoritative for the churches. Why? Because these officers act in His name and by His authority.

The council of Jerusalem did not merely give advice, but pronounced an authoritative decision. It "ordained decrees," "laid a burden" upon the churches and enjoined them to observe certain "necessary things," and the churches were not disobedient to the will of the council.

## CONF. XXXIII:3

The third section contains an affirmation and a denial. It affirms the fallibility of all synods and councils, and denies that the final appeal in matters of faith and practice is to be made to them. All this, of course, is aimed at the Roman Catholic Church, which holds that infallibility resides somewhere in the church. They disagree as to the seat of infallibility. Some locate it in a general council; others in the pope. Protestants stoutly and confidently assert that it resides in neither, basing their statement upon the evidence of history. Both popes and councils have acted contrarily to each other. Surely infallibility is not inconsistent with itself. An infallibility which contradicts itself destroys itself. The records show that a fallible council declared a fallible pope infallible. Can two fallibles make an infallible?

## CONF. XXXIII:4

The last section of this chapter delimits the jurisdiction of synods and councils. The line between the state and the church is distinctly drawn. They exist alongside each other and are in contact at many points; yet there is no collision or conflict so long as each keeps to its side of the dividing line. While the ends of the two institutions are distinct in nature, they are not contradictory, but complementary. These two powers, both ordained of God, are not intended to destroy, but mutually to uphold and preserve one another. The Confession as strongly denounces all popish intermeddling with civil affairs, as it resists any Erastian interference of the civil magistrate in matters purely spiritual and ecclesiastical.

The state and the church may profitably co-operate for the security and advancement of objects common to both; but let each keep within its own proper sphere. Here is the church on the right and here is the state on the left, in the same locality. Over the door of each is a word to the other: "Keep out!" The intruder or intermeddler is a troublemaker. There is a law against him.

# CHAPTER XXXIV

# Of the State of Man After Death, and Of the Resurrection of the Dead

CONFESSION OF FAITH XXXIV:1-3
LARGER CATECHISM 84-85, (86), 87 · SHORTER CATECHISM 37

| THE WESTMINSTER CONFESSION OF FAITH | THE WESTMINSTER LARGER CATECHISM | THE WESTMINSTER SHORTER CATECHISM |
|---|---|---|

**Q. 84.** *Shall all men die?*

A. Death being threatened as the wages of sin,[1] it is appointed unto all men once to die;[2] for that all have sinned.[3]

(1) Rom. 6:23.
(2) Heb. 9:27.
(3) Rom. 5:12.

**Q. 85.** *Death being the wages of sin, why are not the righteous delivered from death, seeing all their sins are forgiven in Christ?*

A. The righteous shall be delivered from death itself at the last day, and even in death are delivered from the sting and curse of it;[1] so that although they die, yet it is out of God's love,[2] to free them perfectly from sin and misery,[3] and to make them capable of further communion with Christ in glory, which they then enter upon.[4]

(1) I Cor. 15:26, 55, 56, 57; Heb. 2:15.
(2) Isa. 57:1, 2; II Kings 22:20.
(3) Luke 16:25; II Cor. 5:1-8.
(4) Luke 23:43; Phil. 1:23.

THE bodies of men, after death, return to dust, and see corruption;[1] but their souls (which neither die nor sleep), having an immortal subsistence, immediately return to God who gave them.[2] The souls of the righteous, being then made perfect in holiness, are received into the highest heavens, where they behold the face of God in light and glory, waiting for the full redemption of their bodies;[3] and the souls of the wicked are cast into hell, where they remain in torments and utter darkness, reserved to the judgment of the great day.[4] Besides these two places for souls separated from their bodies, the Scripture acknowledgeth none.

(1) Gen. 3:19; Acts 13:36.
(2) Luke 23:43; Phil. 1:23; II Cor. 5:6, 7, 8.
(3) Luke 16:23; Rom. 8:23. See under figure 2 above.
(4) Luke 16:23, 24; II Pet. 2:9.

(Q. 86. *What is the communion in glory with Christ, which the members of the invisible church enjoy immediately after death?*

(A. The communion in glory with Christ, which the members of the invisible church enjoy immediately after death, is in that their souls are then made perfect in holiness, and received into the highest heavens, where they behold the face of God in light and glory; waiting for the

**Q. 37.** *What benefits do believers receive from Christ at death?*

A. The souls of believers are at their death made perfect in holiness, and do immediately pass into glory;[1] and their bodies, being still united to Christ,[2] do rest in their graves till the resurrection.[3]

(1) Luke 23:43; Luke 16:23; Phil. 1:23; II Cor. 5:6-8.
(2) I Thess. 4:14.
(3) Rom. 8:23; I Thess. 4:14.

THE WESTMINSTER
**CONFESSION OF FAITH**

THE WESTMINSTER
**LARGER CATECHISM**

THE WESTMINSTER
**SHORTER CATECHISM**

full redemption of their bodies, which even in death continue united to Christ, and rest in their graves as in their beds, till at the last day they be again united to their souls. Whereas the souls of the wicked are at their death cast into hell, where they remain in torments and utter darkness; and their bodies kept in their graves, as in their prisons, until the resurrection and judgment of the great day.)

2. At the last day, such as are found alive shall not die, but be changed:[5] and all the dead shall be raised up with the self-same bodies, and none other, although with different qualities, which shall be united again to their souls forever.[6]

(5) I Thess. 4:17; I Cor. 15:51, 52.
(6) I Cor. 15:42, 43, 44.

Q. 87. *What are we to believe concerning the resurrection?*

A. We are to believe that, at the last day, there shall be a general resurrection of the dead, both of the just and unjust;[1] when they that are then found alive shall in a moment be changed; and the self-same bodies of the dead which are laid in the grave, being then again united to their souls forever, shall be raised up by the power of Christ.[2] The bodies of the just, by the Spirit of Christ, and by virtue of his resurrection as their head, shall be raised in power, spiritual, and incorruptible, and made like to his glorious body:[3] and the bodies of the wicked shall be raised up in dishonor by him as an offended judge.[4]

3. The bodies of the unjust shall, by the power of Christ, be raised to dishonor; the bodies of the just, by his Spirit, unto honor, and be made conformable to his own glorious body.[7]

(7) Acts 24:15; John 5:28, 29; Phil. 3:21.

(1) Acts 24:15.
(2) I Cor. 15:51, 52, 53; I Thess. 4:15, 16, 17; John 5:28, 29.
(3) I Cor. 15:21, 22, 23, 42, 43, 44; Phil. 3:21.
(4) John 5:28, 29; Dan. 12:2; Matt. 25:33.

# EXPLANATORY NOTES

THE last two chapters of the Confession, the thirty-fourth and the thirty-fifth, belong to the department of eschatology, which means the doctrine of the last things. The last things here mentioned are death, intermediate state, resurrection, and judgment.

## L.C. 84

The Larger Catechism teaches that death is not something that just happens: it is ordained of God, on account of sin.

## L.C. 85

This Catechism raises and answers the question: Why do the justified die, seeing all their sins are forgiven in Christ? To the answer of the Catechism it may be added that death is a part of the discipline appointed unto saints. Their Saviour endured the humiliation of death; through death He overcame death. The servant is not above his Lord. God is engaged in the business of making character, and character is not made by magic but by means, and death is a part of the means. A curriculum of suffering and death breaks down pride and develops humility. The end here justifies the means.

## CONF. XXXIV:1; (L.C. 86); S.C. 37

The intermediate state is the state between death and the resurrection. What is it like? All should be interested in this question. All our friends and loved ones who have departed this life are in that state; and all now living will soon be there, if the Lord delays His coming.

The intermediate state is alike for all in two respects:

1. It is for all a state of separation of soul and body.

2. It is a state of consciousness, for the souls of men neither die nor sleep. But as there are two kinds of characters there are two kinds of consciousness. In the case of the righteous the intermediate state is a state of blessedness, of conscious bliss; while in the case of the unrighteous it is a state of misery.

The Standards do not recognize the existence of an intermediate place. They acknowledge only two places for souls separated from their bodies: the name of one is hell, and the name of the other is heaven. All those in the intermediate state are in one or the other of these places. The intermediate state differs from the final state in degree rather than in kind. In the former state the man is not all there, whereas in the latter state he is all present, the two parts of his being having been reunited. The reunion of souls and bodies takes place in the resurrection.

## CONF. XXXIV:2

The Standards teach a general resurrection of the dead, both of the just and unjust. Coincidently with the resurrection of the dead occurs the transformation of the living, both kinds.

## CONF. XXXIV. 3; L.C. 87

Both the Confession and the Larger Catechism indicate the diverse destinies of the righteous and the wicked. Why does the Confession refer the resurrection of the unjust to Christ and the resurrection of the just to Christ's Spirit?

# CHAPTER XXXV

# Of the Last Judgment

CONFESSION OF FAITH XXXV:1-3
LARGER CATECHISM 88-90 · SHORTER CATECHISM 38

THE WESTMINSTER
## CONFESSION OF FAITH

THE WESTMINSTER
## LARGER CATECHISM

THE WESTMINSTER
## SHORTER CATECHISM

GOD hath appointed a day, wherein he will judge the world in righteousness by Jesus Christ,[1] to whom all power and judgment is given of the Father.[2] In which day, not only the apostate angels shall be judged; but likewise all persons, that have lived upon earth, shall appear before the tribunal of Christ, to give an account of their thoughts, words, and deeds; and to receive according to what they have done in the body, whether good or evil.[3]

(1) Acts 17:31; Matt. 25:31-34.
(2) John 5:22, 27.
(3) Jude 6; II Pet. 2:4; II Cor. 5:10; Rom. 2:16; Rom. 14:10, 12; Matt. 12:36, 37; I Cor. 3:13-15.

2. The end of God's appointing this day, is for the manifestation of the glory of his mercy in the eternal salvation of the elect;[4] and of his justice in the damnation of the reprobate, who are wicked and disobedient.[5] For then shall the righteous go into everlasting life, and receive that fullness of joy and refreshing which shall come from the presence of the Lord:[6] but the wicked, who know not God, and obey not the gospel of Jesus Christ, shall be cast into eternal torments, and punished with everlasting destruction from the presence of the Lord, and from the glory of his power.[7]

(4) Rom. 9:23; Eph. 2:4, 5, 6, 7.
(5) Rom. 2:5, 6; II Thess. 1:7, 8.
(6) Matt. 25:31-34; II Thess. 1:7; Psa. 16:11.
(7) Matt. 25:41, 46; II Thess. 1:9; Mark 9:47, 48.

Q. 88. *What shall immediately follow after the resurrection?*

A. Immediately after the resurrection shall follow the general and final judgment of angels and men,[1] the day and hour whereof no man knoweth, that all may watch and pray, and be ever ready for the coming of the Lord.[2]

(1) II Pet. 2:4; Rev. 20:11, 12, 13.
(2) Matt. 24:36, 42, 44; Luke 21:35, 36.

Q. 89. *What shall be done to the wicked at the day of judgment?*

A. At the day of judgment, the wicked shall be set on Christ's left hand,[1] and upon clear evidence, and full conviction of their own consciences,[2] shall have the fearful but just sentence of condemnation pronounced against them;[3] and thereupon shall be cast out from the favorable presence of God, and the glorious fellowship with Christ, his saints, and all his holy angels, into hell, to be punished with unspeakable torments both of body and soul, with the devil and his angels forever.[4]

(1) Matt. 25:33.
(2) Rom. 2:15, 16. See context.
(3) Matt. 25:41, 42.
(4) Matt. 25:46; II Thess. 1:8, 9; Luke 16:26; Mark 9:43, 44; Mark 14:21.

[ 229 ]

| THE WESTMINSTER CONFESSION OF FAITH | THE WESTMINSTER LARGER CATECHISM | THE WESTMINSTER SHORTER CATECHISM |
|---|---|---|

**LARGER CATECHISM**

Q. 90. *What shall be done to the righteous at the day of judgment?*

A. At the day of judgment, the righteous, being caught up to Christ in the clouds,[1] shall be set on his right hand, and, there openly acknowledged and acquitted,[2] shall join with him in the judging of reprobate angels and men;[3] and shall be received into heaven,[4] where they shall be fully and forever freed from all sin and misery;[5] filled with inconceivable joy;[6] made perfectly holy and happy both in body and soul, in the company of innumerable saints and angels,[7] but especially in the immediate vision and fruition of God the Father, of our Lord Jesus Christ, and of the Holy Spirit, to all eternity.[8] And this is the perfect and full communion, which the members of the invisible church shall enjoy with Christ in glory, at the resurrection and day of judgment.

(1) I Thess 4:17.
(2) Matt. 25:33; Matt. 10:32.
(3) I Cor. 6:2, 3.
(4) Matt. 25:34, 46.
(5) Eph. 5:27; Rev. 7:17.
(6) Psa. 16:11; I Cor. 2:9.
(7) Heb. 12:22, 23.
(8) I John 3:2; I Cor. 13:12; I Thess. 4:17, 18; Rev. 22:3-5.

**SHORTER CATECHISM**

Q. 38. *What benefits do believers receive from Christ at the resurrection?*

A. At the resurrection, believers, being raised up in glory,[1] shall be openly acknowledged, and acquitted in the day of judgment,[2] and made perfectly blessed in the full enjoying of God[3] to all eternity.[4]

(1) I Cor. 15:42, 43.
(2) Matt. 25:33, 34; Matt. 10:32.
(3) Psa. 16:11; I Cor. 2:9.
(4) I Thess. 4:17. See preceding context.

**CONFESSION OF FAITH**

3. As Christ would have us to be certainly persuaded that there shall be a day of judgment, both to deter all men from sin, and for the greater consolation of the godly in their adversity:[8] so will he have that day unknown to men, that they may shake off all carnal security, and be always watchful, because they know not at what hour the Lord will come; and may be ever prepared to say, Come, Lord Jesus, come quickly.[9] Amen.

(8) II Cor. 5:11; II Thess. 1:5, 6, 7; Luke 21:27, 28; II Pet. 3:11, 14.
(9) Mark 13:35, 36, 37; Luke 12:35, 36; Rev. 22:20. See Matt. 24:36, 42, 43, 44.

# EXPLANATORY NOTES

THE last chapter of the Confession and of this Harmony is about the last judgment. The solemnity of the subject makes the heart of this annotator ache as he writes about it.

## CONF. XXXV:1; L.C. 88

The Larger Catechism at its 88th question tells us that the general and final judgment shall come immediately after the resurrection.

The first section of the Confession contains five points of teaching:

1. The fact of the judgment. God hath appointed a day wherein He will judge the world in righteousness.
2. The agent of the judgment. By Jesus Christ, to whom all power and judgment is given of the Father.
3. The subjects of the judgment. Apostate angels and all persons that have lived upon the earth.
4. The matters to be judged: thoughts, words, deeds.
5. The sentence to be pronounced.

The sentence will be in kind and measure according to deeds done in the body.

## CONF. XXXV:2; L.C. 89-90; S.C. 38

These statements deal with the object and issue of the judgment. The object is the manifestation of the glory of God's mercy and justice. The issue of the judgment will be twofold. In the case of the righteous the judgment will issue in their full and final reception into the presence of the Lord, where there is fullness of joy and life abundant and everlasting. In the case of the wicked it will issue in their expulsion from the favorable presence of God, and the fellowship of Christ, angels, and redeemed men, into outer darkness with the devil and his angels forever. He that hath ears to hear, let him hear!

Larger Catechism question 90 should be carefully considered for its fullness of statement and additional ideas. What ideas does it add to the foregoing?

It is worthy of note that the Shorter Catechism at question 38 states succinctly what is done for the righteous in the judgment, but omits all mention of the wicked.

## CONF. XXXV:3

The analysis of the last section of the Confession yields three points of teaching in regard to the day of the final judgment:

1. The certainty of it.
2. The uncertainty of it.
3. The design of both the certainty and the uncertainty. State the design in each case.

The Confession ends, as the Bible ends, as I want these notes to end, with the prayer: "Come, Lord Jesus, come quickly. Amen."